Spanish Studies

AN INTRODUCTION

Bill Richardson

School of Applied Language and
Intercultural Studies,
Dublin City University

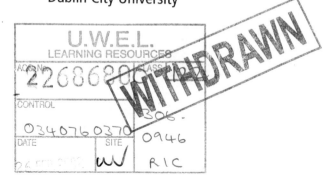

ARNOLD

A member of the Hodder Headline Group
LONDON
Co-published in the United States of America by
Oxford University Press Inc., New York

First published in Great Britain in 2001 by
Arnold, a member of the Hodder Headline Group,
338 Euston Road, London NW1 3BH

http://www.arnoldpublishers.com

Co-published in the United States of America by
Oxford University Press Inc.,
198 Madison Avenue, New York, NY 10016

British Library Cataloguing in Publication Data
A catalogue record for this book is available from the British Library

Library of Congress Cataloging-in-Publication Data
A catalog record for this book is available from the Library of Congress

ISBN 0 340 76037 0 (hb)
ISBN 0 340 76038 9 (pb)

1 2 3 4 5 6 7 8 9 10

Production Editor: Anke Ueberberg
Production Controller: Iain McWilliams
Cover Design: Terry Griffiths

Typeset in 10/12½pt Sabon by
Phoenix Photosetting, Chatham, Kent
Printed and bound in Great Britain by
MPG Books Ltd, Bodmin, Cornwall

What do you think about this book? Or any other Arnold title?
Please send your comments to feedback.arnold@hodder.co.uk

Contents

In memory of my parents, Rachel and Albert

Preface

This book is the fruit of a period of study leave from Dublin City University in the academic year 1999–2000, supported by a grant from the Spanish Ministry of Foreign Affairs. In another sense, of course, it is the fruit of over 25 years' professional and personal involvement with Spain and all things Spanish. The numerous conversations and discussions I have had with Spanish people and with observers of the Spanish scene and – more importantly, perhaps – the hospitality shown by Spanish people towards me, have contributed enormously to the generation of whatever insights may be offered in this book into how Spain is or how Spanish people 'make meanings'.

Various specific points addressed in the book were discussed with or generously commented on by Matías Bedmar, Alvina Byrne, Gabrielle Carty, Antonio Celada Rodríguez, Don Cruickshank, María Dolores Fresneda, Rosemary Graham, Louise M. Haywood, Leo Hickey, John Hurley, Catherine Lowry, Ian Macpherson, María Angeles Martín, Eva Mateo, Ignacio Montes, Lesley Murphy, Patricia O'Byrne, Kènia Puig, Eamonn Rodgers, Anne Walsh, Catherine Way and Alejandro Zarza.

Fiana Griffin, Leslie Davis, Fernando Prieto and Carlos Uxó read the draft manuscript and made invaluable suggestions for amendments and improvements. Mags Lehane at DCU Library and Santiago Díaz-Jove Blanco at the Library of the Cervantes Institute, Dublin, were enormously helpful, as was Elena Seymenliyska at Arnold. Further editorial assistance was provided by Aurora Palacín and Michael O'Sullivan.

To all the above, and to students and former students of Spanish at Dublin City University – especially those Applied Languages students who have discussed the topics covered in this book in my seminar on 'Cultural Difference' – I offer heartfelt gratitude and appreciation.

Finally, biggest thanks of all to my wife, Marion, without whose support it would not have been possible to undertake this task.

Acknowledgements

Ediciones Hiperión for Ana Rosetti, 'Chico Wrangler', from *Indicios vehementes* (1985); Editorial Anagrama for an extract from Josefina R. Aldecoa, *Historia de una maestra* (1996), for an extract from Xavier Rubert de Ventós, *De la identidad a la independencia* (1999), and for an extract from José Antonio Marina, *La selva del lenguaje* (1998); Berg Publishers for the table on page 35 from José Álvarez Junco, 'The nation-building process in nineteenth century Spain', published in C. Mar-Molinero and A. Smith (eds), *Nationalism and the nation in the Iberian Peninsula: competing and conflicting identities* (1996); Visor Libros for the poem 'El cerdo' from Luisa Castro, *Los hábitos del artillero* (1990); Grupo Planeta for an extract from Miguel Delibes, *Los santos inocentes* (1989); the heirs of Antonio Machado for extracts from the poem 'Retrato', published in *Poesías completas*, Austral, Madrid, 1971; Juan Ballesta and *Cambio16* for the cartoon on page 113; the author and El País Ediciones for extracts from 'Europa, patria querida' by Vicente Verdú (*El País Digital*, [http://www.elpais/p/d/especial/domingo/euro6.htm]); the author and El País Ediciones for an extract from *La vida desnuda* by Rosa Montero, Aguilar/El País Ediciones, 1994; Museo del Prado for permission to reproduce the picture on page 86 ('The nobleman with his hand on his chest'); Córdoba Cathedral for the image of the Mosque at Córdoba on page 16; Mikel Urmeneta and Kukuxumusu for the illustration on page 127; Ramón Masats and *Carta de España* for the photograph on page 189; the Museo Nacional Centro de Arte Reina Sofía for permission to reproduce Picasso's 'Guernica' on page 211; the author and Alianza Editorial for a passage from *Hispanoamérica* (1986) by Julián Marías; the author and Alianza Editorial for a passage 'España, una sociedad vital y desmoralizada' from *La sociedad española 1992–93: informe sociológico* (1992) by Amando de Miguel; the author and Editorial Debate for an extract from 'Una historia de amor' by Manuel Vicent published in *Crónicas urbanas* (1984); the author and Editorial Alfaguara for an extract from *Son de mar* by Manuel Vicent (1999); the author and Editorial Destino for an extract from Camilo José Cela, *La familia de Pascual Duarte* (1971).

Illustrations

Introduction: What Does It Mean to Be Spanish?

. . . man is an animal suspended in webs of significance he himself has spun . . .
Clifford Geertz (1993: 5)

This book aims to present Spanish life and culture through an exploration of ten basic thematic areas of universal relevance. These are: Spaniards' identity in the world; 'Spanishness'; the significance of place in people's lives; language; classic Spanish icons and archetypal figures; love, sex and issues of gender; money and the economy; the formation of the Spaniard at home and in school; religious belief; and death.

The scope is deliberately broad and the range eclectic. This reflects the conviction that students of Spanish language and culture wish to have an overview of the culture they are studying and are interested in exploring Spain from many different angles. The student of languages in the twenty-first century is as likely to read a sociological text as a literary one and will be as interested in the everyday lives of Spaniards as in the historical background needed to understand certain aspects of contemporary Spanish life.

Here, the objective is to provide an introduction to all of these areas and an initial exploration of a wide range of issues of relevance to Spain today. The approach taken is based on the assumption that culture is centrally about whatever is meaningful in people's lives and that the meaning can take many forms. Meanings may be derived from major cultural artefacts (for instance, well-known works of art and literature), just as they may also relate to popular cultural forms and to the everyday experience of living in a particular place at a particular time. A neat summary of the range of concerns likely to be of interest to anyone wishing to gain an insight into the lives of any group of people is provided by the classic UNESCO definition:

> Culture may now be said to be the whole complex of distinctive features, spiritual, material, intellectual and emotional, that characterize a society or social group. It includes not only the arts and letters, but also modes of life, the fundamental rights of human beings, value systems, traditions and beliefs.
>
> (quoted in Gallagher 1998: 154)

Spain is an exciting country, and there is a huge – and growing – interest in Spanish Studies. The popularity of Spanish and its status as one of the most widely spoken languages in the world are likely to ensure that the study of the cultures linked to that language continues to develop. The study of Spanish culture and society is valuable and rewarding; with its relation to the Spanish language and its central importance within the mix of cultures linked to that language, Spain becomes even more interesting and is even more likely to exercise a fascination over the minds of those who approach it from outside.

In a book such as this it is not possible to offer an in-depth study of the whole range of relevant areas; it is hoped, however, that the selection of sub-topics related to each area will place the themes in their Spanish context sufficiently well for them to provide a springboard for additional exploration, and the short readings at the end of each chapter will give further insight into how the themes may be approached. To help the reader to study the topics in greater depth, a set of suggestions for further reading – in either print or electronic form – is offered at the end of each chapter.

1

Hispanic v. European Identity: Where is Spain?

1.1 INTRODUCTION: BETWEEN EUROPE AND LATIN AMERICA

One of the aims of this book is to explore the issue of Spanish identity, and one way to begin exploring identity is to consider questions about people, place and time: Who? Where? When? To explain who we are, we need to situate ourselves in a possible group or groups to which we 'belong', to identify a location or locations that are special to us, and to see ourselves in a particular historical period and in relation to the historical periods that came before ours.

Basic human truths obviously also apply in the case of Spanish people: every individual is unique; there are no easy ways to summarize complex human cultures; and human happiness may be pursued universally but is only ever attained partially. People everywhere undertake the same endeavours and strive to satisfy similar needs: for food and shelter, for love and affection, for security and self-fulfilment. In discussing the various topics addressed in this book, our starting point will be the recognition of this reality, and any reflections offered on the 'Spanish' dimension of these topics are informed by an awareness that the nuances that apply to Spaniards also apply to people anywhere, especially when we wish to comment on cultural difference.

The obvious answer to the question 'Where is Spain?' is 'In south-western Europe.' However, we could ask whether this is where Spaniards see Spain, and whether it is where they have always seen it. One competing answer is 'In the Hispanic world.' There are, therefore, at least two possible major 'ethnic' groupings to which Spanish people could be said to belong, and one of these is defined in terms of place (geographically Spain is attached to the European land-mass), while the other is defined in terms of time (given the historical reality of the colonial relationship between Spain and its former overseas territories, mainly in Latin America).

Whether Spaniards look towards Europe or Latin America, they can perceive ties to both those places: Spain is both European *and* Hispanic. The emphasis in Spain over the last few decades has been on Europe, to the detriment of the

'Hispanic dimension'. Since 1986, Spain has been a member of the European Union (EU) (at the time, the European Economic Community, or EEC), and so has been perceived, both inside and outside the country, as an integral part of contemporary Europe. The shift in emphasis in Spain is well demonstrated by the responses given to two surveys conducted just two years apart by the newspaper *El País* (reported in November 1997). Each survey asked:

> In general, do you believe that Spain has more in common with the countries of the European Union or with the countries of Latin America? With which set of countries does it have more common interests? And with which set of countries should Spain be more closely linked in the future?

There was a symmetrical shift of opinion between 1995 and 1997: while, in 1995, 49 per cent of respondents felt that Spain had more in common with Latin American countries and 36 per cent felt that it had more in common with the countries of the EU, in 1997 only 37 per cent favoured Latin America and 48 per cent favoured Europe. About ten years after their country had become a member, Spaniards' sense of identification with the countries of the EU was rapidly becoming stronger. Yet the very fact that 37 per cent of the population felt a stronger attachment to Latin America than Europe in 1997 indicates that the bond between Spain and Latin America is still deeply rooted. The drift 'away' from Latin America is confirmed, however, by the respondents' perceptions of difference between Spain and Latin America, as indicated by their answers to the question: 'Would you say that, in general, there are more similarities than differences between Spain and Latin America, or vice versa?' In 1995, 60 per cent felt that there were more similarities than differences, but this dropped to 49 per cent in 1997, while the figure for those who felt there were more differences than similarities between Spain and Latin America rose from 34 per cent to 42 per cent in the period.

While these statistics are obviously not conclusive, it is reasonable to infer that *both* Europe and Latin America are places with which Spaniards feel a special affinity, and that there is a growing tendency for Spaniards to feel more strongly attached to Europe and less attached to Latin America. The *El País* report summarized the situation in its headline in the following terms: 'España quiere a América Latina, pero cada vez menos' ('Spain is fond of Latin America, but less and less so').

Increased cultural integration into Europe in the form of a stronger identification with the countries of the EU may well be a concomitant of greater *economic* involvement: financial transfers from the EU in the form of European Structural Funds gave much-needed lifeblood to the troubled Spanish economy of the mid-1990s. While this may help to explain the increased identification with Europe, we should not forget that, before the mid-eighteenth century, Spain had been a significant force in Europe, and that during the sixteenth century it had been *the* major power in Europe and the world.

In this chapter we shall explore some of the historical links between Spain and Latin America, the European dimension of Spanish culture, the notion of Europeanization (especially as it is reflected in the writings of José Ortega y Gasset) and the increased integration of Spain into Europe in recent decades. Two readings at the end of the chapter offer contrasting commentaries by Spanish writers on Latin America and Europe respectively; these are preceded by a feature on one of the most 'universal' of Latin American authors, Jorge Luis Borges.

1.2 LANGUAGE AND COMMUNITY: SPAIN AND THE NEW WORLD

The term 'Hispanic' can be understood as referring to everything connected with Spanish language, culture and identity anywhere in the world. In fact, however, the term is frequently employed with the meaning 'anything to do with Spanish language and culture which is external to Spain'. In particular, it is most generally used in reference to the cultures and peoples of Latin America (particularly in terms of their 'Spanish' dimension), or to the 'Spanish' element of the culture of places such as the Philippines. This link between Spain and the Hispanic parts of the world is both problematical and very real.

The most obvious dimension of that link, and perhaps also the most significant one, is language. Spanish is the mother tongue of about 350 million people, and most of these Spanish speakers – about 85 per cent – live in Latin America. Spanish is an official language in some 19 Latin American countries and in most of those countries, it is spoken by a majority of the population. Partly because of this, it enjoys a high status, although, by and large, the privileged position of Spanish is simply a consequence of the fact that, for historical reasons, a Spanish-speaking elite holds significant political, social and economic power.

In some cases the dominance of Spanish has resulted in an almost exclusive use of Spanish in a country (e.g. Argentina, Uruguay or Nicaragua). In other cases, Spanish is just one of several languages. Mexico, for instance, has some 250 languages, mainly of the Aztec family. A number of Mayan languages survive in Guatemala, and Quechua and Aymara are spoken in Peru and Bolivia, respectively. None of these, however, has the high status of Spanish in those countries; the only native American language with comparable status is Guarani, which is spoken by the vast majority of people in Paraguay – including its educated middle classes – and which is officially accorded the status of 'national language' along with Spanish. On the other hand, hundreds of native American languages have died out completely, reflecting the historically weak position of the indigenous cultures of the continent.

The damage inflicted on the indigenous languages of Latin America is part of a pattern of destruction wrought by Europeans since the Conquest. The

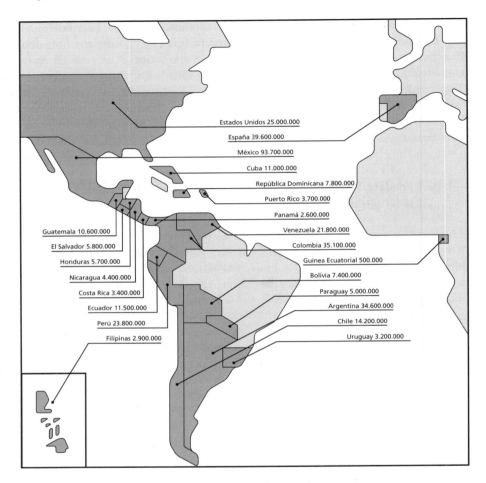

Estados Unidos 25.000.000
España 39.600.000
México 93.700.000
Cuba 11.000.000
República Dominicana 7.800.000
Puerto Rico 3.700.000
Panamá 2.600.000
Guatemala 10.600.000
Venezuela 21.800.000
El Salvador 5.800.000
Colombia 35.100.000
Honduras 5.700.000
Guinea Ecuatorial 500.000
Nicaragua 4.400.000
Bolivia 7.400.000
Costa Rica 3.400.000
Paraguay 5.000.000
Ecuador 11.500.000
Argentina 34.600.000
Perú 23.800.000
Chile 14.200.000
Filipinas 2.900.000
Uruguay 3.200.000

Figure 1: Distribution of native speakers of Spanish

dominant picture that emerges from the story of the Conquest itself and of the subsequent colonization is one of exploitation, greed and ruthlessness, combined with the devastating effects of disease. Estimates vary as to how many people were already living on the continent when the Europeans arrived, but there may have been as many as 100 million. Their ancestry stretched back about 35,000 years to when the very first settlers set foot on American soil, and, by the time Europeans arrived in the fifteenth century, the different groups of inhabitants had developed a wide variety of cultures, some of which were as advanced in their way as contemporary European ones.

The most outstanding pre-Columbian cultures were probably the Incas, the Maya and the Aztecs. The Incas were the dominant civilization in the area which we now call Peru. Their 'capital city', Cuzco, was built to very high technical standards, on a par with those of the most advanced European constructions of the time. The Maya were prominent in southern Mexico, Guatemala, Belize and Honduras. They had an elaborate system of culturally related independent states, based on a combination of advanced agricultural activity and urban settlements. They had devised a highly sophisticated writing system, using some 800 individual signs or 'glyphs'. The Aztec empire covered much of what is now central and southern Mexico during the fifteenth and sixteenth centuries, with a population of some 5–6 million people. They had developed an elaborate calendar based on a combination of a ritual calendar of 260 days and a solar calendar of 365 days. The Aztec priests kept careful track of both calendars, believing it important to understand the relation of each day to a particular god, so that their appeals to those gods (which often involved sacrifice of animals and humans) would be successful in terms of obviating disasters.

In certain respects, then, these civilizations may be said to have actually surpassed that of Europe, but, as Alan Riding reminds us, we need to be careful not to idealize pre-Columbian cultures:

> To romanticize the Indians from the monumental ruins and folklore remnants evident today is to distort the lot of most Indians even before the Spanish Conquest. Then as now, the majority suffered under an inequitable social system: they fought and died as foot soldiers; they sustained the superstitions that gave rise to the ruling theocracies; they worked the fields, carried water and built the temples and pyramids; they ate only corn tortillas and beans; and they lived in wooden and adobe huts not far from the stone palaces occupied by their masters. Successive conquering lords gave them different gods to worship, but their lot rarely changed. After the Conquest, it was just another god who arrived, in whose name the Indians were subject to new exploitations.
>
> (Riding 1985: 22)

From the start, the dominant European and Spanish attitude towards the indigenous inhabitants of America was one of exploitation, to the point of enslavement. This appears to have been true even of Christopher Columbus, despite the fact that on occasion he wrote in an idealistic vein of these 'Indians', as they were soon called, on the mistaken assumption that what had been found by the first explorers were Asian islands and archipelagos. Columbus referred to the indigenous population in his writings as *gente harto mansa* and praised their good looks and docility, but was nonetheless willing to tolerate their exploitation. Some of the Spaniards, to their credit, protested at the harsh treatment the Indians received, while the majority of the settlers simply took advantage of their strong position and determinedly advanced their own cause, without a thought for the havoc being wreaked on the resources available to them in the New World, not the least of which were, of course, human ones.

One Spanish settler, Juan Pijoan, made the point very explicitly in the late sixteenth century when he referred to the Indians as a resource to be used for the benefit of the Spanish: 'Al indio ... no hay que tratarle como bestia, ni como esclavo, ni aun como humano; es un divino depósito que Dios ha confiado a los españoles' (quoted in Rubert de Ventós 1987: 55).

Laws were passed by the Spanish Crown in an attempt to copper-fasten the fair treatment of Indian workers, the *Leyes de Indias*. These contained an unambiguous injunction against the practice of slavery, as can be appreciated from the following extract:

> Likewise we order that no person, whether in war or peacetime, may take, appropriate or seize, nor sell or exchange as a slave, any Indian, or hold one as such, even if it is done during a just war, for the purpose of purchase, ransom, barter or exchange, nor for any other reason.
>
> (*Leyes de Indias* 1526)

Defence of just treatment for the Indians came also from Spanish priests and monks, most notably the Dominican friars who accompanied the first settlers, many of whom were horrified at the abuses they witnessed. The best known of these was Bartolomé de Las Casas (1474–1566), who started out as a conventional Spanish priest and a settler himself, but was converted to the Indians' cause. Las Casas devoted his life to this cause, and there were other men like him (albeit a minority) who raised their voices in protest at what was happening, even if the efforts of such enlightened people were largely in vain. The bulk of the Indian population suffered under the tyranny of their Spanish masters as they toiled in the fields and mines. While the wealth they extracted was largely shipped back to Spain and on to other parts of Europe, the indigenous population declined under the harsh conditions to such an extent that by the end of the sixteenth century their numbers had dropped by perhaps as much as 90 per cent (Kirby 1992: 16).

Ideologically, the Europeans of the late Middle Ages justified their imperial expansion on the grounds that the colonization would bring Christianity to the people of the conquered territories. From the start, friars and priests were sent to the colonies to convert and instruct the Indians in the 'true faith'. The degree of coercion employed in such conversion varied from group to group and from individual to individual. The conquistadors were officially obliged to demand of the Indian population that they subject themselves to the Spanish monarch and that they should convert to Christianity. This legal device, the *Requerimiento*, often meant simply that a document stating these demands was read to the Indians – a document written in a language they did not understand – whereupon they would be attacked and subjugated.

The process of creating an 'Hispanic community', then, was begun on the basis of an encounter between two very different (and, militarily, very unequal) cultures. The relationship between the two was forged in blood and exploitation, under the shadow of the Christian Cross, on terms laid down by the Spaniards, and within the intellectual and moral framework of sixteenth-century European thought.

1.3 HISPANIC NATIONS: DEMOCRACY AND DEVELOPMENT

The issues surrounding the relationship between Spain and Latin America came under scrutiny in a special way in the run-up to 1992, when Spain announced plans to celebrate the 500th anniversary of the 'discovery of America'. From what has been said already, we can appreciate how inappropriate the use of the term 'discovery' seemed to many Latin Americans at the time. It seemed to imply that what was important about Latin America began only at the point of its discovery by Europeans. Even the shift in the terminology used by Spanish official bodies – from *descubrimiento de América* to *encuentro de dos culturas* – could not mask the fact that challenging issues needed to be addressed, not the least of which was the collective memory of the reduction of the indigenous population during the early decades of the conquest. Although it is possible to refer euphemistically to what happened as an 'encounter', the reality of maltreatment and exploitation remains in the historical memory of the region, just as it must be a factor colouring the thinking of observers from other parts of the world, including Spain itself.

The tradition of exploitation laid down by the first settlers was continued by their successors in the social elite of most Latin American countries. Even after independence, which happened for most of the Spanish colonies had gained their independence in the early nineteenth century, the European upper classes of Latin American society formed a wealthy minority who ruled unscrupulously over the majority of the population. For the most part, the movements for independence in Latin America were led by such *criollos*, or creoles (Latin Americans of European descent), who had no desire to revolutionize the societies in which they lived. Their aim was, rather, through independence, to remove the burden of taxes and the trading constraints imposed by a distant metropolis, and free themselves from the political control of the Spanish Crown. Frequently, peasants and workers fared even worse in the post-independence period than before: quite often, no attempt at all was made to treat them humanely once the link to Spain had been broken.

The writings of Latin American authors reflect the cultural conflicts that existed, and, to some extent, still exist between Spain and her ex-colonies. The rejection of the Spanish legacy found forceful expression in several writers who themselves belonged to the elite of *criollo* culture. One example is the Argentine author Juan Bautista Alberdi (1810–84). Alberdi wrote essays and newspaper articles condemning the influence of Spain on Latin American thinking and behaviour. He saw Spain as the source of despotic and reactionary ideas, and felt he detected the continued influence of these ideas in his own country. While acknowledging that individual Spaniards may have been worthy of respect and affection, he associated Latin American despotism with Spanish attitudes and 'Spanishness', *españolismo*. Witness this extract from his tirade against all things Spanish, published in the newspaper *La Moda* in April 1838:

> For us, the era of the Spaniards and the era of the tyrants were one and the same thing . . . . The Spaniards enslaved us . . . . We clearly retain many aspects of the colonial epoch, because we have maintained Spanish beliefs and behaviour. It is within this general notion of *españolismo* that we have come to understand all that is reactionary, because today every backward idea, habit and custom that we have is of Spanish origin.
>
> (Alberdi 1999; my translation)

But within the relatively small circles of the educated classes in postcolonial Latin America, there was a tension between, on the one hand, a desire to reject the cultural baggage of Spanish identity and, on the other, a countervailing tendency to mimic European mores and to laud European sociocultural values as superior to the supposed 'savagery' of the indigenous masses, or even of the culture of the *criollos*. The issue becomes crystallized in Latin American cultural history at the moment in 1845 when a contemporary of Alberdi's, Domingo Faustino Sarmiento (1811–88), also from Argentina, published *Facundo*, the story of a provincial *caudillo* and leader of an army of irregular soldiers. In this book, Sarmiento ostensibly sets out to express his dislike of this *hombre de campo*, Facundo Quiroga, and appears to side with the 'civilized' city-dwellers who consider themselves superior to the 'savage' countrymen. However, his high regard for what he thought of as the Argentinian's autochtonous (non-European, non-Spanish) values is evident in his admiration for the skills and courage of the *gaucho*, the cowboy of the pampas who despises the sedentary life and engages in a struggle for survival in completely natural surroundings.

This theme – the opposition between 'civilization' and 'barbarism' – became a leitmotif in Latin American writing for more than a century, and is reflected indirectly in some of the leading artists and writers of twentieth-century Latin America, much of whose work reveals a preoccupation with the issue of how 'European', 'Hispanic' or 'American' Latin Americans should be. Generalizations conceal the complexity and diversity of the cultural production of this vast and varied territory, with its huge population. Nonetheless, a preoccupation with the issue of dictatorship and/or the influence of European thinking are reflected in, among other work, the novels and stories of major authors such as the Argentinians Jorge Luis Borges (see Feature 1.7) and Julio Cortázar, the Colombian Gabriel García Márquez, the Peruvian Mario Vargas Llosa and the Cuban Alejo Carpentier. There is no doubt that some novelists are avowedly American in orientation rather than European, including, for instance, Mariano Azuela and Juan Rulfo in Mexico, and Jorge Icaza in Ecuador. By the same token, there are major literary figures from Latin America who have produced poetry imbued with a sense of the multiple ethnicity characteristic of certain parts of that continent (e.g. Nicolás Guillén from Cuba or Ernesto Cardenal from Nicaragua). The majority of the writings of the cultural elite, however, have been Eurocentric in that they have reflected European cultural concerns, at least until relatively recently.

At the same time, one of the key characteristics of Latin American identity is the strength and depth of the process of racial intermixing that has taken place there since early colonial times. The first settlers in Latin America were predominantly male, with only a small percentage of women, so that relationships between European males and indigenous women soon became an established pattern. This process of miscegenation ultimately had positive consequences in terms of its contribution to forming bonds between the races, although there were very likely some immediate *negative* consequences in terms of the exploitative nature of the relations between the sexes at the time. A possible long-term negative consequence of the imbalance between dominant male partners and the relatively powerless females may be the *machismo* which has been a recognized feature of much of Latin American society, where male chauvinist attitudes have only recently begun to be undermined. Contact between the races included the mixing that took place with people of African origin. Most black people in Latin America have their origins in the groups of Africans imported as slaves to serve colonists over the course of two centuries. The pattern of settlement and colonization was such, however, that out of these basic stocks emerged a mix which produced *mestizos* (people of mixed European and indigenous blood), *mulattos* (i.e. the product of European and African blood), and other combinations and gradations of different types. Such intermingling was quite unlike the dominant pattern in the British colonies, for example, where there tended to be a rigid separation between the foreign colonial presence and the broad mass of the indigenous population (e.g. in India, Kenya or Nigeria). It was also unlike the pattern of European settlement in most of North America, where the trend was for entire settler families to occupy the new territories, and where a policy of reducing Indian communities to a minimum was brutally – and successfully – carried out. However, we should not imagine that an idyllic, peaceful or egalitarian coexistence was the norm in Latin American colonies. As mentioned previously, indigenous communities were exploited and reduced, and mulattos and blacks suffered racial discrimination, even if there were no elaborate legislative structures in place to reinforce such practices. And the reality of creole social and political dominance was and still is a fact of life in Latin America.

The Spanish Crown had the good fortune to have been persuaded by Columbus and his sponsors to finance the initial expeditions. Spanish subjects carried the sword and the Cross to America in a process which brought considerable economic and cultural benefit to Spain, while establishing a type of linguistic hegemony over a vast new territory, a hegemony which continues to be advantageous to the so-called *madre patria* today.

The expanded European world-view which resulted from the Conquest could be said to have reinforced western cultural dominance to the point where the global influence of such thinking has become increasingly obvious. The indigenous cultures of America were connected – violently, and with much suffering and loss – to a wider cultural community. This dramatic encounter between two worlds is still working itself out in the twenty-first century, through a process of struggles and conflicts and the attempt to impose honourable values and democratic principles in the countries of Latin America. In the post-1992 era, Spain and Latin America appear to have rediscovered each other and perhaps to value more what is positive in the legacy of contact between the two, notwithstanding – or perhaps because of – the fact of Spain's increased commitment to Europeanism, and increased political and economic integration in the EU. Within the Union, Spain has often acted as a point of political and economic contact with Latin America, supporting cooperation projects between the EU and the subcontinent, and helping to ensure that Europe is continually reminded of the historical debt that she owes it.

Most contemporary Spanish people have gone beyond seeing Latin America as merely a rather large part of that 'glorious' collection of Spanish-speaking peoples who can be grouped under the label 'Hispanic', even if such sentiments are sometimes evident on occasions such as the annual celebrations surrounding the *Día de la Hispanidad*, or 'Columbus Day', 12 October. The Spanish perception of Latin America, when positive, still relies on a sense of a link based around language, although usually without colonial delusions. Certain Latin American countries – notably Argentina, Mexico and Cuba – occupy a special place in the hearts of Spaniards: in a 1998 survey, for instance, these three countries emerged at the top of the list of countries 'por el que más simpatía siente Vd.', as well as being the ones which were considered 'más amigo de España' (CIS 1998: 11-13). In the same survey, Argentina was deemed to be, by far, the one Latin American country 'más similar a España', just as it was also the one 'al que más le gustaría ir a vivir' (ibid.: 10, 12). In its negative aspects, the Spanish image of Latin America is that shared by other Europeans: of a subcontinent struggling with issues of development and social inequality and prone to political instability and economic insecurity – and this is true despite the political and economic progress achieved in Latin America in recent decades.

1.4 SPAIN AND EUROPEAN CULTURE

As with any other European country, there are dimensions to Spain's culture which give its Europeanness a Spanish 'accent'. From the appearance of its people (predominantly white Caucasians) to the languages spoken (predominantly derived from Latin), to the organization of its society, its art and literature, its industry and commerce, and to the nature of the political culture of the country, Spain is recognizably European. Like the travellers to Spain during the Romantic era, we could choose to accentuate the 'differences', the exotic and the unusual, in order to present an image of Spain which would distinguish it from other European countries. If we seek such exotica we can find them: in the flamenco music of Andalusia, in the existence of a non-Indo-European language, Basque (many of whose speakers would baulk even at being called 'Spanish'), or in customs and habits which are 'foreign' to the mainstream of European culture, such as bullfighting or the spectacular Holy Week processions. But, although these are important and relevant topics (some of which will be discussed later), we need also to focus on those aspects of Spanish life and culture which mark Spain as being similar to, rather than different from, the rest of Europe. Finding the correct balance between the study of difference and the recognition of similarity is an important part of the task faced by any student of Spain and things Spanish. Let us therefore focus (albeit briefly and somewhat arbitrarily) on some of the historical links between the culture of Spain and the wider culture of Europe, viz., Franco-Cantabrian cave paintings, Spain's Roman heritage and Islamic Spain.

1.4.1 Franco-Cantabrian art

Even in prehistoric times, Spain was linked culturally with the rest of Europe. If we take the longest possible temporal perspective on human culture in the Iberian Peninsula, we can appreciate that the development of early civilization in the Stone Age was a process that took place without any regard for what we now think of as national frontiers (or, indeed, concepts of Europeanness). We know that between about 10,000 and 30,000 years ago, parts of the Peninsula, and in particular the coastal regions, were inhabited by groups of people whose basic means of survival was hunting. These groups were related culturally to other people who have left evidence of their existence in the south of France and in other parts of Europe. Pictures painted by these Paleolithic people can be found in the caves which they inhabited, and these cave-paintings represent the earliest evidence of artistic activity in Spain. The Cantabrian region in the north is particularly rich in sites of this type, having over thirty of them. The best-known examples of this Franco-Cantabrian art are found in the caves of Altamira, at Santillana del Mar (Santander).

The Altamira pictures contain paintings of animals and symbols related to hunting, including bison, deer, boars and mountain goats, horns and skins. They also include engravings of human figures with heads of birds, as well as painted hand impressions and hand outlines. The dominant images are the colour pictures of large bison, executed in black, red and violet, for which the artists made use of the natural contours of the rock on which they were painting, using it to give the animals a sense of volume. The result is a series of pictures which express a tremendous vivacity and which reveal a high level of sophistication in the artists who produced them.

These paintings were produced by groups who lived at subsistence level, so that it is very unlikely that time would have been devoted to such activity unless the people concerned believed that it could have a practical purpose. According to Bozal (1973, I: 15), art had a magical function for these people, and, given that the pictures vibrate with such a sense of life, it was probably associated with rudimentary religious rituals believed to have the effect of improving the group's success at hunting. It is possible that such painting was carried out as part of a funeral rite, and, since paintings are frequently partly superimposed on one another, each may have been produced as part of a particular ceremony or act, and may have lost its significance at the termination of that ritual. The quality of the paintings would suggest that the artists were specialized in their work, and when we consider that specialization would not have been common in early civilizations of this type, this suggests that, for these groups of people, producing such pictures was a highly significant cultural acitivity.

1.4.2 Spain's Roman heritage

Millennia later, the Peninsula formed part of another cultural group, that of the Roman Empire, the dominant political and military power of its time. Two thousand years ago, Spain was an essential part of that empire, and Roman remains are now to be found virtually all over the country. The Latin spoken at the time was to evolve later into Castilian and the other vernacular languages of Spain (with the exception of Basque), and Roman administrative practices and forms of communication were to impact on the lives of the various Celtiberian groups who inhabited the territory. This included, for instance, the creation of roads, some of which remain to this day. One such is the *Vía de la Plata*, which was built to transport silver from the north of Spain to the south coast for shipment to Rome. This road originated in Gijón (Asturias), and passed through Oviedo, León, Astorga, Zamora, Salamanca, Cáceres, Mérida and Zafra, ending up in Seville. Later, in medieval times, during the heyday of the pilgrimages to Santiago de Compostela, the road was used by people travelling in the opposite direction, towards Galicia, from North Africa and the East.

The most outstanding architectural monument dating from Roman times, however, is probably the aqueduct at Segovia, a massive stone structure (28 metres wide and 800 metres long) used to convey water to the cities of the northern meseta. This is an outstanding work of engineering, which has lasted intact for 2000 years, and it is likely to outlast even major twentieth-century constructions, despite its erosion by atmospheric pollution.

Spain's link with this major European empire, centred in Rome, is further exemplified by Seneca the Younger (4BC–AD65), a 'Roman' writer and politician born in Córdoba. He lived in Rome from his early childhood and became heavily involved in public affairs. He was the leading intellectual figure of his period, particularly in the time of the Emperor Nero (AD54–68), and is now remembered for his plays and for his many essays on philosophy and morality. His pre-eminence during his lifetime provoked the enmity of some of his contemporaries, however, who secured his downfall and disgrace in AD65, when he was ordered to commit suicide. His writings constitute a significant body of work within the tradition of Classical Latin literature, and they formed a particularly influential part of Latin culture in the Middle Ages.

1.4.3 Al-Andalus

If we wish to identify a link between Spain and Europe which illustrates the positive contribution made by Spain, the impact of Al-Andalus – Muslim Spain – over a period of several centuries must be taken into account. Moorish control over Spanish lands began in the eighth century with the rapid conquest after 711 of large areas of the Peninsula, and the Muslim presence continued until the fall of the Kingdom of Granada in 1492. The territory of Al-Andalus expanded and contracted considerably during those seven centuries, but the period of greatest splendour occurred during the Omeya Caliphate under the Caliphs Abd al-Rahman III (912–61) and al-Hakam II (961–76). It was during this time that Córdoba became not only the focal point of a major Islamic empire stretching from Asia to the Iberian Peninsula, but also one of the most important centres of learning in Europe. It was to Córdoba that scholars came from France and England to study medicine, philosophy and science. While Europe generally languished in poverty and squalor, Al-Andalus was a cultured and sophisticated society. Both materially and intellectually, tenth-century Al-Andalus was more advanced than other contemporary societies: in Córdoba,

> there were half a million inhabitants, living in 113,000 houses. There were 700 mosques and 300 public baths spread throughout the city and its twenty-one suburbs. The streets were paved and lit. There were bookshops and more than seventy libraries.
>
> (Burke 1985: 38)

In the city's great central library there were over 400 000 titles, more than in the whole of France. Furthermore, major advances were achieved in the fields of law, mathematics, architecture and astronomy, and the writings of classical Greece and Rome were preserved in Arabic translations, to be mined eventually when Europe emerged from the Dark Ages at the beginning of the Renaissance period.

The contribution made by this learning towards the development of Europe is incalculable. In sum, in the words of Richard Fletcher:

> The creative role of Islamic Spain in the shaping of European intellectual culture is still not widely enough appreciated ... . Europe's lead in resourcefulness and creativity, the vital factor in the history of the world for the six centuries preceding our own, was founded in large part on intelligent grasping at opportunities offered by the civilisation of Islam; and that proffer came through Spain. Islamic Spain was not just an exotic bit of orientalia quaintly moored in the Iberian peninsula which has left behind some pretty flotsam for tourists to take photographs of. It played a significant part in the formation of the Old World's civilisation.
>
> (Fletcher 1992: 8)

Most notably, there was a far greater level of cultural tolerance in Al-Andalus – tolerance between Muslim, Jew and Christian – than in Christian Spain or in the rest of Europe at this time. Islamic Spain offered Europe technical and scientific advances and an example of tolerant coexistence, its contributions ranging from something as specific as the mathematical concept of zero to the broad contribution of facilitating the emergence of the European Renaissance. Islamic society was far from perfect – it was a very unequal society, and one devoted to warfare – but, when compared with the European society of the time, at least during the tenth century and probably for some time before and after, it achieved a level of culture and civilization beyond what was general in Europe.

Figure 2: The Mosque at Córdoba. Córdoba Cathedral was built in 1253, incorporating a pre-existing mosque which dates back to the late eighth century; the mosque, in turn, had been built on the site of a Visigothic church. The mix of Christian and Islamic styles – and the tension between them – is evident in the combination of elements from the two traditions to be found throughout the building.

Spain's contribution to Europe extends far beyond the artistic and scientific achievements of Al-Andalus. Over the centuries, Spain's input into European culture has included the production of the first European novel, *Don Quixote*, and the artistic achievements of, for instance, Velázquez, in the seventeenth century, or Pablo Picasso, the most influential artist of the twentieth century. And further examples of how Spain has been a locus of European culture also abound, whether we think of the art of El Greco (the Greek Domenico Teotocopulos, who lived and worked in Spain from 1575 till his death in 1614), or of the many Golden Age poets (Garcilaso de la Vega, Juan Boscán, Luis de Góngora, etc.), whose work was imbued with the spirit of the Italian Renaissance, although, once again, what they produced would have had its own distinct flavour.

The examples cited here have been confined to the area of 'high art'. One could equally mention the influence, at the level of popular culture, of the *gaita* music of Galicia or the *flamenco* of Andalusia. Links between Spain and the rest of Europe have been manifold through the ages, and, although the place occupied by Spain – both geographically, next to Africa, and culturally, with its tradition of cultural multiplicity – has necessarily been unique and different, the country has played a significant role in European history and has been instrumental in taking European culture to other parts of the world.

The example of Spain reminds us that change and diversity are as much a part of Europe as they are a part of any other dynamic cultural entity: there is, therefore, no one monolithic 'European culture' which could be defined in terms of ethnicity, religion, territory or cultural production. Europe is a fluid concept, at times implicitly defined in cultural terms, at other times assumed to fit within certain administrative and political boundaries. However the frontier between Europe and 'non-Europe' is defined, Spain clearly belongs with Europe, and Europe without Spain would be unthinkable.

1.5 EUROPEANISM AND ORTEGA Y GASSET

In 1985, on the eve of Spain's joining the European Community, her Minister for Defence, Narcís Serra, said that becoming a member would mean 'Spain's return to where it belongs historically, culturally and geographically: the West European world' (quoted in Heywood 1995: 270). The very use of the word 'return' in what Serra said betrays an interesting truth about Spain's integration into the Community: that in fact Spain had in some sense become 'separated' from the Europe of which it had previously formed such a significant part.

The significance of its earlier involvement was political and military as well as artistic and cultural: Spain in the sixteenth century had possessions which included parts of Italy, the Low Countries and Austria in Europe, along with its vast colonies in the New World. A combination of circumstances, including external military and political hostility and weak territorial integration internally, along with poor management of its resources, led to a severe decline in status during the seventeenth century. From that period on, Spain was increasingly viewed as being on the margins of Europe: the major centres of cultural and political activity were located elsewhere on the continent, particularly in England and France. Both the political upheavals which led to the disappearance of the old European absolutist regimes in the late eighteenth century and the industrial revolutions of the nineteenth were events that Spain witnessed from a distance, so that the country felt itself to be outside that arena, just as other Europeans viewed Spain as being somehow 'different' from the European mainstream.

There were, of course, real ways in which Spain *was* different from the European mainstream: traditional social attitudes persisted when changes were taking place in other countries, the country clung determinedly to an orthodox Catholicism in the face of Protestant reforms which swept over much of northern Europe from the sixteenth century, and there was a historical connection with Islam which turned Spain, for many Europeans, into a country closely identified with Africa. In the nineteenth century, Spanish people came to see Europe as a symbol of modernity and progress. As such, it was viewed either as desirable and conducive to social and economic advancement, or as threatening and alien to the true spirit and traditional values of their country. Most intellectuals recognized the centrality of Europe to Spain and urged their compatriots to learn from European social and political models, although there were also those who felt that the distinctiveness of Spain's character was something which should be maintained and defended. By the end of the nineteenth century, when Spain lost the last of her colonies in a disastrous war with the USA in 1898, *europeísmo* – an intellectual stance which favoured closer approximation to mainstream European values – seemed the inevitable direction for social and political modernization to take.

The philosopher José Ortega y Gasset (1883–1955), for instance, was an ardent *europeizante*. Ortega saw 'Europeanization' as a means for resolving Spain's problems; but he was also concerned about the direction that Europe in general was taking. He had no sympathy with the notion that Spain should be thought of as occupying a special position separate from Europe. He himself had spent several years studying in Germany and had been highly influenced by major European thinkers, especially Heidegger and Husserl. He saw Europe as having a natural role to play as cultural leader of the world, although he regretted what he saw as the decline being experienced in Europe in the early twentieth century. His ideas about this decline were crystallized in his book *La rebelión de las masas* (1929), in which he lamented the lack of a well-educated group of leaders within European society who would give Europe a direction and a sense of destiny which he felt it had lost. He believed he was witnessing the rise of what he called 'mass-man', people who had all the conveniences of the modern world and a higher standard of living than had been possible previously, but who were uneducated and uncultured, intellectually lazy and materially spoilt, and who were thus unfit to provide European society with the leadership it needed. With society thus rudderless, there would be a danger that only mediocre or fanatical and totalitarian leadership would prevail. The points he makes in connection with this idea are subtle and complex, and, at times, he appears to espouse an elitist conception of society, since he puts much emphasis on the need for enlightened, educated leadership. However, his view was that the difference between a superior minority and the broad mass of people was not a difference based on social class, but merely a difference in sensibility and in the degree of effort that people were willing to put into improving their society. The kind of fragmented, drifting society that Ortega believed predominated in Europe generally he also detected in Spain itself. But if Spain were to lift itself out of the morass which he and others believed it to be in, the only option, in Ortega's view, was to identify more closely with Europe generally.

The flaw which Ortega believed he detected in modern sensibility was excessive individualism: true meanings came, in his view, from the interaction between self and circumstance. Without context, neither an individual person nor a nation could achieve their destiny. This implied that Spain must recognize its relationship with the rest of Europe as being part of what gave it a meaning and a purpose. In Ortega's view, both the development of his own country and the progress of Europe as a whole were part of a project that needed to be undertaken, and, in both cases, success would only be achieved by dedication and hard work.

At the turn of the twentieth century, this theme of Europeanization was gaining currency and numerous influential books and articles were published, urging Spaniards to become 'more European' and thereby to bring about the regeneration of their country. Among these was Joaquín Costa's *Regeneración y europeización de España* (1900), and it was largely on the basis of Costa's book that Ortega developed his ideas on the identification of Europe with regeneration. Such regeneration would be a process whereby Spain achieved the success she deserved, not by imitating other European countries such as England, France or Italy, but by developing a new form of culture which would be different from the cultures of those countries and would be truly Spanish:

> What do we care about foreign things, the number of ethnic and historical forms that culture may take in other places? Precisely when we postulate the europeanization of Spain, we want nothing other than the obtention of a new form of culture different from French culture, different from German. . . . What we want is the Spanish interpretation of the world.
>
> (quoted in Marias 1970: 169)

Ortega identified Europe with the idea of regeneration and the ongoing project of building on the age-old traditions of philosophical and scientific thinking which had ultimately led to the technological advances of the modern world. Europe was, for him, not the *things* which resulted from these technical advances – the railways, the good hotels, and even the laws and the good police force – but the science which lay behind them. As Julián Marías (1970: 167) puts it in a summary of Ortega's thoughts: 'Europe is not civilization, but that from which all this comes.' And Spain can only be regenerated, according to Ortega, if she takes on this process of Europeanization:

> Regeneration is inseparable from europeanization: this is why, as soon as the reconstructive emotion, or anguish, or shame, and yearning were felt, the europeanizing idea came into being. Regeneration is the desire; europeanization is the means of satisfying that desire. Truly it has been seen very clearly from the beginning that Spain was the problem and Europe the solution.
>
> (quoted in Marias 1970: 166)

Ortega continued to be an ardent Europeanist throughout his life. In the wake of World War II, Ortega was more convinced than ever of the special role that Europe was destined to have in the world, but the shame of the war had, in his view, exposed the dangers of a narrow-minded nationalism, a nationalism without a sense of direction and without a worthy national project which would ennoble it. For their nationalism to be a positive and creative force, European nations needed to recognize that they were European, i.e. that they belonged to that wider cultural realm which was Europe, and that that element of their identity needed to be acknowledged.

Ortega's endorsement of Europeanism, although it was more committed and more fully thought-out than that of others, was certainly not unique. As suggested earlier, during the course of the nineteenth and twentieth centuries, most progressive Spanish intellectuals favoured a similar approach, and lamented the isolation of Spain from the international scene generally and from Europe in particular. But, as Preston and Smyth (1985: 25) have pointed out, some Spanish intellectuals were far more inclined to emphasize Spain's differences from Europe and to mythologize its 'special' position. These included, for instance, Miguel de Unamuno (1864–1936), the novelist Benito Pérez Galdós (1843–1920), who talked about 'the image of a nation *sui generis*, a natural force uncontaminated by Europe'; and, in the twentieth century, the intellectual Américo Castro (1885–1972), who maintained that 'the Spaniards lived alongside Europe, but ultimately they were . . . alien to it'. In the period when Spain was ruled by the dictator Francisco Franco, European ideas were treated with suspicion by his regime, and the traces of Europeanism in Spain were officially reviled by the ruling military, who claimed that the cultural principles espoused by European countries generally were 'un-Spanish' and alien, especially with respect to religion and the organization of the state. These attitudes were part of the attempt by the regime in the 1940s and 1950s to inculcate a xenophobia which would set Spanish people against other Europeans, the aim being ultimately to ensure the survival of the dictatorship through the rejection of democratic ideas. By the 1960s, although their head of state continued to express hostility to the outside world, the vast majority of Spaniards had come to accept that closer integration with the rest of Europe was not only inevitable but also economically and politically desirable.

1.6 INTEGRATION INTO EUROPE

Although drawing closer to Europe is not the same thing as becoming a member of the EU, there is no more powerful signal of Spain's rejection of isolationism than the integration of the country into European structures. Spain's entry into the European Economic Community (EEC), as it was then known, was marked by protracted and difficult negotiations. Since then the country has consistently followed pro-European policies, and opinion polls have repeatedly shown that Spaniards are among the most enthusiastic supporters of the notion of European unification.

Some of the key steps along the path to Spain's integration into the structures of the Community are as follows:

1962 An initial application for membership of the EEC from the Spanish Minister for Foreign Affairs was rejected on the grounds that the Community could not accept as a member any state whose government was not democratically elected.

1970 A purely economic agreement was negotiated between Spain and the EEC. This allowed for significant reductions in tariffs on goods traded between the two, with tariffs for goods exported from Spain to the EEC reduced by 26 per cent, and, in recognition of the poor state of the Spanish economy, a reduction of between 40 per cent and 60 per cent on tariffs for goods imported into Spain from the EEC.

1977 In the wake of the first free general elections in the new democracy, the Spanish government applied officially in July to join the institutions of the Community. The application received a non-committal response from the EEC countries: there were particular concerns over the possible economic impact of the entry of Spanish agricultural goods (fruit, vegetables, olive oil, wine) into the Community.

1978 Despite these misgivings, approval in principle was given in December for the entry of three new members, Spain, Portugal and Greece. However, it was clear that the Community would need to come to some agreement on the management of its own economic affairs before negotiations on entry could be completed.

1980   In June, France called for negotiations on Spanish entry to be frozen until the EEC had finalized plans for reform of its economic structures. The French continued to resist Spanish entry over the next four years, but the Spanish effort to join continued.

1982   Spain made a major concession in the negotiations, by agreeing that Value Added Tax would be imposed in Spain immediately after her entry into the Community. In June, Spain became a member of NATO; although not officially related to the negotiations for entry into the EEC, this move was seen as an indication of Spanish willingness to cooperate as fully as possible with other European countries, since most of the EEC countries were members of this military alliance.

1985   The Accession Treaty was finally signed in Madrid on 12 March, although some of the conditions stipulated for Spanish entry were quite harsh. For example, Spanish fruit, vegetables and olive oil would not come within the remit of the Community's Common Agricultural Policy (CAP) until ten years after the country joined the EEC, which meant that Spanish farmers would not enjoy the advantage of price supports in those areas for that length of time.

1986   Spain officially joined the Community on 1 January. The immediate economic consequences of entry were difficult: not only had adjustments to be made in relation to the agricultural products mentioned above and the fishing industry – Spain's entry had the effect of increasing the Community's fishing fleet by almost half – but Spanish industry generally had to introduce radical changes in order to modernize and streamline its activities. Older, more traditional sectors such as steel and shipbuilding suffered major consequences, such as loss of employment, company closures, forced early retirements, etc. In the aftermath of entry, and as a result of this streamlining and of increased foreign investment, however, Spain's economy experienced a boom, and the country generally was euphoric about entry into the EEC and about its future prospects.

Spain has been one of the more enthusiastic members of the EU since the mid-1980s, and Spanish people have repeatedly emerged as more pro-European than most EU citizens, with an above average level of commitment to further European integration. In November 1999, for example, Spain came in fifth place (of the 15 EU countries) in terms of its citizens' support for EU membership (European Commission 2000: 26).

Spain has played an increasingly important role in the EU. The first phase of European Economic and Monetary Union (EMU) was agreed during the Spanish presidency at the Madrid summit of 1989, and it was the Spanish Minister for Finance, Carlos Solchaga, who secured agreement from the EU members to postpone the introduction of the second phase until 1 January 1994. In October 1996, the Spanish Prime Minister, José María Aznar, proposed that the EU should become a single jurisdiction to facilitate the pursuit of criminals across European frontiers by the various national police forces, and he even advocated that Europol should be developed into a federal police force within the Union. In the late 1990s, Spain managed to fulfil the stringent economic criteria laid down for participation in the EMU – including strict limits for inflation, interest rates and the public debt – and was among the group of countries which set up the Euro-zone area in January 1999.

FEATURE: BORGES, A UNIVERSAL LATIN AMERICAN?

The Argentinian author Jorge Luis Borges (1899–1986) embodied the connection between European and Hispanic culture, as he was a Latin American writing in Spanish, but one who was profoundly influenced by European culture. He is best remembered for his short stories, especially those which combine elements of realistic detail with mind-boggling concepts drawn from his imagination and his readings in philosophy and literature. Two of the best-known stories (both contained in the anthology *Ficciones*, first published in 1944) are 'Tlön, Uqbar, Orbis Tertius' and 'The circular ruins'.

'Tlön, Uqbar, Orbis Tertius' is the story of an attempt to create an imaginary world, one in which the basic assumptions which we make about how things are and how things happen do not apply. Drawing on the ideas of the eighteenth-century philosopher George Berkeley, Borges invents a 'world', Tlön, in which the relationship between cause and effect does not hold: in it, it is impossible to know for certain that anything really exists, we have no guarantee that our perceptions of the world are anything more than mere perceptions. For the people of Tlön, 'el mundo … no es un concurso de objetos en el espacio; es una serie heterogénea de actos independientes. Es sucesivo, temporal, no espacial' (Borges 1972: 21). Borges takes the core idea of Berkeley's idealism and manufactures a fantastic tale around it, carrying the basic notion to an absurd conclusion, all the time toying playfully with his own story and with its various elements.

'The circular ruins' opens with the depiction of an anonymous man arriving at a clearing in a jungle and setting about the 'task' of creating a man – a task of invention which the protagonist undertakes by dreaming. In a succession of dreams, he manages to conjure up, in detail, another human being. As is typical of the stories in *Ficciones*, the fictitious individual who is the product of the man's imagination is somehow projected into the 'real' world of the story which is being written by Borges, and the dreamer sends his invented 'son' off into the world, hoping that he will never realize that he is not real and only the figment of someone else's imagination. At the end of the story, the dreamer himself suffers the fate of discovering his own lack of reality, and is shocked and horrified at this revelation.

Borges manages to surprise us with his ability to invent fictional worlds, but he does so self-consciously, playfully mocking himself and his own role as creator of these fictions. He delights in manipulating notions of space and time, but his principal concern is with the ways in which we can be surprised by our own identities and with undermining the idea that the reality we see around us is solid and immutable.

Borges' thinking was essentially European. For him, the intellectual tradition of Latin America was the European tradition. He had little knowledge of, or interest in, the pre-Columbian cultures of the continent. As a youth he was educated in Europe and the many references he makes to authors who actually lived – as opposed to his numerous inventions – reveal this European bias. Being both European and Latin American may have given him precisely the opportunity he needed to imagine himself as a 'universal' writer, concerned with basic universal themes, and adept at selecting the most appropriate and interesting details from the immense body of world literature and culture.

READINGS: JULIÁN MARÍAS, 'RAZA', AND VICENTE VERDÚ, 'EUROPA, PATRIA QUERIDA'

1. Julián Marías, 'Raza'

In the following passage from his book *Hispanoamérica* (1986), the Spanish philosopher Julián Marías (b. 1914) looks at Latin America through Spanish eyes – i.e. through European eyes – and reflects on the notions of race and ethnicity. Witnessing the ethnic diversity of Peru, he is reminded of the limitations of European definitions of mankind, but acknowledges how our ethnic identity correlates, in many contexts, with our cultural and material destiny in life.

El racismo es, según se mire, una teoría falsa, una estupidez o un crimen. De acuerdo. Pero no vayamos a olvidar que hay razas. También el nacionalismo es un error, con frecuencia grotesco, que no excluye la realidad de las naciones. Lo malo son los 'ismos', es decir, el espíritu de abstracción, que esquematiza, desorbita y falsea los datos y los problemas reales.

He pensado esto en el Perú, donde se me ha revelado con extraña fuerza esa misteriosa realidad que es la raza. El hombre olvida demasiado su animalidad; bueno está saber que lo que en el hombre es propiamente humano no se puede reducir a lo biológico; pero a condición de no perder de vista el animal en que vamos metidos, que, en cierto modo, también somos. Y esto se advierte cuando se topa con otro modo de animalidad, es decir, con otra raza. Los latinos – eso que se llama latinos – solemos parecer a los hombres nórdicos unos animales vivarachos y gesticulantes, de negra mirada cálida y un temblor inquieto en las manos que aletean al hablar. Tal vez simios. Yo descubrí no hace mucho, en un coche de ferrocarril, entre Munich y Heidelberg, el parentesco de los escandinavos con el corzo, el ciervo y el reno. Un matrimonio sueco mostraba su refinada humanidad inserta y engastada en las líneas ágiles, herbívoras, huidizas, un poco inexpresivas, de Bambi y Falina. Y ahora, en el Perú – en Lima, en el Cuzco, en Ollantaitambo –, la cosa es más grave y más dramática.

No; no me refiero al 'indigenismo', ni a lo que se llama la condición social de los indios en relación con los mestizos o los blancos. Eso también es grave, pero no tanto. Pienso en esa condición circunstancial del hombre, en virtud de la cual se encuentra adscrito a un modo de ser, a una situación; histórica, social, económica; y antes todavía, racial. Al contraste de los indios, de seca piel cobriza, de rasgos inmóviles – allí sólo tiembla y se estremece el suelo –, de ojos cuajados en muerta negrura hace tres mil años, se ve hasta qué punto está el hombre – ese drama inquieto, ese proyecto irreal que quiere ser y no es; esa pretensión novelesca, día a día inventada –, hasta qué punto, digo, está empastado en su raza, moldeado en ella, vertido, desde luego, el hirviente licor alcohólico de su afán en el barro de un ánfora precisa. Ya está, para siempre, indio quechua, negro, chino – o blanco –; pero esto apenas lo advertimos: sólo al vernos en la oscura obsidiana ('espejo de incas') de nuestros hermanos sujetos a distinto yugo étnico.

Los niños oprimen el corazón. ¿Simplemente porque son pequeños, tiernos e inermes? ¿Acaso porque andan descalzos e indeciblemente sucios por las callejas del Cuzco, a 3.300 metros, o miran con ojitos asustados desde la bolsa en que los lleva a su espalda una hermanilla minúscula? No; no es eso, no es sólo eso. No siempre son pobres, ni sucios; los indios son con frecuencia coroneles con seis galones de oro, sable y casco de acero; o millonarios; los niños nos miran a veces desde las ventanillas de un Cadillac. Pero al verlos, en lujosa calle limeña, en la aldeíta perdida entre los Andes – como en un cuento –, o cuando van a leer, con graciosa seriedad, en la deliciosa biblioteca infantil, pienso que ese puro futuro, esa indecisa irrealidad que hay que inventar, esa esperanza, tiene ya pie forzado: indio quechua, mulato, zambo, 'salto atrás'... los doce o catorce nombres que los peruanos conocen y usan para expresar ese destino inapelable.

¿Y nosotros? También, también. También estamos ya adscritos al ser 'latino' o escandinavo, ario impuro, celtíbero o lo que se quiera; pero al permanecer interiores a nuestra raza, la olvidamos y vivimos como si fuésemos simplemente hombres. Y de este error de óptica, de esta ingenuidad que ignora la limitación de la propia raza nace el racismo.

(Marías 1986: 12–14)

2. Vicente Verdú, 'Europa, patria querida'

In the following article, written in early 1999, at the moment when Spain and most of the other countries of the EU took a further major step towards European monetary union through the creation of a common currency, the Euro, the Spanish writer Vicente Verdú (b. 1942) reflected on the theme of European unity and on how real a *cultural* unity there may or may not be in Europe.

Uno de los mitos mejor construidos en nuestro presente es el de la europeidad.

Renovado, flamante, económicamente atractivo, lustrosamente internacional, panorámicamente ameno, el mito de ser europeo ha superado al anhelo español de pertenecer a Europa. Ser europeo es un grado de la traslación más; o un simulacro de transustanciación mediante el cual la españolidad se revalida, como la moneda, por una entidad común y a estrenar junto a los demás colegas. Ahora bien, ¿efectivamente es así? Los europeos, no en cuanto divisas sino en cuanto ciudadanos, ¿han llegado a un nivel de convertibilidad apto para la estabilidad de los intercambios? Obviamente, no. Ni en las costumbres, ni en la axiología, ni en los gustos, ni en las maneras de bailar, de casarse o de cenar, los del sur son igual a los del norte, los del este a los del oeste y los del centro a todos los demás.

Hay una línea, espiritualmente trazada, que divide con nitidez el área llamada del vino del área de la cerveza. Los consumos reales de uno u otra no tienen ya mucho que ver, pero la idiosincrasia sí. El pub irlandés o la cervecería alemana disponen configuraciones relacionales distintas a la de las tabernas españolas y portuguesas. Las tapas, por ejemplo, en España hacen entender un consumo entretenido de la bebida, interrumpen la secuencia de los tragos y dan a saber que la reunión de la barra no tiene el fin único de consumir alcohol sino de reunirse en torno a él. La compulsiva manera con la que los británicos y los alemanes se emborrachan ha sido inconcebible hasta hace poco en España y sólo ahora se sigue por los más jóvenes que, como en otras cosas, recibe con mayor facilidad la influencia anglosajona que propagan los media. En Italia, en España, en Francia o en Portugal la cultura del vino emborracha de una manera aparentemente menos suicida de lo que hace presumir la borrachera de cerveza que, en algún momento, escenifica no sólo la idea de una intoxicación sino también la voluntad de ahogarse.

Los mediterráneos se parecen en un vitalismo dionisiaco que enciende mejor el vino, y también en una luz de extroversión que dista de hallarse en Helsinki. A la altura de la cerveza, en el meridiano del Tirol aproximadamente, empieza un catálogo de argumentos familiares que difieren sustantivamente de los que se registran bajo esa cota. La familia es más decisiva al sur y en esto baña de una realidad afectiva peculiar a una y otra zona. En España, en la Italia meridional o en Portugal, los miembros de una casa se sienten parte de ese grupo con una intensidad que raramente desaparece del centro de las vidas. La enfermedad, la penuria, el paro, la adversidad matrimonial, tiene en el sur asistencias familiares que se han ido disipando en el norte. Los hijos en Holanda, en Bélgica o en Alemania se emancipan cuando van a la Universidad mientras en España o en Portugal, en muchos casos, no acaban de emanciparse nunca. En Italia, como en España, abundan las pequeñas empresas familiares en las que participan los hijos, los hermanos, los cuñados, los primos, mientras esta fórmula va deshaciéndose a medida que se escala en la orientación septentrional.

La familia está fuera y dentro de la empresa, se encuentra presente en el ocio y en el trabajo, en los viajes y entre las ocupaciones o los deberes, lo que en poco se parece a lo que se siente en Finlandia. Los divorcios han aumentado en España, pero su tasa es de una proporción ínfima si se la compara con los de Alemania o los de Francia. Como consecuencia, la composición de familias mecano, formadas con hijos de uno y otro matrimonio, son allí más frecuentes y las clases de arraigo menos pendientes de la parentela que de los intereses funcionales. O, simplemente, de los intereses.

El dinero cuenta en todas partes, pero hay partes donde esa importancia se disimula menos y, lejos de pertenecer a las cuestiones rebozadas de pudor, su condición aparece desnuda en las propuestas. Los protestantes se han liberado antes que los católicos del sentido negativo de lo material y, en concreto, de la consideración de la vileza monetaria. Para las separaciones, para las uniones, para las ocupaciones, el dinero cuenta más a sus allegados, a sus tierras y a sus viviendas que los del norte, más portátiles, traslaticios o internacionalistas, según se estime. Los dramas del cambio de domicilio, de pareja o de ocupación son más frecuentes y en consecuencia menos dramáticos que en el sur. También, en consecuencia, los delitos están teñidos de esta circunstancia. En el sur se mata más por celos, por el terruño, por defender lo establecido que se asocia a una identidad irrenunciable. En el norte, la identidad se va obteniendo cada vez con mayor celeridad, no de lo recibido, sino de lo que se adquiere. Y en esa dirección camina la globalización del mundo y discurrirá, sin duda, el porvenir de Europa.

(*El País Digital*, www.elpais/p/d/especial/domingo/euro6.htm)

FURTHER READING

Beardsell, P. R., *Europe and Latin America: the identity of the other* (Manchester, Manchester University Press, 1996).
A useful introduction to the cultural links between Europe and Latin America.

Elliott, J. H. (ed.), *El mundo hispánico: civilización e imperio; Europa y América; pasado y presente* (Barcelona, Crítica, 1991).
Offers an interesting account of Spain's imperial relations with the New World.

Fletcher, Richard A., *Moorish Spain* (London, Weidenfeld & Nicolson, 1992).
Offers an interesting and very comprehensive account of Muslim Spain.

Ministerio de Administraciones Públicas, *Directorio de la Unión Europea*, http://www.map.es/directorio/union.html
Useful information on the EU in Spanish.

Ross, Christopher, *Spain 1812–1996: modern history for modern languages* (London, Arnold, 2000).
A very accessible account of two centuries in Spanish history.

Williamson, Edwin, *The Penguin History of Latin America* (Harmondsworth, Penguin, 1992).
A handy single-volume history of Latin America.

2

Spanishness: How Spanish are the Spaniards?

2.1 INTRODUCTION: SPAIN AND 'NATION-NESS'

Cultural boundaries do not coincide with the frontiers of the nation-state, and this is even more obvious in our age of globalization in business and communications. The developments in communications media mean that people – the young in particular – are more likely to think of themselves as citizens of the world or of a supranational entity such as 'Europe' than they used to. This is the case for Spain as much as it is for anywhere else.

And yet we must not exaggerate the decline in allegiance to national identity. The tragedy of ethnic conflict in the Balkans and the triumph of the French soccer team in the 1998 World Cup are examples of the continuing validity of national and ethnic sentiment. The former was an instance where the boundaries of ethnic identities had failed to coincide with the frontiers of a nation-state, while the latter was a case where sporting success reawakened patriotic sentiment in a country with well-fixed borders (although players from French overseas territories added an innovative, multicultural dimension to the team, to which the French people responded enthusiastically). These examples remind us of the reality of the concept of national identity, however complex and open to multiple interpretations that concept may be. Being 'French' is different from being 'Spanish' or 'English', even if nationals of France, Spain and England can be very similar to each other, and even if, within each of those states, there are many who are indifferent to the notion of such nationalities, or even hostile to it.

The question 'How Spanish are the Spaniards?' is an immensely difficult one; in effect, it asks for a description of 'Spanishness'; an assessment of the degree to which the label 'Spanish' can be applied to Spaniards and the various aspects of their culture with which we are concerned. The complicated issue of Spanishness can reasonably be addressed by focusing on the concept of nationalism in the Spanish context and by asking what Spaniards are like. The three main sections in this chapter, therefore, address, respectively, the meaning of Spain as a nation; some attempts – both by Spaniards and by overseas visitors – to articulate what Spanish people are like; and the emergence in recent decades of Spain as a 'fully mature' nation in all its modernity.

For historical reasons, the very notion of 'Spanishness' has something of a bad name. Most importantly, this is because of the attempts that were made during the Franco years to manufacture a kind of 'glorious Spanishness', resonant of imperial greatness and suffused with spuriously heroic virtues, military values and macho supremacy: Spain as the guardian of noble traditions, setting its face against the decadence of the rest of the developed world. Such ideas have now been fairly comprehensively discredited, and there is an increased appreciation among Spaniards of the worth of other countries and cultures. But one of the curious – if understandable – negative effects of this rejection of Francoist propaganda is that it has become unpopular to express *any* appreciation of Spanishness at all. It seems much easier in the new Spain to articulate an allegiance to Catalan or Basque identity, or a fondness for being Galician or even Andalusian, than to express an attachment to (much less, a pride in) being Spanish. While this can be readily understood as a consequence of the dominance of a new set of democratic values based around equality, fairness and the absence of coercion, to talk of 'Spanishness' as if it were the *españolada* of Francoist propaganda or the anachronistic evocation of Hispanic imperialism is surely to miss the point. First and foremost, being a Spaniard entails belonging – with stronger or weaker bonds of attachment – to a community which calls itself Spanish. This community is an historical and cultural reality which has created an identity with a certain currency in the wider community of nations, states and cultures. As a nation, Spain is, in the term coined by Benedict Anderson (1983: 6), an 'imagined political community . . . imagined as both inherently limited and sovereign'. Better, perhaps, to say that there is an imagined community which can call itself 'Spanish'. Its historical background is linked to the spread of the Spanish language, the centralization of territorial administration in nineteenth-century Spain and the imposition of a centralized educational system delivered through Spanish.

With Anderson's definition of 'nation', we are a long way from the notion that there are characteristics and qualities which are quintessentially Spanish or French, German or British. While we may recognize that certain nationalities tend more than others to behave in certain ways, discussions of the 'character' of a nation or a people are unlikely to be conducted in the same way as before. In the eighteenth and nineteenth centuries, there was a trend among certain linguists and philosophers (e.g. Johann Gottfried Herder and Alexander von Humboldt) to equate one culture with one language and one group of people, and to see aspects of the people's character in their language, and characteristics of the language in the people. On this view, the German language and its people could be dubbed rigid and formal, French meant subtle reasoning, and English was synonymous with hypocrisy, pragmatism and diffidence! Spaniards (and their language) could be deemed passionate, conservative, proud and individualistic. And so it went, for each cultural group.

Such characterization leads almost inevitably to over-simplistic national stereotyping, where groups of people are thought of in reductionist terms as having a set number of qualities, and as being inevitably prone to certain weaknesses: the 'excitable' Italians, the 'drunken' Irish, the 'devious' Moroccans. That the picture presented by a stereotype is inaccurate is surely self-evident; it is true, nonetheless, that the caricatures they present are frequently harmless. But they are invariably misleading, and sometimes can be very dangerous indeed. Here is how one expert on interculturality articulates that danger: 'Stereotypes limit our understanding of human behavior and of intercultural discourse because they limit our view of human activity to just one or two salient dimensions and consider those to be the whole picture' (Barna 1993: 156). It is worth remembering, however, that some degree of stereotyping, or at least, an oversimplified representation of what other people are like, is inevitable and may be a natural human stratagem: in a complex world, language – and our apprehension of other people – require simplicity. Since we cannot know everything about anything or anyone, we need to be able to operate with somewhat simplified conceptions of cultures and ethnic groups; at least for certain purposes, we function on the basis of rough approximations and broad generalizations. No matter how useful such simplifications may be, however, thinking in stereotypes is potentially disastrous when combined with situations of conflict and inter-group competition, and can exacerbate such conflicts to the point where they become violent. Seeing economic migrants one-dimensionally as simply a threat to 'our' jobs can precipitate racist behaviour towards those migrants; seeing Jewish people as alien money-grubbers can precipitate massive extermination and the ultimate violence of war, based on irrational mass hatred and acquiescence in evil.

The seed of conflict can be as simple and undramatic a mistake as misreading another person's culture or attributing motivations to the other person that are not actually there. There are many such clichés associated with Spanish culture, and many icons, images and cultural products which are treated in a stereotyped fashion as being 'essentially Spanish'. Misreading things such as bullfighting, *zarzuela*, flamenco, *turrón*, El Cid or even sandy beaches and interpreting them as being what Spain is 'really' about may seem merely a trivial error, and is just that in most circumstances. The longer-term hidden danger of not having a proper understanding of such phenomena or of how they are used, however, is ultimately the universal peril associated with not knowing what cultural difference means.

2.2 SPAIN THE NATION

The concept of nationalism is not only notoriously difficult to define; it also carries ambivalent connotations. On the one hand, it can be the source of a noble patriotism which influences citizens to make sacrifices for the common good and which spurs people on to great economic and cultural achievements; on the other hand, it can be a negative force, a reaction against liberal conceptions of the state, a cause of fanaticism and totalitarianism and a prelude to violence and war.

As mentioned earlier, the notion of the nation as an 'imagined community' leads us to think of nationalism as being about the process of 'imagining a nation'. In other words, a 'nation' comes to be created by a group who feel that they have sufficient cultural and historical bonds in common for them to aspire to being united politically. A variety of factors can facilitate this, including language, a common religion, shared ethnicity and a common (real or imagined) set of myths about the origins of the people. Both Benedict Anderson (1983) and Eric Hobsbawm (1990) point to the instrumental role played by the invention and spread of the printing press, the development of navigation and increased literacy in laying the foundations for national movements in the late Middle Ages and the early modern period. These ensured that channels of communication between large numbers of people were sufficiently sophisticated for a shared sense of identity to begin to develop. But in the Spanish case, for instance, what was developing was a 'proto-nation', not a nation. Under the Hapsburg kings in the sixteenth and seventeenth centuries, a kind of dynastic unity was achieved, but this was only the beginning of a sense of 'nation-ness' in Spain, in the sense of 'the personal and cultural feeling of belonging to a nation' (Anderson 1983). As Álvarez Junco (1996: 89) points out, Spain may be one of the oldest political entities of this sort established in Europe, but the country still consisted at that time of an alliance of separate kingdoms, with varying systems of legislation and their own autonomous institutions; these kingdoms even maintained customs borders between themselves. On the other hand, as Javier Tusell (1999) argues, it is possible to suggest also that nations are not just the product of people's fertile imaginations: if Spain was 'imagined' as a nation, it is because there was already some sense of common identity and a shared cultural and ethnic background that could be appealed to, an historical memory which was common to all of the people of *las Españas*, no matter how 'plural' Spain may have been: 'No puede existir identidad colectiva sin memoria, por selectiva que sea, ni proyecto común sin pasado histórico compartido, por más que le rodeen mitos objetivamente falsos' (Tusell 1999: 24). As early as the sixteenth century, therefore, an entity was being forged which could claim to be able to command the allegiance of the communities inhabiting the scattered and diverse regions of Spain. The arrangement put in place under the Hapsburgs combined a nascent sense of national identity with the defence of orthodox Catholicism and a belief in the primacy of the Castilian language. This enabled subsequent generations of 'centralists' to assert an identification between the notion of being Spanish, the idea of being a Catholic and the use of Castilian. This centralizing tendency was reinforced and turned into a key element of policy by the monarchs of the House of Bourbon, whose dynasty has been in place in Spain since the beginning of the eighteenth century.

In modern times, the existence of both the 'Spanish nation' and the 'Spanish state' is beyond question, although the degree of acceptability accorded to each of these notions can vary enormously. The arrangement currently in place for the political administration of Spain – the *Estado de las Autonomías* as set out in the 1978 Constitution – is largely deemed acceptable by the overwhelming majority of Spaniards, the principal exceptions being certain nationalist groups in the Basque Country and Catalonia. The structure of the state works well, but only by allowing some ambiguity in relation to the definition of the Spanish nation. While most Spaniards are happy enough to use the functions of the state apparatus – whether in terms of obeying its parliament, being subject to its legal system, paying taxes or carrying a Spanish passport – the level of identification with Spain as a nation is actually much lower. Many Catalans, for instance, only reluctantly carry a Spanish passport and miss no opportunity to stress that they are Catalans, not Spaniards.

There is a real tension, therefore, between a sense of Spanish identity on the one hand and an identification with the Autonomous Community one lives in on the other. This is well demonstrated by the responses given by young Spaniards (aged 15–29) to a question on identity included in a CIS survey conducted in 1997. The question was: 'Which of these sentences do you agree with most?' The respondents' preferences were as follows (in the statements, 'X' stands for the relevant *gentilicio*, i.e. the term denoting a person from a particular Autonomous Community in Spain – Basque, Andalusian, Murcian, etc.):

I consider myself exclusively Spanish	9.5%
I consider myself more Spanish than 'X'	10.0%
I consider myself as Spanish as 'X'	54.7%
I consider myself more 'X' than Spanish	18.2%
I consider myself exclusively 'X'	6.0%
No opinion	0.6%
No reply	1.0%
	(CIS 1997a: 3)

Just over half of those surveyed (54.7 per cent) showed an equal commitment both to being Spanish and to belonging to their Autonomous Community, and, although very few (6 per cent) described themselves as committed exclusively to their region – and we might guess that the majority of these lived in the Basque Country or Catalonia – considerably more felt a stronger sense of affinity with their Autonomous Community than with Spain.

The predominant attitude towards the plurality of nationalities, cultures and languages of Spain is now positive and nurturing, both officially (in terms of financial and legal support from central government and autonomous governments) and in everyday practice (e.g. in the increased use of vernacular languages and the increased consumption of regional cultural production in the form of books, radio and television). Spanish 'Nationalism' (with a capital 'N') has consistently been associated with hostility towards those cultures of the Peninsula which were not Castilian or were unwilling to be Castilianized. This negative view of regional identities – manifest in its most vicious form in the Franco dictatorship – tolerated only a monolithic Castilianized Spanishness, with a prominent place for the Catholic dimension of that culture, and anything which departed from this vision was seen as a threat to the unity of the state. State and nation were to be coterminous, and nothing persisting within the boundaries of Spanish territory had a right to be deemed 'non-Spanish', so the assertion of non-Spanish cultural identities within that territory could only be seen as an aberration.

In practice, in modern Spain, the plurality of cultural identities possible within an overarching concept of Spanishness is both established on a legal basis within the constitution and acknowledged in practice within the various parts of Spain. Article 2 of the Spanish Constitution articulates both the commitment to Spanish unity and support for the rights of the 'nationalities and regions' which form part of the state:

> La Constitución se fundamenta en la indisoluble unidad de la Nación española, patria común e indivisible de todos los españoles, y reconoce y garantiza el derecho a la autonomía de las nacionalidades y regiones que la integran y la solidaridad entre todas ellas.
>
> (Art. 2)

The various Autonomous Communities share a common basic legal framework as set out in this Article, although each operates on the basis of its own autonomy statute. Culturally, however, their diversity is reflected in the fact that each stands in a somewhat different relationship to the centre, with some (such as the *Comunidad de Madrid* and the provinces of the two Castiles) forming a kind of 'core' of highly Castilianized provinces; others (such as Cantabria or Extremadura) constituting a moderately Castilianized group of territories which are unlikely to express any discontent about their relationship with central government; a non-Castilianized group with a strong sense of their own cultural difference (including, for example, Andalusia or Asturias), and, at the extreme, the 'historical nationalities' of the Basque Country, Galicia and Catalonia (with, perhaps, the communities of Valencia and the Balearic Islands), which display an accentuated sense of their difference from Castilian Spain, to the extent that, at least in Catalonia and the Basque Country, people will sometimes reject altogether the notion that they are Spanish. The Canary Islands are a special case: most Canarians identify strongly with Spain, although they recognize that the geographical distance between them and the mainland makes them somehow 'different'.

One of the important complicating factors which impinge on the notion of Spain as a unified nation is the diversity of its geography. Nation-states characteristically emerge as a group of contiguous communities come together to form a territorial unit, but the limits to the territory included are always, to some extent, arbitrary. The most obvious geographical unit in the part of the world which we are discussing is, of course, the Iberian Peninsula, and, towards the end of the sixteenth century, a kind of dynastic unity was achieved on the Peninsula with the union of Castile and Aragon and the incorporation of the Portuguese Crown within the Spanish one; but this dynastic unity was never perceived as indicating a cultural unity or a 'national' entity. This alone is a reminder of the arbitrary nature of national boundaries and of the less than complete homogeneity within any nation-state. The very nature of the Peninsula's terrain as a whole has been a factor in prolonging cultural diversity and disunity. Communication between the different parts of this large mountainous land-mass was always difficult before the advent of modern technology, and one crucial factor in the emergence of a sense of nation-ness in the nineteenth century was the arrival of the railways. Given such geographical diversity, it is not surprising that loyalties should tend to extend only to limited areas of the Iberian land-mass rather than to the Peninsula as a whole. Nor should we be surprised that the acceptance of a sense of common nationhood has been brought about, at least partially, by the use of force.

Implicit also in the notion of nationality is a sense of a shared history, but here again, Spanishness presents a complex and variegated picture. A simplistic thesis would be that Spanishness arose from the unification of the Christian kingdoms and principalities during the period of hostility towards the Muslim south – the so-called Reconquest – and that this then continued with the expansion of this kingdom – the Spain of the Catholic Monarchs – as they proceeded to conquer the kingdom of Granada, followed by an overseas expansion which led to the establishment of a major world empire, and that, eventually, a natural process of contraction occurred which reduced Spanish influence again to the Peninsula, leading to a gradual consolidation into the modern nation-state of Spain. However, a truer picture of the nuances attendant on this 'shared' historical heritage can be gained from looking at how it is possible to construct two opposing 'readings' of these events. Álvarez Junco (1996), for instance, does this by means of the table opposite, which demonstrates some of the differences between a 'liberal-progressive' interpretation of the history of Spain and a 'National-Catholic' one.

Álvarez Junco suggests that these two competing visions of the story of Spain as a nation eventually gave rise to a version which combined features of both, and emphasized the supposed noble independence and heroism of Spaniards, prepared to defend their bountiful land against the incursions of any foreign invader. But this mythology failed to provide a worthy cause for the development of Spain's economic base: it was a sterile force which harked back to the past rather than ensuring that people would have reasons to look to the future, to feel that they were engaged in a nation-building project which could inspire confidence and effort.

Nationalism became a potent force in nineteenth-century Europe and nation-states emerged in a context where those nation-states could be perceived to be cohesive economic and political units, functioning within industrialization and modernization. But, in the Spanish case, industrialization came late, and when it did come it was haphazard, uncoordinated and unevenly distributed, which led to great social and regional imbalances. Consequently, the national political situation of Spain was frequently unstable and, for many, lacked legitimacy because there was little consensus about the form which the state should have. It eventually reached the high point of its stability in the twentieth century under General Franco, but this was achieved only through coercion, corruption and the suppression of liberties. It also entailed the construction of a lopsided vision of Spain, one that pandered to the establishment powers – the *poderes fácticos* – especially the armed forces and the Church, and entailed emphasizing the more traditionalist view of Spanish history (the view represented as 'National-Catholic' in Álvarez Junco's table).

National Histories of Spain	Golden Age	Decadence	Redemptive Ideal
Liberal-Progressive	Middle Ages: Cortes, fueros, democratic town councils Religious tolerance	Hapsburg: Foreign absolutism Repression of the Comunidades of Castile Suppression of local fueros	Freedom, democracy (federalism, in some versions)
National-Catholic	King Reccared Ferdinand III Catholic Kings Philip II Counter-reformation Council of Trent Golden Century Mystics and theological plays Anti-Islamic wars European hegemony of the Hapsburgs	17th century: 'feebleness' of the last Hapsburgs. 18th century: 'Anti-Spanish' Bourbon reformism. 19th century: revolutions, a-religious drift.	Unity 'on all fronts' (political, religious, linguistic, racial) Strong crown (without interference in religious matters)

Two versions of Spanish history: 'Liberal-Progressive' v. 'National-Catholic'

(Álvarez Junco 1996: 102)

2.3 *LO ESPAÑOL*: DESCRIBING 'SPANISHNESS'

The very existence of 'national traits' is itself questionable, and never more so than in an era when globalization and internationalization have brought more cultures into contact with each other, and to a greater extent, than ever before. The diminution in the importance of national boundaries and state frontiers has meant that differences between groups are more likely to be marked by ethnocultural factors than by traditional notions of national culture. Ethnic groups are most commonly thought of as being minority cultural groups within a situation where another culture dominates – this is frequently associated with the idea of the oppression, to a greater or lesser extent, of the minority ethnic group, and with the notion of a struggle against the dominant group. Increasingly, however, ethnicity is being thought of in positive terms, as cultural identity where there is a more or less harmonious relationship between an identifiable group and a wider political or cultural entity. Thus, ethnicity is increasingly a relevant concept in relation to the position of nations within supranational structures – as in the case of the nation-states of the EU – and in relation to the status of subnational groups within a traditional nation-state – as, for instance, of the regional cultures existing within the Spanish state.

In fact, in Spain, what often holds the greatest appeal is the most local area possible, the *patria chica*, the very village or small locality that people come from. Richard Ford (1796–1858), author of the *Handbook for Travellers in Spain*, recognized this and alluded to it in the opening of his book. Explaining how difficult it was to generalize about the country he was presenting, he said:

> Since Spain appears, on the map, to be a square and most compact kingdom, politicians and geographers have treated it and its inhabitants as one and the same; practically, however, this treatment of the Peninsula is impossible, since both the political and social instincts of each once independent province vary the one from the other, no less than do the climate and productions themselves.
>
> (Ford 1898: 2)

He suggests that, although it is possible to find Spaniards who boast about Spain itself, their hearts are not really in it: 'every single individual in his heart really only loves his native province, and only considers as his fellow-countryman . . . one born in the same locality as himself'.

Ford was a keen observer of Spain and the Spanish people, although his views were coloured by the Romantic vision of cultural difference which predominated in his time. He lived in Spain in the mid-nineteenth century and travelled extensively around the country. His *Handbook* was a practical guide which offered basic information on travel and accommodation, along with a discussion of points of artistic and historical interest. He also offered his readers – typically, Victorian English gentlemen – his personal commentary on Spain and Spanish people. He lived in an age typified by a reaction against the highly rational, rather stuffy Enlightenment thinking of the period which preceded it, which had been based on order and balance; Romantic travellers like Ford sought out what was different and unusual. Like many of his contemporaries, Ford saw Spain as an exotic country, 'peculiar', picturesque and full of passionate people. When they arrived at the French–Spanish border, travellers like Ford already had a fantasy image of Spain in their heads, and whatever they saw during their stay only served to confirm this view. For them, Spain was a mix of anachronism and poverty, sensuality, peasant servility and the exquisite manners of the aristocracy. They focused on whatever was strange or extreme, exaggerating the differences between this 'curious country' and the comfortable, rational Europe from which they came, and describing its details in the most colourful terms possible. Francisco Calvo Serraller offers the following summary of the approach they adopted:

> It is easy . . . to list the clichés about Spain which these European Romantics believed in: the natural world in preference to the city; old towns with little winding streets over the straight lines and monumental architecture of more recent urban developments; exotic ruins rather than the blandness of the new; picturesque local customs rather than cosmopolitanism; colourful popular traditions – i.e. folklore – rather than the boring uniformity of polite bourgeois behaviour; a world of risk and adventure rather than a feeling of comfort and security; the excitement of strong religious convictions rather than rational political thinking, etc.
>
> (Calvo Seraller 1995: 20; my translation)

The Spain depicted by these Romantic writers and artists was populated by swarthy gypsies, passionate young men with daggers in their cummerbunds, peasants leading gaily decorated donkeys through picturesque plazas and down tortuous winding streets, or by tradition-bound aristocrats, exemplars of pride, piety and honour. But the most striking and most frequently repeated image is of the beautiful, wild Spanish woman, especially the woman from Andalusia, a gorgeous creature with rosy-red lips and jet-black hair. This *andaluza* attains mythic status, as Calvo Serraller demonstrates with an extract from the writings on Andalusia of the French traveller Antoine de Latour, who, in the 1840s, described how he went in search of 'this Oriental woman taken out of a languid harem and given new life by the more civilized and intelligent atmosphere of the West; this model of southern beauty, where even passion is restrained by a more spiritual religion' (Calvo Seraller 1995: 61). Latour goes on to describe his disappointment when, on going to an Andalusian dance in the expectation of seeing it full of such beauties, he in fact finds that the dance is no different from anything he might have seen elsewhere in Europe. The creatures he encounters are not exotic beauties but ordinary people dancing as awkwardly as anyone else might. And to all of this his reaction is to exclaim: 'This is no longer Spain . . .'.

If Spain was exotic, Andalusia was the most exotic part, for the simple reason that it displayed more evidence of the Moorish past than anywhere else. The *andaluza* was, in Latour's telling phrase, 'esta mujer sacada de Oriente', but Andalusia as a whole represented what was most interesting and most exotic for Ford, Washington Irving (the American author who lived in Spain in the early nineteenth century and published his *Tales of the Alhambra* in 1832), Latour and many others. Andalusia connected Europe directly with the East; it *was* the East: indeed, the implication was that, just by crossing the Pyrenees, you could enter an oriental land. The clichéd vivid colours and heightened sensations of the Orient were to be found in a land which had for centuries been largely ignored by the European aristocracy. In the eighteenth century, the gentleman's 'grand tour' of Europe had included obligatory stops in locations of artistic renown in France, Italy and the Netherlands, but a visit to Spain was both unnecessary (because of its supposedly marginal artistic interest) and possibly dangerous (because of the country's reputation for brigandry). But the poverty and backwardness which had formerly caused the country to be ignored were seen, in the Romantic era, as assets: in the new vision, Spain was an oriental and exotic location.

Spain, for the Romantics, was a 'place apart', a place which did not quite form part of Europe. It had most, if not all, of the qualities which Edward Said attributes to the East in his classic discussion of the subject, *Orientalism* (1978). Said's book is anti-colonial in tenor, and his focus is that large group of countries in Asia and the Middle East which were formerly colonies of Europe. Spain was, of course, a colonizing and not a colonized country, but, for the Romantics (as well as for many who came after them), it displayed the relevant characteristics: it was socially backward, bound by tradition, pre-modern, and with a tendency towards despotism in politics. Above all, it was picturesque, it was exotic, and it was *different*. But, like the 'real' Orient, it could be seen as having had a pre-eminent status in the past, as carrying a baggage of historical greatness, and could be viewed as a place where ancient, natural values were preserved, values superior to the supposedly artificial ones of more advanced (i.e. more urban and more industrialized) European societies.

Perhaps the single most outstanding trait commented on by observers, both Spanish and foreign, is that 'non-centralizing' tendency that Richard Ford mentioned, and which is variously described as 'individualism' or 'lack of civic spirit'. In our times, the writer and long-time Spanish resident Ian Gibson (1992: 174) has noted the Spaniards' lack of a sense of civic responsibility, and their apparent inability to make any effort for the good of the community at large. In a similar vein, John Hooper (1995: 334) quotes a member of the Spanish National Symphony Orchestra who explained that the main difficulty associated with playing music in a Spanish orchestra was that 'everyone has his or her own conception of *la*'.

The anthropologist Julio Caro Baroja favours the term 'personalism' to describe his fellow-countrymen, meaning that Spaniards are keenly aware of the *person that is each* one of us. The consequence of this, for him, is that each one reserves his or her most acute awareness of person for themselves:

> Yo siempre he creído que el español no es individualista, sino personalista, que es distinto. Es un hombre que tiene una conciencia tan viva de su persona, que no conoce nada más que su persona. A la vez, tiene una especie de ímpetu tan arrollador para no enterarse de que existen los demás, que asusta.
>
> (quoted in de Miguel 1990: 35)

The inability to put oneself in another's place, to take others into consideration, is often commented on. Fernando Díaz-Plaja (1966: 86-7) offers the example of a group of women who arrive late at the cinema and disturb everyone by commenting loudly on the film as they take their seats, after which they gradually become absorbed in what they are watching. When, a few minutes later, another group of women enter and do the same thing, the first group complains loudly about the second group's lack of consideration.

Certainly, Spaniards – Díaz-Plaja among them – have a facility for making scathing comments about their compatriots, as well as about other people. How much of this can be taken as anything other than idiosyncratic reactions to subjective experience is difficult to say. In the early 1960s, when Franco was still very much in power in Spain, and his dictatorship was aggressively peddling its propaganda about the supposed superiority of all things Spanish to the people of Spain and the outside world, there was no shortage of commentators to provide supportive arguments. In 1960, for example, in a book called *El español y su complejo de inferioridad*, Juan José López Ibor argued that the Spaniard was ethically superior to other Europeans. 'The Spaniard is, essentially, an ethical man. Any mere woman from the remotest Castilian village retains in her breast, like a sacred relic, more ethical values than most Europeans' (quoted in de Miguel 1990: 36; my translation).

Under a military dictatorship, the appropriate praise for the citizenry is to depict them as ethically superior, with an implicitly masculine set of values which raises them to levels far above the supposedly degenerate *masa europea*. Even a 'mere woman', and even one from an obscure Castilian village, once she is Spanish, is morally superior to the weak and corrupt foreigners who inhabit the rest of the continent! The obsessively masculinist portrayal of Spanish people's virtues and the implication that other (wealthier) European countries are morally inferior and 'effeminate' strike us now as ridiculously anachronistic and narrow-minded.

Perhaps where the 'essentialist' approach to matters of cultural difference is seen most clearly nowadays is in the context of media commentary, when the focus is not on Spanish character as such, but on some other topic altogether. One example is sports journalism, a field of discourse where national stereotypes are evoked in abundance. Hugh O'Donnell (1994) examined the use of such stereotyping in sports reports published in newspapers from 15 different European countries, including reports on football matches played in the World Cup competitions of 1990 and 1994. His analysis shows how southern Europeans (and Latin Americans) are generally portrayed as being naturally talented but also lazy, deceitful and undisciplined, in comparison with their northern counterparts. Hence, footballers from Mediterranean countries and from Latin America are thought of as having 'flair' – there were recurring references to creativity and to 'Latin American magic' – but they were prone to failure because of their hedonism, their hot tempers and their lack of discipline. Without sufficient 'technique' (which was associated, above all, with the German and Nordic sportspeople), their otherwise impressive 'magic' was not enough to ensure success. This was especially the case with Spanish players, since it was associated (in the minds of many reporters, at least) with lack of effort, superstitious religiosity and inefficiency!

2.4 A MODERN DEMOCRATIC STATE

Given Spain's complicated history, and given the perception of the country as being 'different', there is a sense in which Spain has only fully matured as a modern nation in the last few decades. Certainly, Spain was still carrying the heavy burden of its past – in terms of outdated traditions and an anachronistic political system – until at least 1975, the year of General Franco's death. The most obvious manifestation of that burden was the persistence of the Franco dictatorship and the continued survival of the General himself as Head of State. It is difficult to say whether the dictator's shadow has truly been removed from the country yet, although it was certainly still present in 1981, for instance, when elements of the Spanish armed forces attempted to carry out a *coup d'état* and tried to seize power from the democratically elected parliament. The attempt was unsuccessful, but it may have caused Spaniards to increase their resolve to pull their country away from those forces which were blocking its progress towards full modernity.

In the mid-1980s, there were those who looked back on Spain's transition to democracy with some scepticism, asking if what had taken place had been merely a formal change, without substance, a kind of sham whereby the same groups who had occupied powerful positions before were now masquerading as democrats, but were still controlling affairs for their own benefit. This view ignored the reality of the profound change that had taken place: after all, the change from a totalitarian to a democratic system was not inevitable, and it was achieved with difficulty and in the face of opposition from the many forces within the old Spain implacably opposed to democracy.

Even the enormous economic progress achieved in the 1960s was not necessarily going to be accompanied by social and political liberalization. There is no doubt that economic progress assisted the process of liberalization, but there was no automatic route from economic development to democratization, and the Francoist architects of the economic boom did not envisage any such transition, nor did they wish for it.

The economic miracle of the 1960s resulted from a stringent set of policies put in place by the ministers in charge of economic portfolios in Franco's government. These were members of the religious organization *Opus Dei*, men committed to the continuation of a repressive political regime and dedicated to maintaining the influence of the Catholic Church on the behaviour of Spanish people.

These were among the most liberal ministers in the cabinet; many others were virulently authoritarian, and urged the violent repression of dissent at every turn. For decades, privileged Spaniards – those adept at identifying with a corrupt regime – at every level of society had invested an enormous effort in ensuring that they had a favourable position for themselves and their families. Franco's dictatorship was a highly personalized one: it was not based on a particular ideology, a coherent set of political beliefs or a well thought-out view of how the world ought to be. Rather, it revolved around one individual, Franco himself, and the only loyalty required of those around him was that they should be faithful to him. From that core, there spread out a network of corruption and personalized power, which ensured that success and material rewards went to those whose allegiance to the regime was soundest. It was this 'philosophy' which ensured that favours were done for those who were closest to Franco; but this also enabled the regime to take a hardline stance in relation to demands for liberalization. Until his death, Franco continued to execute his opponents; notoriously, two members of the Basque terrorist organization ETA (*Euzkadi ta Askatasuna*) and three members of the left-wing organization FRAP (*Frente Revolucionario Antifascista y Patriota*) were executed on 27 September 1975, just two months before Franco died. The tradition of violent repression of dissent was so strong within the Civil Guard and the police that brutal methods of crowd control by those groups continued for several years after the death of the dictator, especially in 'rebellious' regions such as the Basque Country.

Despite the rearguard action of the ultra-right-wing defenders of Francoism, democracy prevailed in the 1970s and 1980s. It was supported and sustained by a mood of liberalism among ordinary people, by the street activism of left-wing groups opposed to the regime, by modernizing tendencies in business and industry, by the ideological defection of the Catholic Church which had been distancing itself from the regime since the early 1960s, and finally by a commitment to change on the part of the monarchy, in the person of Juan Carlos Borbón (as Prince of Asturias and Franco's nominated heir from 1969 onwards, and as King Juan Carlos I from the moment of his coronation two days after Franco's death in November 1975).

The various factions within the regime in the 1970s found themselves having to adjust to a situation where groups that were strictly illegal (notably the PSOE (*Partido Socialista Obrero Español*) and the PCE (*Partido*

Comunista de España)) were being incorporated into the process of decision-making. In July 1974, the *Junta Democrática* was formed, which brought together the PCE, the pro-Communist trade union group *Comisiones Obreras*, and others who favoured a complete break with the old regime, i.e. a *ruptura*. A group formed the following year (in June 1975), called *Plataforma de Convergencia Democrática*, was led by the PSOE and included the moderate Basque nationalists, the PNV (*Partido Nacionalista Vasco*). The demands made by the latter group were less radical, but both groups shared a willingness to engage in unofficial contacts with the regime. With ETA violence continuing, on the one hand, and with the constant danger of a right-wing backlash from the hardline military, on the other, it became increasingly obvious that there was a need for a strong centre-ground in the political arena and for a convincing leader who could hold the process together.

At first, it did not seem that such a leader was forthcoming. Franco's friend and hardline military colleague Admiral Luis Carrero Blanco had taken over effective control of the government from 1969, being promoted to President of the Council of Ministers in 1973, with Franco himself continuing as Head of State. Carrero Blanco undoubtedly had the strength of character and the right-wing convictions to ensure a continuation of Francoism after Franco, but he was assassinated by ETA in December 1973. He was succeeded as head of the government by another loyal Francoist, Carlos Arias Navarro, who appeared unsure of which direction he should take and vacillated as a leader. His reluctance to introduce the radical reforms being called for by the anti-Francoist opposition created an explosive situation of strikes and street demonstrations.

It was Arias who had the task of announcing to the world that Franco had died, on 20 November 1975, but his inability to take control of the situation in the months that followed culminated in King Juan Carlos' request that he resign, which he did in July 1976. His successor as prime minister was Adolfo Suárez, an appointment which caused a sensation, given that Suárez was relatively inexperienced, being only 43 years old. His record proves that he was the right person for the position, however, since he moved rapidly and skilfully to dismantle the Francoist apparatus of government and replace it with democratic systems. The key to his success was his adroit ability to negotiate with parties and individuals from all backgrounds and of all political persuasions. His Francoist credentials were convincing, as he had been Governor of Segovia under Franco and had also headed up Spain's national television service, TVE (*Televisión Española*). King Juan Carlos recognized that Suárez had the ideas and the ability needed at that time, and used his influence to manoeuvre him into the position of prime minister.

The first major step in the dismantling of Francoism was the passing, by the Cortes, of the Political Reform Law, a package of measures which would lead to the formation of a new Cortes, based on democratic elections and the rule of law. Meanwhile, measures to legalize trade unions were brought in and political parties were operating increasingly openly. Most of the military leadership and many right-wing politicians, however, were still opposed to the legalization of the Communist Party, but, with the leadership of the PCE signalling its willingness to accept the notion of working with the monarchy – an idea which would normally have been anathema to republican communists – it was becoming clear that they would necessarily be a part of the new political order. Accordingly, Suárez unexpectedly announced that the Communist Party was to be legalized at Easter 1977, a decision which provoked the anger of the military and of many on the political Right, but a measure which enabled the full panoply of political opinion to compete legally in the first free elections held in Spain in 40 years, the national elections of 15 June 1977.

Out of those elections a new coalition party, the *Unión de Centro Democrático* (UCD), headed by Suárez, formed a government, although the biggest single party, in terms of the votes they commanded, was the PSOE, who therefore led the opposition. With this mandate, Suárez was in a secure position to continue with his reforms and to oversee the drafting of a constitution. The process of creating a new constitution, one which could command the allegiance of the diverse shades of social and political opinion in the new Spain, was a tortuous one. The principal difficulties revolved around the form of the state (especially the issue of autonomy for the regions) and the status of the Catholic Church. In the end, both issues were resolved to the satisfaction of the majority of the members of the Cortes.

In relation to the demands for regional autonomy, the solution was the inclusion within the constitution of 'Title VIII', which provided a mechanism allowing for the creation of Autonomous Communities. Title VIII included two possible routes to autonomy: under Article 151, the historic communities of Catalonia, Galicia and the Basque Country could proceed quickly to acquire self-governing powers; Article 143, on the other hand, provided a device whereby provinces in other parts of Spain could group together, propose autonomy for themselves and call for a referendum, by which autonomy would be granted once the proposal was approved by a majority of the electorate in each province. The result was that, by 1983, all Spanish territory (with the exception of the North African enclaves Ceuta and Melilla) had been divided into Autonomous Communities, each with its own regional government.

With regard to Church–state relations, the solution – a rather unpalatable one for the Church – was to declare (in Article 16) that Spaniards had a right to practise any religion, or none, although the Catholic Church had the consolation of at least being explicitly mentioned in the article. The constitution was passed by a large majority in December 1978 – 88 per cent of those who voted approved of it – with the result that Spain finally had a legal framework for putting a fully democratic system in place. Accordingly, new elections were held in March 1979, again won by the UCD coalition.

The events of the transition were unfolding rapidly, but there were two ongoing problems which could have been disastrous for the process. First, Spain's economy continued to experience severe difficulties, with very high inflation and rising levels of unemployment. Secondly, rapid democratization and devolution of power to the regions had not been enough to encourage Basque separatists to desist from their terrorist campaign: deaths from ETA violence actually *rose* between 1975 and 1980. These factors fuelled the ambition of the hardline Right to roll back the democratization process, and intransigent elements within the military conspired to attempt to do this. The phenomenon of *golpismo* culminated in an attempted coup on 23 February 1981, when the parliament building was stormed by a group of civil guards under the command of Lt.-Col. Antonio Tejero. These held the Cortes deputies hostage for some eighteen hours, until they finally surrendered after it became clear that the King was not supporting the coup and after he had ordered the military authorities to remain loyal to the Constitution. Through the night of 23–24 February, the Spanish people followed the progress of events on radio, acutely aware of the danger that the country might be plunged back into authoritarian rule and violent repression. The *tejerazo*, as the attempted coup came to be known, gave the country an enormous fright, and galvanized people into action designed to ensure that democracy would succeed.

The relatively peaceful transition to democracy in Spain became a model for other countries, including those of Latin America, South Africa and Eastern Europe. The political changes were part of a wider process of social transformation in Spain, out of which emerged a country with a highly liberal ethos and a firm commitment to democracy, a new nation, radically different from the Spain of the 1950s.

FEATURE: 1992, *EL AÑO DE LAS MARAVILLAS*

A nation changes and develops over time. Towards the end of the twentieth century, Spanish people had a sense that their country was undergoing a process of renewal. With new political structures and a modernized economy, the social and cultural climate of Spain was being altered profoundly, and there was a tangible sense of optimism. This reached a peak in the *año de las maravillas*, 1992, the year of the Barcelona Olympic Games, the Universal Exposition in Seville (Expo-92) and the fifth centenary of the 'discovery' of America in 1492. All three of these major international events served to showcase the new, modern Spanish nation to the world, although all of them were culturally complex in their own right.

The Olympic Games were secured for Barcelona six years before the event by enormous efforts on the part of the Catalonian authorities and the mayor of Barcelona, Pasqual Maragall, and with the financial support of the Spanish government. The jubilant Catalonians set about preparing for the Games by putting in the necessary infrastructure, including the construction of stadia in the city and the surrounding area. Some 400 000 million pesetas were spent on urban renewal projects and other developments in order to ensure that the athletes, journalists and spectators attracted to the city by the Games could be housed adequately and that they would take a favourable impression of the city away with them. The investment made had the practical purpose of accommodating the extra visitors and the further purpose of demonstrating to the outside world that a country which had had a tradition of poverty and backwardness had now come of age and could organize such an event to the highest possible standards. The result was very impressive, with a successful and well-run series of athletic events and a spectacular opening ceremony.

Expo-92 ran from 20 April to 12 October 1992 and consisted of a huge exhibition occupying a vast campus located in the city of Seville, with some sixty-eight pavilions housing presentations from over a hundred countries around the world. The show was aimed at both developing trade and promoting the image of the various countries involved and at projecting the connections between modernity and historical heritage. The theme of the exhibition was 'Discovery', reflecting the significance of the 500th anniversary of Columbus's voyage, but it also had a strong technological emphasis. While it was aimed at an international audience, most of the visitors to Expo-92, who came at the rate of 200 000 per day, were in fact Spanish, so that the fair served as a way of presenting Spain in its international context to Spaniards themselves.

The fifth centenary of Columbus's voyage of discovery was an opportunity to rediscover and critically re-examine the ties between Spain and Latin America. Initially couched as the anniversary of 'the discovery of America', the extensive programme of events eventually went under the rubric of an *Encuentro entre dos mundos*, after some outspoken criticism of blatantly postcolonialist attitudes. Rational reassessment of the actions of the conquistadors led to an increased appreciation of the wrongs they had committed. This was complemented by other conciliatory gestures made by the Spanish authorities, including a major exhibition of Islamic art, held in the Alhambra in Granada, and another exhibition, 'La vida judía en Sefarad', which displayed artefacts relating to the lives of the Jews who had been expelled from Spain in 1492 and who had migrated to Central and Eastern Europe.

The success of these events, combined with the designation of Madrid as 'cultural capital of Europe' for 1992, sent an optimistic signal to the outside world that Spain had finally become an unequivocally modern country, with a heightened sense of its own destiny and the confidence to participate fully in the new Europe which itself was forming in that year.

READING: AMANDO DE MIGUEL, 'ESPAÑA, UNA SOCIEDAD VITAL Y DESMORALIZADA'

One of Spain's most renowned sociologists, Amando de Miguel, has written many books and articles about Spaniards and Spanish society. In 1992, he coordinated a study which was published under the title *La sociedad española 1992–93*. This was an extensive portrait of Spain at the beginning of the 1990s, based on the results of a major survey of the attitudes and opinions of thousands of students of the Complutense University in Madrid. He approaches the discussion of Spain with vast knowledge and a fine eye for detail, but not without irony and humour. The following passage consists of extracts from one of the introductory chapters in that book.

Somos una nación vital, dinámica, atenta a profundos cambios, pero un país medio, como corresponde a nuestra extensión, longitud y latitud. Como síntesis de los cambios ocurridos en estos últimos tiempos, se podría concluir que los españoles, de medio siglo para acá, hemos abandonado el quehacer ancestral de matarnos unos a otros (tradición que sólo conservan algunos, contadísimos, vascos; por eso mismo hiperespañoles) y hemos pasado a constituir una población libre, tolerante y bien alimentada, que lleva una vida más bien aburrida. El aburrimiento se corrige con el máximo posible de fiestas y de ruido. La alimentación contiene excesos y flagelaciones. La estudiada tolerancia admite no pocas intransigencias. La libertad está presta a ceder a la seguridad. En definitiva, estamos ante una sociedad compleja y contradictoria . . .

Este es el diagnóstico de un buen conocedor de la realidad española: 'España ha dejado de ser una sociedad altamente conflictiva. Corremos el riesgo de convertirnos en una sociedad básicamente pasiva, más o menos satisfecha a nivel individual, sin grandes ambiciones colectivas e incluso individuales, aparte del bienestar, una sociedad un tanto gris' (Linz 1990: 664). El tono gris de la vida nacional lo da no sólo la ausencia de enconados conflictos, sino la composición dominante de su estructura social, en la que son cada vez más espesos los estratos medios: los poseedores de una vivienda, de un puesto fijo de trabajo, de algún título educativo, de un automóvil . . .

Una creencia muy extendida es la de que el desarrollo, la urbanización, en suma, la modernización, son procesos que terminan por homogeneizar la sociedad en la que tienen lugar. No es así más que en una lámina muy superficial, la que afecta a ciertas modas y costumbres. De manera conjunta, esas grandes transformaciones lo que producen es heterogeneidad, complejidad. La sociedad española de fines del siglo XX es no ya compleja, sino heteróclita respecto a lo que era hace un siglo. España es hoy una sociedad más compleja que la de antaño porque sus habitantes tienen ante sí más posibilidades de vida que nunca. En el bien entendido que no se entra a valorar si todas esas posibilidades son aconsejables o deseables. Para empezar, el aumento de posibilidades de vida lo es en su forma literal de que un mayor número de habitantes llega a vivir más años. A su vez, en esos años de ahora ocurren más acontecimientos, hay más paisajes y escenarios.

Una sociedad compleja es aquella en la que sus habitantes pueden tejer muy diferentes combinaciones biográficas, pueden hacer y rehacer sus vidas, arrepentirse y desdecirse, todo ello con cierta prescindencia de las circunstancias de su origen. Lo que llamamos pluralismo no es más que esas posibilidades en el aspecto político. En el plano laboral sería el ascenso a través de la ocupación o los estudios. En el orden familiar está la autonomía para casarse o descasarse. En la esfera civil hablamos de la libertad para trasladar la residencia, para contratar, para enriquecerse. Hubo un tiempo, por ejemplo, en que algunas de esas posibilidades, tan elementales, se reducían grandemente para las mujeres o para los grupos más desasistidos. Era una sociedad simple, en la que se hacía difícil desandar lo andado. El vecindario, el matrimonio, el trabajo y tantos otros aspectos de la vida eran vitalicios. Hoy son más provisionales. La complejidad es riqueza y variedad, pero también riesgo y percance . . .

La vieja polémica regeneracionista sobre si los españoles – o los otros pueblos – poseen un verdadero 'carácter nacional' se resuelve con esta irónica interpretación: 'El carácter de los países no es invariable, pero existe; confiere a sus habitantes un cierto aire de familia . . ., es decir, se hace notar' (Pinillos 1987: 14). Es decir, no aparece troquelado el carácter de los españoles como tales, sean vivos o difuntos, puesto que son evidentes las variaciones en el tiempo y en el espacio, pero sí se reconoce ese 'aire de familia', que se manifiesta, por ejemplo, en los estilos de vivir, pensar y sentir. Habrá factores constantes que podamos predicar más de los españoles de hoy y otros, en cambio, de los españoles de un tiempo anterior.

Si alguna constante se puede trazar en las costumbres de los españoles de los últimos tiempos es una especie de ánimo experimental por el que se aprueba lo que viene de fuera, lo que resulta novedoso, lo que contraviene los usos tradicionales. Esta disposición choca con la idea que se tenía de nuestros antepasados, más bien volcados a lo contrario: a 'la tenaz resistencia a las novedades' (Pinillos 1974: 345). Esto era la tradición, pero el juicio que merece el paso por la etapa desarrollista de los años sesenta hace concluir al psicólogo que 'no me parece que el pueblo español presente un exceso de espíritu de resistencia ante lo nuevo, en estos momentos, sino acaso más bien una aceptación "poco discriminativa" de lo nuevo se ha trocado en un entusiasmo por las novedades (incluida la psicología), una ciega aceptación del cambio por el cambio mismo.'

(de Miguel 1992: 30–3)

FURTHER READING

Carr, R., *Modern Spain 1875–1980* (Oxford, Oxford University Press, 1980). A very accessible introduction to modern Spanish history.

Gilmour, David, *The Transformation of Spain: from Franco to the constitutional monarchy* (London, Quartet, 1985). See Part Two for a very good summary of the transition to democracy.

Jordan, Barry and Morgan-Tamosunas, Rikki (eds), *Contemporary Spanish Cultural Studies* (London, Arnold, 2000). Parts I and II address a range of issues relating to culture and identity in modern Spain.

Ministerio de la Presidencia, *Spain 2000* (Madrid, Secretaría de Estado de la Comunicación, Min. de la Presidencia, 2000).

Chapter 2 (pages 29-77) of this official publication offers a brief but intelligent summary of the history of Spain.

Rodgers, Eamonn (ed.), *Encyclopaedia of Contemporary Spanish Culture* (London, Routledge, 1999).

A mine of information on a vast range of issues of relevance to modern Spain.

Sí Spain, http://www.SiSpain.org//

An award-winning website sponsored by the Spanish government, which offers access to a wide range of information on Spain and Spanish culture.

3

Place: Y tú, ¿de qué tierra eres?

3.1 INTRODUCTION: YOU ARE *WHERE* YOU ARE

We are interested in the culture and way of life of a group of people whom we can define by reference to a *place*, a country called Spain. This means we are focusing on a geographical location 'other' than our own, which has a set of meanings associated with it which are different from the meanings associated with the place we are from. Places, in other words, are not mere abstractions, mere locations which can be defined using geodetic coordinates, essentially irrelevant to the lives that we live: *whereness* matters. 'To be human', Edward Relph suggests, 'is to live in a world that is filled with significant places. Place is . . . a profound and complex aspect of man's experience of the world' (Relph 1976: 1).

In our times, the notion of place has become an increasingly important area of concern for a wide range of academic disciplines. Apart from the obvious significance of place and space in geography and history, this notion is seen as having increasing relevance for psychologists, sociologists, philosophers, linguists and other theoreticians. It is of particular concern for two reasons. First, the urbanization of the world's population, with over 50 per cent of people currently living in cities, has brought about a growing tendency for people to feel uprooted. In rural contexts, especially when the population level in an area has been relatively stable over a long period of time, there is a more definite sense of identification with place, a sense of belonging, a feeling that you know who you are because you have a clear idea of where you are from. People living in cities tend to be less certain about where they belong, and the mixed population characteristic of the city leaves the question of a person's 'roots' more open, more flexible, more likely to be a matter of choices to be made by that individual rather than one about which there can be a foregone conclusion.

Secondly, increased communication and mobility between places has further destabilized the relationship between person and place. This trend towards globalization has meant that where something or someone originates from is of less consequence than where they are at any given time. Geographical origin in certain contexts may be of no relevance at all, an obvious example being websites. These exist in cyberspace, and are accessible by computer from any point on the globe, but their 'addresses' are only minimally related to the geographical origin of the material offered on the site. The point about the Web is precisely the facility it offers of being able to 'locate' the information we require with ease, no matter where that information may have come from; it is information which, in a real sense, exists not in geographical space but in virtual space.

Thus the notion of place – in the sense both of 'location' and of 'physical entity' – and the notion of space – the more abstract idea of 'physical extension' or 'context in which persons or things are placed' – are concepts which normally have human significances attached to them. 'Place', says John Clarke (1984: 54), '. . . condenses a whole complex history of economic, social and political processes into a simple cultural image.' Mere mention of the name of a particular place can conjure up a wide range of connotations and associations for people, which can be deeply significant for them. When we say 'Guernica' we are not merely mentioning the name of a town in the Spanish Basque Country: the name immediately brings to mind the mural by Picasso, with its references to destruction and violence and its anti-war message which is universally understood (see Feature, Chapter 10). But only relatively few place-names attain the status of Guernica; on the other hand, countless numbers of places – even some without a name – have meanings which are important to particular individuals or groups of people, being places that hold special memories for them or that they are familiar with and feel at home in.

Place will therefore carry particular significance in every culture, and cultural specificity itself will often be identified with place and the naming of places; in Clarke's words, 'one of the most profound effects of place and space is the way they structure cultural diversity' (Clarke 1984: 54). Thus, the mention of place-names, the description of characteristic places and the act of pledging allegiance to national and subnational entities will often serve as a paradigm for a particular culture, will stand for the culture itself.

Two incursions into the notions of place and space as they apply in the Spanish context are attempted in this chapter. The first is to reflect on the significance of the Autonomous Communities in Spain, which is one of the most important facts about the modern nation that Spain has become, a fact which relates to a geographical entity (i.e. an area or region of space). The second is to offer a range of descriptions and other types of texts which evoke particular places in Spain, characteristic types of places which offer the reader a 'sense of place' in a Spanish context.

However, before we broach those two areas it may be useful to summarize briefly two general points about the relevance of place and space to the Spaniard, as a background to further reflection. These points relate respectively to geographical latitude and to urban v. rural living.

Geographical latitude

Spain is a Mediterranean country, although a large one, with wide variations in climate and culture. Its general location may be related to aspects of how people live their lives: certainly, most Spaniards would feel that they live *en la calle* more than British or Irish people would, i.e. they spend more time out of doors and less time in the house, simply because the climate allows this. Warm summer evenings draw Spanish people of all ages out of their homes, often until quite late at night.

Beyond this, more profound cultural differences may be causally related to latitude. Geert Hofstede (1991), for example, suggests that what he calls 'large power-distance' (the tendency to accept autocratic decision-making) and 'collectivism' (the tendency to identify strongly with the family or group) are qualities more characteristic of cultures found closer to the equator (see 7.5.1). These factors are *not directly determined by climate or latitude*, but they are related, according to Hofstede. The explanation he offers for this is that, in early agricultural societies, people living in more tropical climates did not have to intervene with nature to the same extent as in northern regions in order to produce enough food to eat; therefore, people near the equator had as their rivals not nature herself, but other people. Given this competition with other people, those societies which survived best were those which were organized 'hierarchically and in dependence on one central authority which keeps order and balance' (Hofstede 1991: 45), whereas, in areas where nature was less abundant, the societies that thrived were those in which individuals were taught to fend for themselves.

Living in town

Although there is increasing demand now for houses on the outskirts of towns and cities, most Spaniards are still essentially city-dwellers. Isolated houses in the countryside are certainly not typical of Spain. For many Spaniards, even the idea of living five or ten kilometres from their place of work would be putting an unacceptable distance between themselves and their job. Obviously, this applies much less in the context of major cities such as Madrid or Barcelona than it would in relation to smaller cities and towns, and it is also a pattern which is changing over time. But Spanish towns and even villages still generally give the impression of being crowded places, with people living in small houses, flats and apartments amid the hustle and bustle rather than moving to the outskirts.

Commentators frequently suggest that the Spaniard is inclined to be gregarious, to seek contact (perhaps more than, say, northern Europeans) with other people, and is not typically a lover of solitude: John Hooper has written of 'Spaniards' compulsive sociability' (1987: 95), and, in the same book, described how many of the people who moved out of the centre of Madrid in the 1970s and 1980s to suburban housing estates such as La Moraleja later returned to the city out of sheer boredom.

It is also worth bearing in mind that many Spanish people have moved from rural villages and country areas to large towns and cities in relatively recent times. Massive migration to urban centres – especially to the major cities such as Madrid or Barcelona – took place during the 1950s and 1960s, and this pattern has continued, though in a less marked fashion. On the one hand, this means that many urban dwellers have a strong family connection with a particular village or small town: often, they own a second home there. On the other hand, it has accentuated a tendency among many Spaniards to affect an attitude of superiority towards rural life: one common way of insulting people or patterns of behaviour is to label them *pueblerino*, *provinciano* or (even more pejoratively) *cateto*.

3.2 SPANISH SUBNATIONALISM

Both geographical and historical factors have combined to ensure that Spain is multiple, not unitary. Spaniards tend to identify not so much with the Spanish nation-state as a whole but with geographical units on a smaller scale (see 2.2). This starts at the most local level; as Gibson (1992: 8) suggests, they are loyal above all to their local community, their village or town; after that, they identify with their province, and then the region or Autonomous Community where they live. And the trend is in the direction of an increased identification with the local. Salustiano del Campo (1993, I: 149), for instance, reports on surveys indicating that up to 45 per cent of Spaniards identify more closely with their *localidad* than either with their *región*, with Spain, with Europe or with the world.

Local loyalties are not, of course, unique to Spain, but Spanish people seem more inclined than most Europeans to characterize their own identity as being associated with the particular part of the country where they happen to have been born or brought up. This is the place they feel an affinity with, and this sense of identification with the local area has been a constant theme in Spanish cultural history, not only in the 'historical communities' of Catalonia, Galicia and the Basque Country, but in other parts of Spain as well.

Spanish diversity is legendary: the people, the geography, the climate, the built environment, the historical and cultural background, all tend to vary greatly from one region to another, so that an Andalusian does not usually behave in the same way as a Galician, and a folk song from Valencia sounds very different from an Asturian one. It is too easy, of course, to lapse into descriptions of stereotypes when attempting to describe the people from the various parts of Spain. The more notorious of these stereotypes include the penny-pinching Catalan, the devious Galician (the canny dictator General Franco was from Galicia), the proud and arrogant Castilian, and the lazy, happy-go-lucky Andalusian who is everybody's friend and who is devoted to enjoying life rather than working. These are mainly negative stereotypes, invoked most frequently by Spaniards from outside the regions concerned in moments of anger or frustration. The obverse of them is a set of positive images which idealize the 'national' traits of Catalans, Galicians, Castilians and Andalusians. Thus, Catalans claim that they have *seny* – a practical ability to cope well with the business of living, which includes a clever and necessary ability to manage their money. Galicians, in their own view, are wily and astute, not duplicitous. Castilians may admit to being proud, but this, for them, is associated with their bravery and spirit of adventure, and is borne out by the fact that Castile was the cradle of the conquistadors and the region which dominated the Peninsula through the centuries. Andalusians will claim that their love of the here-and-now is a necessary and beneficial part of their deep humanity.

Furthermore, love of one's own 'backyard' can often be accompanied by a contempt for the backyards of others. Rivalry between regions and the playful use of stereotypes is generally innocuous, of course, and only rarely does it lead to dangerous factionalism. Competition between neighbours is to be found in every part of the world, and the supposed cultural superiority of one group of people over another can be a motivating force for the advancement of the group. What the historical record also shows, however, is that inter-group rivalry can also, tragically, lead to demonization and even military combat. The most striking current example of violent difference in Spain is the situation in the Basque Country, where the separatist terrorist organization, ETA, has claimed that it has a mandate to eliminate all traces of the 'foreign' Spaniard from its territory. It sees the Spanish army and Civil Guard as occupying forces imposing an imperialist will on the Basque people. In elections, only about 15 per cent of Basques vote for the political wing of ETA (*Herri Batasuna*, or *Euskal-Herritarrok*), but this low level of support has not deterred ETA from violent activity.

The father of Basque nationalism was Sabino Arana (1865–1903). He combined an ardent love of his homeland and a philologist's interest in the Basque language with a passionate hatred of all *maketos*, the derogatory Basque term for non-Basque Spaniards. His main concern was with immigrants from other parts of Spain who moved to the Basque Country in the late nineteenth century, when that part of Spain was experiencing a frenetic industrial revolution. In response to the sense of threat posed by the 'strangers' from other parts of Spain – half the population of Bilbao in 1900 were *maketos* – Arana articulated a rabid hatred of non-Basques which is reflected today in the actions and language of ETA.

This vehement, racist form of extreme nationalism is not the norm in either the Basque Country itself or the rest of Spain. Much more typical is a strong sense of identification with the place one comes from defined in terms of a region or a 'sub-region'. It is difficult to generalize about such matters, but one will often encounter Castilians, for example, who express pride in the village or town they come from, or pride in their province, or who have a strong sense of identification with Castile as a whole, with possibly a slightly superior attitude towards Spaniards from other parts of Spain.

One of the Autonomous Communities which have gained a great degree of control over their own affairs in recent decades is Catalonia. This Spanish region exhibits many of the characteristics which we normally associate with the idea of a nation-state, in terms of its geography, history, ethnicity, language, politics and economics. It is larger than many existing nation-states, being over ten times the size of Luxembourg, for example, while it is the same size as Belgium. Historically, it has existed more or less as an identifiable unit since the thirteenth century, with a record of willing or unwilling involvement with Castile and other parts of the Peninsula, but also with an identifiable past which is clearly distinguishable from that of other places. Ethnically, Catalonia is as homogeneous a region as any other state. The chief ethnic division perceived by the inhabitants of contemporary Catalonia is that between those whose family roots are strongly Catalan and those whose parents or grandparents came from outside Catalonia. Most people living there, however, still consider themselves to be as much Spaniards as Catalans. In a survey carried out in March 1998, only 14.5 per cent of respondents described themselves as being exclusively Catalan. While a significant number of those surveyed (27.9 per cent) thought of themselves as 'more Catalan than Spanish', the biggest tranche of all (38.3 per cent) considered themselves to be '*tan español como catalán*' (*El Periódico*, March 1998).

Linguistically, Catalonia has its 'own' language, Catalan, spoken by about six million people. Legal measures have been put in place in recent times to strengthen the position of Catalan, and the language is certainly the most dominant one in the region, although a sizeable minority of the population have Castilian as their mother tongue, and there is consequently some lack of linguistic unity (see 4.3.2).

In politico-economic terms, Catalonia is very capable of surviving without the rest of Spain to support it, having a sound economic base. While it is obviously useful for Catalonian business to have access to the Spanish hinterland with its market of over thirty million people, in an increasingly integrated EU, Catalonia does business freely and effectively with the huge market of Europe in general. Indeed, Catalans from every walk of life seem increasingly inclined to present themselves as simply coming from Catalonia, without reference to connections with Spain. In the run-up to the 1992 Barcelona Olympics, for example, advertisements in British newspapers urged visitors to come to Catalonia for the Games – without mentioning Spain at all.

In general, Catalans are content with the degree of autonomy they have achieved: the headline in *El Periódico* reporting on the March 1998 survey announced that Catalonia was *satisfecha de su autonomía*. Most Spaniards would voice that sentiment, in relation to their feelings about the degree of autonomy achieved in the region where they live.

The initial push for autonomy came from the 'historic communities' of

Catalonia and the Basque Country and, to a lesser extent, Galicia. The 1978 Constitution put mechanisms in place which allowed for Autonomous Communities to be formally constituted (see 2.4). Then came the rush for autonomy in all parts of Spain, the so-called *fiebre autonómica,* as the various remaining parts attempted to work out the new identity they would pursue and with whom they would pursue it. The country ended up with 17 Autonomous Communities (not counting the 'autonomous cities' of Ceuta and Melilla), in a nation-state which is neither a unitary kingdom nor a federation of states – although the powers of the Autonomous Communities are similar in many respects to those of, for instance, the federated states of Germany.

Apart from a small minority on both the right and the left of the political spectrum, Spaniards now fully accept the form of their state, and most would believe that the *Estado de las Autonomías* gives sufficient recognition to their sentiments about their own place, both in terms of Spain as a nation and in terms of an attachment to smaller geographical units.

3.3 A SENSE OF PLACE

Places with political names – countries, regions, Autonomous Communities – are often less important in people's lives than the more familiar, everyday places they inhabit. A particular street, a certain hill, a local square – all resonate with meanings for most people in ways that national entities cannot. Familiar, intimate locales and places connect directly with people's emotions, while national and subnational units remain at a relatively high level of abstraction for many.

The significance of such locations is caught in the brief texts quoted below, which attempt to convey the atmosphere, the sense of place, to be experienced in particular locations in Spain. Although some of these writings evoke specific settings, they are, in the main, descriptions of place that could apply to various parts of Spain, her towns, her cities, or her mountains.

Thus, independently of the political and administrative divisions of the country, the sense of place emerges in these writings as a powerful force which makes a strong impact on the individual writer, imbuing a particular place with a special meaning. It is that meaning which each writer attempts to communicate.

3.3.1 The *plaza*

All Spanish towns – and even many villages – have at least one square, or *plaza,* centrally located, surrounded by shops and businesses, a place which people pass through as they go about their business, but also a place where people meet and gather in bars and cafés. The Spanish square functions both as an open space which relieves the congestion of the town, and as a space to be filled, a place that provides an opportunity to linger, to loiter unchallenged, in company or alone. Public parks, of the British or Irish sort, are relatively rare in Spanish towns: the *plaza* is a place for people to come together, to socialize in the presence of a large number of others and to sense the pulse of the crowd. Traditionally, this archetypal relaxed social activity took the form of the *paseo*, the stroll through the streets (often focusing on arrival at a square), which took place ritually just before mealtimes in Spanish towns. This custom is less prevalent than it used to be, although modern variants of it still persist.

The poem 'En la plaza' (from the collection *Historia del corazón*, 1954) by Vicente Aleixandre (1898–1984) captures the bustle to be experienced in a Spanish square. The poet chooses to immerse himself in the crowd, losing his preoccupation with himself by finding company in the mass of humanity moving about the square, and he urges all of us to seek personal identity in that feeling of common cause with all of human nature, rather than looking for ourselves in the isolation of a solitary existence. Man, Aleixandre suggests, needs this immersion of the senses in the pool of common humanity:

> Era una gran plaza abierta, y había olor de existencia.
> Un olor a gran sol descubierto, a viento rizándolo,
> un gran viento que sobre las cabezas pasaba su mano,
> su gran mano que rozaba las frentes unidas y las reconfortaba.
>
> (Aleixandre 1977: 107)

If we become one with the crowd, we recognise ourselves in other people: 'Allí cada uno puede mirarse y puede alegrarse y puede reconocerse' (ibid.). Surrendering our will to the will of this mass of people brings us more fully to life:

> Hermoso es, hermosamente humilde y confiante, vivificador y profundo,
> sentirse bajo el sol, entre los demás, impelido,
> llevado, conducido, mezclado, rumorosamente arrastrado.
>
> (ibid.: 106)

3.3.2 The beach

Spain has almost 4000 kilometres of coastline, more or less evenly divided between the Atlantic Ocean and the Mediterranean. The sea has always exercised a strong fascination over the minds of Spaniards, despite the fact that, as one of the world's largest countries, much of Spain is distant from the coast and much of the population lives far from it. And yet, Madrid, although it is hundreds of kilometres from the coast, has one of the biggest and most active markets for fresh fish in Europe; and every year, massive numbers of Spanish people make their way to a second residence or a rented home *en la playa*, and live there for weeks, or perhaps months.

For millions of foreigners, and for many Spanish people themselves, the beach is the most characteristic element of a Spanish summer, especially a Mediterranean beach, washed by waters which, for much of the year, are warm enough to swim in. Most of the Mediterranean resorts to which both Spaniards and foreigners migrate are places which, as recently as the 1950s, were quiet fishing villages and ports.

In his novel *Son de mar* (1999), Manuel Vicent evokes the changing atmosphere of a Mediterranean village as it prospers and develops with increasing numbers of tourists over several decades. Early on in the novel he describes a small harbour, flanked by piers on which stalls have been set out. There is no mistaking the relaxed atmosphere of summer festivity in an unsophisticated small coastal town:

> Multicoloured fishing nets stretched along the quay, and between them lay stalls selling ice-cream, *pipas* and sweets; handicrafts were laid out for sale on coloured shawls placed on the ground. Amidst the bustle of the fiesta, groups of young men with rucksacks passed by to board the various boats bound for the island, and on top of this sensation of Mediterranean happiness, where cats strolled lazily along the decks of boats, a small orchestra played, not rock, but melodic songs, sung by a lead singer with sideburns, brilliantined hair, a shirt with leg-of-mutton sleeves, a bulge in his pants and a comb in his back pocket. From atop a bench under the palm trees he sang a bolero which went: *Today, like yesterday, I still love you, my love, with the same passion that my heart feels beside the sea.*
>
> (Vicent 1999: 35–6; my translation)

The fictional town of this novel is recognizably Valencian. It serves as the setting for a tragic story of the love between Ulises, a young schoolteacher, and Martina, daughter of the owner of a local bar: their love is such that, rather than allow themselves to be separated from each other, they choose to drown together in the sea.

3.3.3 The patio

The patio is a courtyard found in the interior of many houses in Spain, especially in the more southern regions. Cool in summer, and relatively protected in winter, it is a place where family, friends or neighbours get together and chat or where children play. It is often an intensely personal place, a place whose meanings are intimate, homely, private.

The poet Antonio Machado associates the patio with his childhood, but his lines below tell us not only that he played in a patio in Seville when he was growing up; but also that the patio has now become an emblem of that childhood itself. Place is closely related to time: for the mature Machado, his childhood consists now of the memories left to him of those early years; memories irrevocably linked to the patio he evokes in this portrait of himself, which appears at the beginning of his collection *Campos de Castilla*:

RETRATO

Mi infancia son recuerdos de un patio de Sevilla,
Y un huerto claro donde madura el limonero;
Mi juventud, veinte años en tierra de Castilla;
Mi historia, algunos casos que recordar no quiero.

. . .

Hay en mis venas gotas de sangre jacobina,
Pero mi verso brota de manantial sereno;
Y, más que un hombre al uso que sabe su doctrina,
Soy, en el buen sentido de la palabra, bueno.

. . .

Y cuando llegue el día del último viaje,
Y esté al partir la nave que nunca ha de tornar,
Me encontraréis a bordo ligero de equipaje,
Casi desnudo, como los hijos de la mar.

(Machado 1971: 76–7)

3.3.4 The local shop

There is still a wide range of small specialist shops in Spain – *panaderías,
lecherías, papelerías, mercerías* – even though many have now disappeared
under the pressure of the supermarkets, department stores and smart shopping
centres that have been built around the country, along with the more recently
arrived hypermarkets on the margins of towns and cities. Even in the centres of
Madrid and Barcelona, however, there are few areas which are completely given
over to business and office use, so that people living in those areas are still able
to sustain at least some small shops selling limited ranges of goods. In the 1950s
and 1960s, such small shops were much more abundant than they are now.

In the novel *Tiempo de silencio* (1961), Luis Martín-Santos (1924–64)
painted a highly critical picture of Spain and, in particular, of Madrid under
the dictator Franco: he depicted a world ridden with class division, corruption
and exploitation, with masses of poor migrants from the Spanish countryside
living in squalor and misery in the *chabolas* on the outskirts of the capital.

In the passage cited below, the story's protagonist, Amador, goes down the
Calle Atocha in old Madrid, observing the huge diversity of articles for sale in
the various shops he passes:

As they made their way down the narrow street, doorways on both sides
were open, with thousands of different types of ready-made goods in the
windows. All you could ever wish for was there, from bargain-priced ladies'
underwear in white, pink and purple, all squeezed against the glass in
jumbled heaps, to square-headed nails, plastic glasses, coloured plates and
gift items such as . . . a brass Don Quixote together with a silver-plated
Sancho Panza mounted with screws on a block of black glass, an inkwell
lined with leather, a glass paperweight with mother-of-pearl shells and a

picture-frame made from little pieces of reflecting glass with a portrait of Ava Gardner in it . . . .

(Martín-Santos 1986 [1961]: 30; my translation)

3.3.5 The garden

Finally, to Heaven – not so much a place, more a state of mind. The garden, or orchard (*el huerto*), famously evoked in the poem 'Vida retirada' by Fray Luis de León (1527–91), is, among other things, a metaphor for Heaven itself. In this poem, León, a learned Augustinian monk, elaborates on escaping from the cares of the world to a place of repose in the country, a theme he borrows from the Latin poet Horace. León describes the *huerto* to which he retreats in terms of an actual place, a quiet country estate called 'La Flecha' outside Salamanca, owned by the Augustinian order.

The orchard in question represents both the choice of spiritual values over materialistic ones, i.e. a rejection of the pursuit of wealth and fame, and a quasi-mystical quest for union with God and an evocation of a vision of Paradise (see O'Reilly 1995). In the poem, nature/God offers harmony and quietude as an alternative to the clamour attendant on worldly ambition.

In the words of Patrick Gallagher (1969: 151), what León is escaping from is 'the senseless clamour leading to spiritual disaster'. The idyllic place to which he escapes, whether a physical reality or an imaginary location of happy fulfilment, or both, is described in concrete terms:

Del monte en la ladera
por mi mano plantado tengo un huerto,
que en la primavera
de bella flor cubierto
ya muestra en esperanza el fruto cierto.

Y como codiciosa
de ver y acrecentar su hermosura,
desde la cumbre ayrosa
una fontana pura
hasta llegar corriendo se apresura.

Y luego sosegada
el paso entre los árboles torciendo,
el suelo de pasada
de verdura vistiendo,
y con diversas flores va esparciendo.

El ayre el huerto orea,
y ofrece mil olores al sentido,
los árboles menea
con un manso ruido,
que del oro y del cetro pone olvido.

FEATURE: CHANGING PLACES – EMIGRATION AND IMMIGRATION

If the notion of 'place' is culturally important, changing one's place of residence, particularly if it involves moving to another country, is of major significance for anyone. As in the case of other countries with long-term economic difficulties, Spain has experienced large-scale emigration which has left a deep impression on her people, especially in regions such as Galicia and Andalusia.

Emigration to the Americas – *a ultramar* – goes back to the time of the Conquest and to the expansion of Spanish power in the region. That steady flow of people across the Atlantic which began in the sixteenth century became a torrent in the latter half of the nineteenth century and the early decades of the twentieth, as Europeans generally were drawn towards the developing economies of countries such as Argentina, Brazil, the USA and Canada. Other Latin American countries also offered opportunities for Spanish people to achieve success, especially Cuba, Mexico, Peru and Chile. In all, in the first three decades of the twentieth century, about three million Spaniards emigrated to America.

A second major phase of emigration from Spain occurred in the period after World War II, especially in the years 1958–73, when one million Spaniards emigrated to other European countries, principally France, Germany, Switzerland and Benelux. This migration was a consequence both of the recovery of the economies of those countries, boosted by the Marshall Plan in the wake of the war, and of the fact that Spain had a surplus of manual workers due to the changes taking place in her economy. The Spanish government set up the *Instituto Español de Emigración* in 1956 to facilitate temporary emigration, which it encouraged on account of the economic benefits it brought, notably in terms of improving the country's balance of payments.

Emigration from Spain to other European countries slowed significantly, however, in the wake of the world oil crisis of 1973 and the general downturn in Western economies. Many emigrants returned to Spain in the 1970s and 1980s, to the extent that the number of Spaniards living in other European countries fell by 33 per cent between 1975 and 1984 (Documentación Social 1987: 69). The return was not always a happy experience, however: having had to deal with the various cultural and linguistic barriers they had encountered in the foreign countries where they had lived, many now found that Spain itself had become a foreign country to them, on top of which they often had great difficulties in finding employment at home.

In recent times, the countervailing tendency – immigration into Spain – has become a much more common phenomenon: Spain is now a labour-importing country, resembling in that respect most other EU countries. Since the 1980s, economic immigrants from Africa, Latin America and Asia have been entering the country in increasing numbers. Currently (in the year 2000), there are about a million foreign residents in Spain, of whom about half are from non-EU countries (many of the latter having entered the country illegally). As the number of foreigners has increased, they have become more visible, with the result that immigration has become an issue for Spanish people in a way that it never was before. There have been numerous instances of ethnic conflict and evidence of an increase in racism and xenophobia, notably in cases such as that of El Ejido (Almería), where a murder committed by a deranged man – who happened to be Moroccan – sparked a series of protests against the local Moroccan community (mainly labourers working in the fruit and vegetable farms in the vicinity), some of which have turned violent. Such tensions clearly demonstrate the difficulties being experienced in coming to terms with the country's new-found multicultural status.

READING: XAVIER RUBERT DE VENTÓS, 'MADRID AND BARCELONA'

In his book *De la identitad a la independencia* (1999), the Catalonian politician and author Xavier Rubert de Ventós (b. 1939) argues against fundamentalist conceptions of identity, and suggests: 'hay muchas maneras de ser catalán o vasco: tantas, cuando menos, como maneras de ser filósofo, homosexual o cristiano'. He advocates recognition of the need for <u>inter</u>dependence between Catalonia and Spain – 'la interdependencia para una verdadera independencia nacional'. In the following extract, he discusses traditional Catalonian perceptions of Madrid and Castilian perceptions of Barcelona, and how these are changing in modern times.

En el marco mundial y europeo de principios del siglo xx, Barcelona y Madrid eran dos ciudades a un tiempo más distintas y más complementarias que en la actualidad. Con el tiempo, sin embargo, se han vuelto más semejantes y más competitivas. Y este hecho no es ninguna paradoja. Mientras Madrid fue titular indiscutible del poder político, económico y militar, se dio un pacto tácito entre los poíticos de Madrid y los señores de Barcelona por el que éstos renunciaban al poder político a cambio del proteccionismo económico y el control policial que el gobierno central les ofrecía.

Por un lado, resulta claro que Madrid ha perdido soberanía económica desde que tanto aquellos aranceles como el tipo de interés o el volumen del déficit vienen hoy definidos en un contexto mucho más amplio – ¿y qué quiere decir, de hecho, 'mandar' cuando ya no se puede 'devaluar'? También ha perdido soberanía política y militar cuando muchas de las directrices que nos afectan son dictadas por flujos de poder o de capital más cercanos al Quartier Léopold o a Manhattan que al Palacio de Santa Cruz o de la Moncloa. Y la cuestión práctica, en tales circunstancias, es saber a qué nivel y con quién es más rentable negociar cada una de las leyes. No quiero decir con esto que la crisis de nuestro tradicional contrato sea el único problema relevante, ni que ésta haya de orientar toda la relación de Cataluña con España. Pero sí he dicho, y lo repito, que la complementariedad de intereses es la condición necesaria, si no suficiente, para la consolidación de una verdadera comunidad nacional. Y que esta complementariedad no es ya lo que era. Por otro lado, Barcelona ha ido ganando un relativo poder de decisión política que en muchos aspectos la ha aproximado al estilo de Madrid. Y la indumentaria podría ser una buena metáfora para comprender el alcance de estos cambios. Hace unos años, en efecto, sabíamos que estábamos en Madrid nada más entrar en un cóctel y ver los vestidos, las joyas, las nalgas encorsetadas y el paso decidido de unas señoras de las que sabíamos inmediatamente una cosa: eran 'esposas de Director General', una especie desconocida en nuestros lares. Pero ha bastado con que la Generalitat dispusiera de una serie de consejerías para que los adornos plateados, el fular de derbi y la marroquinería de hebilla dorada proliferasen tanto que, a primera vista, ya no sabes si el cóctel se celebra en Madrid o Barcelona. Por no hablar del propio talante, entre milhombres y hombre hecho a la fuerza, que favorece el alto funcionario de nuestro país . . .

Barcelona es más 'madrileña': ha ganado poder administrativo y ha perdido 'clase' burguesa; ha consolidado una burocracia y ha perdido el liderazgo cultural en los medios de comunicación. Por el contrario, Madrid es más 'barcelonesa'. Hace tiempo que ha dejado de ser 'aquel pueblo de la Mancha unido a una ciudad residencial': la estepa de los bedeles inalterables, los funcionarios grotescos, los burócratas indocumentados, los indígenas ocurrentes, planchados y repeinados. Hoy es un centro económico y cultural de primer orden que incluso ha sabido (como hizo el neorrealismo italiano en la posguerra) inventar con la *movida* su propio imaginario y comercializar un cine más bueno e incluso más identitario que el nuestro.

No todos los catalanes quieren ver esta nueva realidad. Muchos prefieren vivir aún de viejas imágenes y tópicos congelados, liofilizados y listos para ser inoculados en el cerebro del catalán sediento de causas justas. Son los que citan todavía aquello de 'la ligereza de carácter y la egoísta pereza de los castellanos' (Mañé i Flaquer); 'de una raza que vive, ciertamente, desde hace siglos a nuestro lado, pero que siempre ha sentido un profundo alejamiento espiritual de nuestro pueblo, porque se trata de una raza esencialmente pobre, fatalista, inmóvil, y que siente una especie de repugnancia por la evolución, el trabajo y la prosperidad' (Josep Carner). Al *entre Cataluña y España no hay más salida que el abrazo o el fusil* de Giménez Caballero se corresponden esta suerte de insensateces que suelta todavía, tan contenta, mucha gente de aquí. 'Claro', dicen, 'nosotros somos la *sociedad civil*, y ellos, la *guardia civil*, comparad nuestras "crónicas" con sus "gestas", la nostalgia de su noventa y ocho con el dinamismo de nuestro modernismo y nuestro novecentismo . . . ¿Verdad que la nuestra es la más guapa?' (Son los mismos, supongo, que creen que podemos permitirnos el lujo de no cultivar, e incluso menospreciar en Cataluña, un activo de la importancia cultural y económica de la lengua castellana. Y que tampoco apreciarán que alguien como Enrique Vila-Matas puede apoyar la independencia de Cataluña 'siempre que él pueda escribir en castellano'.)

Y así puede seguirse la canción sin ver lo que tiene uno delante, es decir, que nuestro desarrollo económico y social es mucho más parecido, pero que, precisamente por eso, somos mucho menos complementarios y mucho más competitivos. Las viejas razones de nuestra complicidad ya no pesan como antes. Ni valen ya los viejos tratos entre una periferia económica y culturalmente rica y un centro armado y arruinado pero que conserva el monopolio del poder político. Al ser más semejantes, el conflicto entre nosotros es cada vez más narcisista (el 'narcisismo de las pequeñas diferencias' de que hablaba Freud). Al competir en un mismo mundo, cada día es más probable que una ley de puertos o una 'solidaridad' decretada por ellos resulte ser una rémora para la supervivencia y la competitividad de nuestro país. Con todo, muchos siguen planteando el problema en aquellos viejos términos que no hacen más que perpetuar la prepotencia de los unos, la actitud pedigüeña de los otros y el recelo por parte de ambos lados. Y este es el segundo gran obstáculo que dificulta nuestro entendimiento: un entendimiento justo que pase por la efectiva difusión del poder, por la supresión de toda interferencia estatal en nombre de la simetría y por el reconocimiento de una interdependencia capaz de canalizar flujos reales y no sólo de asegurar paranoicas integridades territoriales.

(Rubert de Ventós 1999: 96–101)

FURTHER READING

Conversi, Daniele, *The Basques, the Catalans and Spain: alternative routes to nationalist movements* (London, Hurst & Co., 1997).
A fascinating study of Basque and Catalan nationalism.
Hooper, J., *The New Spaniards* (Harmondsworth, Penguin, 1995).
Part 6 of this book has useful chapters on the Basques, the Catalans and the Galicians, along with others on the issue of autonomy in Spain.
Mar-Molinero, C. and Smith, A. (eds), *Nationalism and the Nation in the Iberian Peninsula: competing and conflicting identities* (Oxford, Berg, 1996).
Outlines a range of issues relating to the concept of nationalism in Spain.
Ross, C., *Contemporary Spain: a handbook* (London, Edward Arnold, 1997).
Chapter 3 offers a very readable account of the autonomy process.
Temprano, E., *La selva de los tópicos* (Madrid, Mondadori, 1988).
Presents a wide range of views on the stereotypes associated with the different parts of Spain, in an entertaining manner.

4

Language: How do Spaniards Speak?

4.1 INTRODUCTION: LANGUAGE AND IDENTITY

In Chapters 1 and 3 we saw something of the importance of language in relation to issues of identity. As suggested in Chapter 1, one of the fundamental elements of the link between Spain and the countries of Spanish America – perhaps, indeed, the most important one – is that these countries share a language. It is language which, more than any other factor, binds them into some sort of cultural group, a fact acknowledged by both Spaniards and Latin Americans. In a survey carried out in 1994, for example, in Spain, Portugal and ten Latin American countries, language was perceived to be the most important link between Spaniards and Latin Americans, followed, at a distance, by religion (*Cambio16*, February 1994).

Language is a fundamental aspect of our identity. It is not just one more element of our culture, but a basic one. It conveys much of our experience of the world and transmits this from one generation to the next, so our cultural realities are largely linguistic in nature, however we may define those realities. Our customs and traditions, our rites and festivals, our education and socialization, the very existence of mythologies and literature, song, poetry and cinema, down to how we interact with others: all of these are bound up with the use of language. Human beings everywhere inevitably develop the use of and employ language in virtually all the activities they engage in. Its centrality to human experience is such that it is often deemed to be the defining characteristic of human beings: our species is sometimes labelled *homo loquens*.

Our linguistic behaviour is influenced by the particular cultural patterns that surround us, just as the latter influence our use of language. Cultural patterns have an effect on how we express ourselves, on what we tend to emphasize or de-emphasize, on the style of language we adopt, and even on the particular language we choose to use when we are in a multilingual situation. The individual language or languages we speak will themselves assist in establishing those cultural patterns: our cognitive and cultural choices are to some extent constrained by the linguistic means of communication which are available to us, and we evolve, in terms of our personality and our preferences – in other words, in terms of our culture – in certain directions more than in others, depending on the linguistic and cultural context in which we live.

Emotionally and intellectually, language is therefore close to whatever we may think of as our 'core' identity. It is prime among the ways in which we convey our sense of ourselves to the outside world and it is the key to successful interaction with others. Politically and sociologically, particular languages take on special significances for groups and communities: Spain would be unthinkable without the Spanish language, and people in the various parts of Spain where other languages are spoken cleave to those languages as badges of identity. A speaker's manner of expression can reveal traits of his or her personality, and people's use of language can signal aspects of their education and social background, as well as indicating their geographical origin. The particular ways in which language is employed in different contexts can vary from one language-group to another, and the contrasts between such usage in any two languages can help us to grasp how each group manufactures its own meanings.

These issues are the topic of this chapter; the question of how Spaniards speak will be explored by focusing first on some salient features of the Spanish language itself (4.2), then on the multilingual nature of modern Spain (4.3), and, in 4.4, on some of the contrasts between the way communication takes place in Spanish and how it takes place in English. This is followed, first by a feature on one specific area of language use (spatial expression in Spanish and English), and then by a Spanish text on language and humour.

4.2 THE STORY OF SPANISH

The earliest written evidence of the language we call 'Spanish' dates from about AD1000 and consists of glosses or explanations in Spanish of terms and phrases used in Latin documents. For instance, one such document, the *Códice Emilianense*, composed in tenth-century Latin, contains annotations written in both Basque and an early version of Spanish. These glosses were jotted down in the margins of the Latin document by a monk in the monastery of Yuso, in San Millán de la Cogolla (La Rioja), some time in the eleventh century. The 'proto-Spanish' in which these notes were written was just one variety of Romance, which was itself derived from the Latin brought to the Peninsula by the Roman conquerors. This language – Castilian Spanish – was of relatively minor importance in the early Middle Ages, compared with, for instance, Galician and Catalan, both of which were also emerging from Romance.

As Castile progressed from being a mere county within the kingdom of León to being an important kingdom in its own right, the language grew in importance. The territorial advances made by the Christian Spanish against the

Muslims in the twelfth and thirteenth centuries ensured the spread of the language and its increasing dominance in the Peninsula. Castilian was deemed worthy of use for administrative and literary purposes by King Alfonso X (the Wise), who reigned in Castile from 1221 to 1284, and the major literary output produced under his patronage helped to ensure that the language gained a high status as Castile's power increased. The use of Castilian gradually spread, as the use of Latin declined, especially in documents prepared for non-academic purposes, since knowledge of Latin was restricted to an educated elite. With the completion of the Reconquest in 1492 and the subsequent conquests in the New World, Castilian spread even more widely, until it reached the level it is at today.

The basic stock of forms employed in the language is of Romance or Latin origin. This means that both in its vocabulary and in terms of the structures it uses, Spanish strongly resembles its Latin ancestor. The bulk of the Spanish lexicon consists of items derived from Latin, and grammatical features such as the pattern of verb tenses and the use of gendered nouns resemble the Latin systems, although clearly modifications have occurred along the way, including, for example, the use of periphrastic verb structures such as *ir a* plus the infinitive (e.g. 'Voy a contarte un chiste') and the development of two verbs 'to be', *ser* and *estar*.

Certain types of etymological change are especially characteristic of Castilian Spanish. For instance, word-internal consonant clusters in Latin such as *-ct-* and *-lt-* typically evolved into the Spanish *ch*, as in the case of the following words:

lectu	→	leche
multu	→	mucho

The initial consonant groups *pl-*, *cl-*, *fl-* usually became *ll-*, as in these examples:

pluvia	→	lluvia
clave	→	llave
flamma	→	llama

One feature which distinguishes Castilian Spanish from other Peninsular languages is the reduction and gradual disappearance of word-initial *f-* from Latin words, as happened in the following examples:

facere	→	hacer
farina	→	harina

The [*f*] sound in these words changed to an aspirated [*h*] sound, and by the end of the sixteenth century, this aspiration had disappeared, leaving only an orthographic trace in the form of the 'h' which is used in the spelling of words such as these today.

Lexical borrowings were imported from many sources. A range of words, having to do with a wide variety of activities from agricultural and domestic matters to civic institutions and science, were imported from Arabic: frequently, these words begin with the morpheme *al-* (the Arabic definite article). Examples include *albaricoque, almohada, alcalde, álgebra, alambique, alcázar*, etc., although also of Arabic origin are *acequia, Guadalquivir, arroz, naranja, azulejo, taza* and *Ojalá*.

French borrowings entered early on, especially during the eleventh century, when the Reconquest and the Camino de Santiago brought thousands of pilgrims out of France and across the north of Spain, many settling permanently in the Peninsula. Gallicisms in Spanish, dating from this period or from the following centuries, include *homenaje, fraile, vergel, servilleta, batallón, conserje* and, surprisingly, *español*! Later French imports include such 'bourgeois' words as *pantalón, potaje, hotel* and *burgués* itself, while nineteenth-century Gallicisms are frequently drawn from bureaucracy and politics, reflecting the influence of the French administrative system on Spain during that period, with words and phrases such as *cotizar, aval, garantía, parlamento* and *tomar acta*.

With the expansion of Castilian linguistic hegemony to the New World from 1492 onwards, names of hitherto unknown foodstuffs entered the language, such as *patata, cacahuete, tomate* and *chocolate*, as well as words like *cacique, canoa, tiburón* and *huracán*, all taken from indigenous American languages.

Modern Castilian Spanish demonstrates a high degree of dialectal variation, the principal varieties being (other than standard Castilian) the Andalusian, Canary, Extremeño and Murcian dialects. Geographical variation is important, but so also is the variation which occurs at the levels of social class and education. The dialect with the highest prestige is the Spanish of Castile, and the 'best' Castilian is reputedly spoken in Valladolid, although it is associated also with Salamanca, Toledo, Burgos and Palencia. However, we must always bear in mind the point made above: the language actually spoken by particular individuals in specific areas will vary according to their background and education. Given the variations that occur within any one geographical area, the notion of associating 'good Spanish' with a particular place is highly questionable. The linguist Fernando Lázaro Carreter, in an article published in the magazine *Cambio16* (November 1987), maintained that the best Spanish is, axiomatically, that spoken by the best speakers of Spanish, no matter where they are.

One renowned slang version of Spanish, often deemed degenerate, which was highly popular in the 1980s, was called *cheli*. This argot served as a kind of badge of identity among young people in Madrid. Lázaro Carreter (1997: 152) has drawn attention to the tendency among speakers of *cheli* to employ what he calls *términos brutales*. Thus, he says, a young man may proposition a girl by telling her that she has '*unas cachas molonas*' (nice legs), and, pushing this to its conclusion, he may, with her consent, end up *picándosela, clavándosela o tabicándosela* (roughly, 'getting laid'). This variety of Spanish is characterized by the use of a special vocabulary which, like the lexis of most slangs, changes rapidly; some current expressions are *tronco* (friend), *paliza* (a bore), *carroza* (an older person, someone who is past it, no longer hip), *bocata* (sandwich – this word is now in widespread use), *demasiao* (meaning 'great', as in *un coche demasiao*), along with expressions such as *echarse unos pelotazos* (to go for drinks), *me enrolla cantidá* (I really like it) and *ligar bronce* (to get tanned).

In the Canary Islands and Latin America, the varieties of Spanish which predominate share some of the characteristics of the Andalusian dialect, including the *seseo* phenomenon, i.e. a 'z' or 'c' pronounced [s] in words such as *paz* or *cinco*. Apart from differences in pronunciation, there are numerous differences of vocabulary, both between Peninsular Spanish and the Spanish of Latin America and between the various varieties of Spanish spoken in Latin America itself. Thus, in the Canary Islands and in parts of the Caribbean, the word *guagua* corresponds to the Castilian Spanish *autobús*; in Mexico and Colombia, *manejar un carro* is the equivalent of *conducir un coche*; in much of Latin America the adjective *lindo* is preferred to *bonito*.

Looking to the future, many people conclude that the version of Spanish that will increasingly predominate in the world is the Latin American variety, since only about 15 per cent of Spanish speakers are Spaniards, although it is possible that mass communication will ensure the survival and mutual comprehensibility of all the main dialects. The huge number of speakers (about 350 million, in more than 20 countries) places Spanish among the top three or four most widely spoken languages in the world, and means it occupies an important position in international organizations such as the United Nations (where it is one of the six official languages) and the EU, where it is both an official and a working language. It is also the only official language in the vast majority of Latin American countries and, of course, in Spain, although the situation of Spanish is not always straightforward: within Spain, Catalan, Basque and Galician also have official status in the relevant Autonomous Communities, while in Paraguay, Guarani is an official language along with Spanish. In most Latin American countries, however, languages other than Spanish do not enjoy high social prestige, nor are they official. There are 22 national Academies of the Spanish Language in the world, all of which form part of the Association of Academies of Spanish, founded in 1951 with the aim of preserving the unity of the language and fostering its use.

As a world language, Spanish is in competition with English. The latter predominates in business, technology, the media and academia generally around the world, and Spanish – like other languages – needs special support in order to hold its own in these areas. The national Academies are helpful in this respect, as is the work of the Cervantes Institute, set up in 1991 to promote Spanish language and culture. The Institute devotes much energy to developing the study of Spanish as a foreign language, by organizing classes in the 23 countries where it has centres and by fostering research into the methodologies of teaching Spanish as a foreign language.

In the USA, the position of Spanish vis-à-vis English has come under scrutiny and has often been the cause of controversy. There are about 20 million native speakers of Spanish in the USA, people who in American terms are labelled 'Hispanics', although this label is clearly an oversimplification, given the diverse ethnic backgrounds of the people concerned. In recognition of this diversity, members of the group themselves tend to favour the use of the term 'Latinos' instead. But since Latinos are a relatively marginalized and impoverished minority in a country where English predominates, the language they speak, Spanish, has a low status in the minds of many. The result has been a tendency, in certain areas and especially among young people, to favour the use of English over Spanish. This is offset to some extent, however, by the fact that, within certain US states and cities, Spanish is the majority language, and by the fact that hundreds of radio and television stations broadcast in Spanish in the USA. Spanish is by far the most widely taught second language in the USA, with some 70 per cent of high school students studying it. Despite this, or perhaps because of it, many English speakers in that country are wary of the growing use of Spanish, and fear that English may lose its dominant position. The supporters of the 'English Only' campaign claim that the growth of Spanish is undermining 'American identity' and have opposed the use of Spanish as an official language. In California, the state with the highest number of Latinos, this led in 1986 to the passing of an amendment to the state constitution which made English the only official language.

English has had a strong influence on the Spanish of the Americas, giving rise to what is termed 'Spanglish', a mixture of Spanish and English, using Spanish grammatical structures with an English-style lexis. Some of the more colourful terms to come out of this mix are the following:

chequear ('to check')	for	*inspeccionar*
cloche ('clutch')	for	*embrague*
manager asistente ('assistant manager')	for	*subgerente*
mayor ('mayor')	for	*alcalde*

Examples of sentences found in Puerto Rican Spanglish include such expressions as:

Yo no estoy fuleando.	I'm not fooling.
El rufo liquea.	The roof's leaking.
Está ahora en el grin.	The traffic light's just turned green.

(from Nash 1970)

4.3 MULTILINGUAL SPAIN

In European terms, Spaniards are not great linguists: the levels of bilingualism or multilingualism are low by the standards of most EU countries: within the EU, only the Portuguese, Irish and British have lower levels of multilingual competence than the Spanish. Only 37 per cent of Spaniards can hold a conversation in a language other than their mother tongue (the average for the EU being 44 per cent – European Commission 2000: 91). A significant proportion of these is made up of speakers of English as a second language: some 17 per cent of Spaniards claim competence in English (ibid.: 94), and many more have an elementary knowledge of it. Much of the remaining multilingualism can be attributed to the presence of the other, non-Castilian languages of Spain.

In fact, about a quarter of Spain's population are native speakers of languages other than Castilian. Three of these – Basque, Catalan and Galician – are official languages, along with Castilian, in the Basque Country, Catalonia, Valencia and the Balearic Islands, and Galicia, respectively. The official policy of the Spanish state towards these languages, as enunciated in the 1978 Constitution, could not offer a starker contrast with the policy of the regime of General Franco which preceded it. Under Franco, Spaniards were told to *hablar cristiano*, and were informed that languages such as Catalan and Galician were merely inferior dialects of Castilian. In the new constitution, on the other hand, the vernacular languages are referred to as part of the cultural heritage of Spain and are deemed worthy of respect and protection. The balance between commitment to Castilian and respect for non-Castilian languages is reflected in Article 3 of the Constitution, which sets out three clauses in relation to language policy in the Spanish state:

1 Castilian is the official language of the State. Every Spaniard has the duty to know it, and the right to use it.
2 The other languages of Spain shall also be official languages in the respective Autonomous Communities, in accordance with their Statutes.
3 The wealth of the different linguistic identities in Spain is a part of her cultural heritage and shall be the object of special respect and protection.

Since 1978, tensions have arisen in relation to the status and use of Castilian and the vernacular languages mentioned above; these have been most in evidence in Catalonia and the Basque Country. But, in all cases, use of the vernacular languages has spread and the number of speakers appears to be increasing continually. The strength and status of each of the three languages (Basque, Catalan and Galician) are different, as we shall see below.

4.3.1 Basque

For speakers of other languages (and certainly for Spanish speakers), Basque has the reputation of being a difficult language to learn. The structures of the language are very different from those of Spanish, and even the appearance of the language, when it is written down, can be off-putting. Here, for instance, are some examples of Basque words and phrases:

Kaixo	Hi
Zer moduz?	How are you?
Mesedez	Please
Mila esker	Thank you
Ez horregatik	Not at all, you're welcome
Bai	Yes

Euskara, as the language is called in Basque, does not derive from Latin, as the other languages of the Peninsula do, and is therefore much more difficult for speakers of Spanish to learn than Catalan or Galician. The origins of Basque go back thousands of years, and it may well be that the language was quite widely spoken on the Peninsula in the remote past, but it remains a linguistic puzzle, a language unrelated to the Indo-European family of languages (which includes, for example, Spanish and English), and another reminder, as far as Basque nationalists are concerned, of the cultural difference between the Basque Country and the rest of Spain.

Proportionately fewer people speak Basque than either Catalan or Galician: about half a million of the 2.1 million people living in the Spanish Basque Country (although the language is also spoken in Navarre and in the French Basque region).

Until recently, the Basque-speaking community was confined to the rural areas of the Basque Country. The language did not have the prestige associated with Catalan in Catalonia, and was not spoken by the industrial or commercial bourgeoisie, who were happy to deal with Madrid and the rest of Spain in Castilian. Although Basque nationalists have advocated the use of the language since the early nineteenth century, it was less important as a symbol of nationhood than Catalan was in Catalonia. Early nationalists in particular (such as Sabino Arana) were more inclined to emphasize what they saw as racial differences between Basques and non-Basques. Nonetheless, Arana himself did study Basque and even published philological and etymological essays on it.

Under the repressive policies of the Franco regime, publication in Basque virtually dried up and it was dangerous to speak Basque in public, although, in the later stages of the dictatorship, this repression eased, with the result that some few publications were permitted and some private *ikastolas* (all-Basque schools) were allowed to be set up.

In post-transition Spain, and especially since the enactment of the 1982 Linguistic Normalization Act, assistance has been available at official levels to support the more general use of Basque in education and administration. Basque-language education is now widespread within the region, although the situation of the language is still uncertain, especially given that it is so difficult to learn and that it displays huge dialectal variation.

4.3.2 Catalan

Of the three principal 'minority' languages in Spain, Catalan is the one with the largest number of speakers: about six million in Catalonia alone, without counting Valencia (where a variety of Catalan is spoken by most of the 3.5 million inhabitants) or the Balearic Islands (with a population of about 750 000). Catalan speakers can also evoke a long literary tradition associated with the language which goes back to medieval times, with such outstanding figures as the philosopher Ramón Llull (d. 1315) and the Valencian poet Ausias March (1397?–1459). This tradition was revived in the context of a reawakened national consciousness in the middle of the nineteenth century with the cultural movement known as the *Renaixença*, which gave us the work of writers such as Jacinto Verdaguer (1845–1902) and Joan Maragall (1860–1911).

The similarity between Catalan and Castilian is so great that even the following verses, a lament on the death of his beloved, written by Ausías March in the fifteenth century, can be fairly readily understood by anyone competent in Castilian today:

> Morta és ja la que tant he amat,
> mas jo són viu, veent ella morir:
> amb gran amor no es pot bé soferir
> que de la mort me pusca haver llunyat.
>
> (quoted in Keown 1999: 157)

Catalan also has the strongest legal framework of the three vernacular languages. Since the restoration of the system of Autonomous Communities in the late 1970s, three important pieces of legislation supporting the use of Catalan have been passed. The first was the Catalan Statute of Autonomy (1979), which explicitly stated that Catalan was the *lengua propia* of Catalonia. The second was the *Llei de normalització lingüística a Catalunya* of 1983, which set out the principle that children should have the right to an education through Catalan at all levels, from early schooling through to university, and introduced the notion of 'immersion programmes' in Catalan for Castilian-speaking children. The third was the *Llei de política lingüística* of 1998, which further strengthened the position of Catalan in the areas of education, administration, business and the media, and reinforced the legal position of those who insisted on giving preference to Catalan over Castilian. Although in both of the latter legal instruments the rights of Castilian speakers are specifically protected – children and adults have the right to use Castilian and to be educated in Castilian – the thrust of the legislation is to favour Catalan by emphasizing its special position as the *lengua propia* of Catalonia. In the Preamble to the 1998 Act, Catalan is described as having been 'negatively affected by many events in the history of Catalonia, leading to a situation where its survival is in doubt'. It continues:

> This has been due to various factors, including political persecution . . . and the legal imposition of Castilian during more than two hundred and fifty years; the political and socio-economic conditions which have produced

demographic changes in recent decades, and also, in common with other European subaltern languages, the limited range which it has in a world where, in the fields of communication, information technology and culture, globalization is a key factor.

Catalan is seen by the legislators of the Generalitat as a language under siege. There are references to the history of repression of the language and culture of Catalonia by Madrid governments. There is an allusion to the increase in the numbers of speakers of Castilian in Catalonia over recent decades, which was due to the huge influx of migrants from other parts of Spain (particularly Andalusia) in the 1960s and 1970s. Catalan is also seen as being threatened by the increased globalization of modern society, presumably due to the widespread use of English in the media.

It is against this background that we need to see the Catalonians' desire for legislation which would provide extensive protection and support for the language, which is what the 1998 Act, in particular, does. Repeatedly, the Act makes reference to the fact that Catalan is the *lengua propia* of Catalonia, and draws out the implications of this in terms of the practical support that should be given to Catalan.

The Act thus ensures that Catalan is used increasingly widely in all areas of life in Catalonia. While it guarantees the rights of Castilian speakers, the brief it hands to the Catalonian authorities is the extension of the use of Catalan to all those organizations that have dealings with the public. In the educational sphere, it forbids the separation of students into groups on the basis of language, thereby placing an onus on both the teaching profession and the student body to develop sufficient competence in both languages for them to be able to teach or study through them. The aim is that Catalan should become the normal vehicle of expression at all levels of the educational system (Art. 20) and that, by the end of compulsory schooling at the latest, children, no matter what their usual language was when they commenced their schooling, should be able to use both official languages fluently and correctly (Art. 21). Certainly, for those who would prefer the exclusive use of Castilian, there is no alternative but to become competent in Catalan. In theory, this Article presumably also means that every school in Catalonia must ensure that its students also emerge with full competence in Castilian.

Resentment against these language policies, and, in particular, against the provision of fines to be imposed on companies and other organizations which fail to support Catalan strongly enough, is growing in Catalonia. It is a special problem for many Castilians resident there. Currently, however, such resentment does not appear to be either widespread or very radical. Associations have emerged to defend the interests of Castilian speakers, such as the *Asociación por la Tolerancia y contra la Discriminación* and the *Acción Cultural Miguel de Cervantes*, but, as Clare Mar-Molinero (1997: 158) suggests, 'whilst clearly there is significant opposition from an articulate minority in Catalonia about the present language policies, it would appear that the majority are still happy with the situation'.

4.3.3 Galician

Galician, which closely resembles Portuguese, is also quite similar to Castilian, and Castilian and Galician have had a mutual influence on each other over the centuries. Muslim influence on Galicia was slight, and consequently there is little evidence of Arabic in Galician, and those words of Arabic origin which exist in the language have entered through the influence of Castilian. The Latin which predominated in the north-west of the Peninsula has been described (Díez 1977: 272) as a more conservative variety than that found elsewhere in Spain, with the result that certain changes typically found in Castilian are not found in Galician. Hence the persistence of the characteristic diphthongs found in Galician such as -ei- and -ou- , which derive from Latin diphthongs and which have given the simpler Castilian vowel sounds -e- and -o-; examples include the diphthongs in words such as *camareiro* and *outro*.

Galician, like Basque, was preserved mainly in rural areas; unlike Basque, however, it has also had a strong literary tradition dating back to the Middle Ages. King Alfonso the Wise wrote in Galician as well as Castilian, as did many other medieval writers, especially poets. A steady output of Galician writing continued down through the centuries, although the Galician literary revival began in earnest only in the early nineteenth century. This movement – known as the *Rexurdimento* – produced writers such as the poets Rosalía de Castro (1837–85) and Eduardo Pondal (1835–1917). Castro's poems often express a sweetly melancholic sentiment, frequently associated in the minds of other Spaniards – and of Galicians themselves – with the terrain and the character of this wet and windswept land. The term often employed to refer to this sentiment is *morriña* – meaning a kind of nostalgia or a yearning for home – a word which has itself passed from Galician into Castilian. Here is a small sample of Castro's lyrical ability (along with a translation into Castilian), from her collection *Cantares gallegos* (1863):

> Iréi, mais dame un biquiño
> antes de que de ti me aparte,
> que eses labiños de rosa
> inda non sei cómo saben.
>
> [Iré, mas dame un besito
> antes que de ti me aparte,
> porque esos labios de rosa
> aún no sé ni cómo saben.]

(Quesada Marco 1987: 140)

Galician has existed in a typical diglossic situation, i.e. where one language – in this case, Galician – is spoken quite widely at lower socio-economic levels, while the other language – Castilian – is the language of power and influence. The use of Galician has spread, however, in recent decades, with the impetus given it by the positive attitudes encouraged in the new democracy and by the passing of the Galician Linguistic Normalization Act of 1983. The language is now widely spoken within the educational system as well as being used for administrative purposes. The relative ease with which it can be learned by Castilian speakers has facilitated these developments, but the linguistic policies pursued by the Xunta de Galicia have been much less aggressive than those pursued in Catalonia. Currently, over two million people (some 90 per cent of the Galician population) have some competence in one of the three dialects of the language, and there appear to be good prospects for a general pattern of bilingualism developing in this Autonomous Community.

4.4 COMMUNICATIVE CONTRASTS: SPANISH AND ENGLISH

The question posed at the beginning of this chapter was: 'How do Spaniards speak?' One short and simple answer (though clearly an inadequate one!) would be: 'Loud and fast'. To the English speaker's ear, Spanish as spoken by Spaniards can often seem like a torrent of words gushing out at very high volume and speed, and Spanish speakers can often appear to the unpractised ear as displaying the kind of speech characteristics that English speakers would associate with angry disputation, even when what is taking place is 'normal' conversation. Needless to say, to describe all Spaniards as 'loud, fast talkers' would obviously be to project a caricature. In fact, many different factors will affect the rate and volume of speech in any language, including variables such as personality, social context, the number of speakers involved in the conversation and, possibly, region: to cite just one example of the latter, Leonese people, for instance, have a reputation for being *parcos en la lengua* (i.e. sparing in their use of language), while Andalusians are characterized as being chatty and voluble. A more realistic account of how Spaniards use language would clearly need to include a description of which grammatical structures are preferred by Spanish speakers, which linguistic devices are employed to carry out the various speech acts, when and in what circumstances particular speech acts occur and many other elements of language use covering phonetic, syntactic and pragmatic aspects of language. Offering such an account is clearly beyond the scope of this book; nonetheless, a small random sample of some of the more striking features of communicative contrast between Spanish and English is presented below, under the following headings: (1) courtesy, politeness and cordiality; (2) argumentation styles; and (3) non-verbal aspects of communication (i.e. gesture and body posture).

4.4.1 Courtesy, politeness and cordiality

Speakers of a foreign language often need to be careful about their use of the language, because of the twin dangers of either appearing discourteous or appearing excessively polite. Spanish speakers of English sometimes seem abrupt and overly direct in their manner because of their tendency not to include expressions such as 'please' and 'thank you' in their speech to the extent that native speakers of English do, and they can also find themselves accused of 'giving orders' when they employ direct imperatives ('Give me the X', 'Do it this way') in the Spanish manner, rather than attenuating their request with more indirect forms ('Would you mind doing X, please?'). Expressions of gratitude and direct imperatives are both available within the range of expressions and structures in the two languages, of course, but the degree to which each is used and the circumstances within which they are used vary from one language to the other.

In former centuries, aristocratic Spaniards in particular were noted for the elaborately polite formulations they employed in addressing one another, and much thought and care were required in order not to offend. When visits took place between members of the upper classes, strict rules of linguistic behaviour were observed, at least until third parties had removed themselves from the scene. Here, for instance, is the advice that Richard Ford gives to Victorian English gentlemen who are contemplating a visit to a Spanish counterpart during their stay in Spain:

> When you get up to take leave, if of a lady, you should say, *A los pies de V. (usted), Señora*, 'My lady, I place myself at your feet;' to which she will reply, *Beso á V. la mano, Caballero*, 'I kiss your hand, Sir:' *Vaya con Dios, que V. lo pase bien*, 'May you depart with God, and continue well'; to which you must reply, *Quede V. con Dios*, 'May you remain with God.'. . . On leaving a Spaniard's house, observe if he thus addresses you: *Esta casa está muy á la disposición de V. cuando guste favorecerla*, 'This house is entirely at your disposal, whenever you please to favour it.' Once thus invited, you become a friend of the family. If the compliment be omitted, it is clear that the owner never wishes to see you again.
>
> (Ford 1898: 42)

Despite the quaint antiquity of the linguistic behaviour described here, at least one aspect of it still survives, though in less elaborate form: the formula *Estás en tu casa* is still widely used to welcome guests into Spanish homes, and it is generally an indication of genuine hospitality.

Leo Hickey (1991) has examined patterns of politeness in the everyday use of British English and the Spanish of the Peninsula and has concluded that the contrast between the two is that Spaniards are more inclined to show 'positive politeness' and Britons are more concerned with 'negative politeness'. In line with the approach set out in Brown and Levinson (1987), positive politeness refers to compliments, expressions of reassurance, admiration, approval and the like, while negative politeness refers to the need not to appear intrusive, to express regret for minor impositions or requests for services, etc. He suggests that 'compliments and expressions of praise or appreciation are a normal part of Spanish social behaviour' (Hickey 1991: 5), with the result that we frequently hear Spaniards utter a statement of the sort *¡Qué X eres!*, where the X slot could be filled by any positive-sounding noun or adjective, such as *buena persona, inteligente, puntual* or *hábil*. Similarly, Spaniards readily use appreciative or reassuring phrases such as *Te aprecio mucho*, or *Mi mujer te admira*, etc. Such expressions would be likely to appear exaggerated or hypocritical to an English speaker (especially a British speaker of English). If Britons use positive politeness, they tend to be slightly embarrassed about it and use somewhat jokey expressions to cover their embarrassment, expressions such as 'I'd be lost without you' or 'You're a genius.'

What British people think of as politeness or good manners usually refers to negative politeness, i.e. the avoidance of verbal behaviour which would appear offensive or face-threatening. This manifests itself in the abundant use of 'please', 'thank you' and 'sorry', which seems so strange to Spaniards. The circumstances in which such expressions are used – brushing past someone, asking a shop assistant for attention, etc. – would normally strike the Spaniard as being very trivial cases of intrusion, a part of the normal business of living, and not instances which should give rise to the need to apologize, to thank or to request favours.

Negative politeness is based on the idea that one should 'keep one's distance' and not intrude on the personal space of another person. But what one culture perceives as a politeness, another culture may see as aloofness. Anna Wierzbicka (1991) maintains that, in Poland, for example, cordiality is deemed a 'cultural value', and that the English tendency to maintain one's distance is often viewed by Poles as a lack of interest or enthusiasm. Spanish people, too, seem to value positive expressions of cordiality, and English speakers can seem to 'lack passion' when they speak Spanish unless they inject energy and enthusiasm into their voices. Affectivity may be conveyed by tone of voice, although presumably other, more strictly linguistic markers are also of relevance here, such as the availability in Spanish of familiar forms of address (*tú, vosotros*), where English has only 'you'. As Wierzbicka (1991: 47) suggests in relation to the contrast between Polish and English, the English pronoun 'you' is democratic but it also serves to keep everyone at a distance; presumably the same distinction applies between Spanish and English, and when familiar forms are combined in Spanish with other markers of affectivity (including, for instance, the use of diminutives), we can begin to understand how English speakers of Spanish may come across to Spanish people as 'cold'.

4.4.2 Argumentation

There are cultural variables also at work in the way in which we converse and the manner in which we intervene in discussions. Broadly speaking, English speakers seem to opt for more orderly interventions and interruptions, waiting until their interlocutor pauses or even finishes what they are saying before interjecting to voice an opinion, while speakers of Spanish are more inclined to allow what they say to 'overlap' with what another person says.

Marisa Cordella (1996) has demonstrated some of the differences between how native speakers of Spanish and Anglophone speakers of Spanish use the language in the context of argument. She observed three groups of students discussing gender issues: one group (G1) were Argentinian and Chilean speakers of Spanish; the second group (G2) were English-speaking learners of Spanish who had lived for one year in a Spanish-speaking country; while the third (G3) was a group of English native speakers who had not spent a significant amount of time in a country where Spanish was spoken. The interventions of G1 and G2 were more 'confrontational' in style, in that speakers tended to intervene before other speakers had finished what they were saying. These groups would pose quick questions, seek clarification, propose a different point of view or even finish the speaker's sentences much more frequently than G3 would. This latter group (the English speakers without much practice of the use of Spanish in authentic situations with native Spanish speakers) were inclined to allow speakers to complete their utterances, tended to contradict and challenge less than G1 and G2, and displayed more orderliness in turn-taking overall.

While it is tempting to offer a value judgement on this behaviour (along the lines of one cultural group being 'more polite' than another), Cordella's study suggests that this would be a mistake. The overlaps and challenge questions and the 'latching' of one piece of talk on to another was not viewed negatively by those who were interrupted in groups G1 or G2. Rather, such verbal 'confrontations' were seen by these speakers as making a contribution to the ongoing discussion and as evidence of the listeners' lively interest in what the speakers were saying. Hence, while theorists of linguistic politeness (such as Brown and Levinson 1987) might categorize overlaps as 'turn-taking violations' and consequently 'face-threatening', the experiment described here would lend support to the view that there are significant cultural differences in relation to what is regarded as cooperativeness, politeness or face-threatening behaviour. In particular, overlaps are less likely to be seen as interruptions in Spanish than in English.

4.4.3 Non-verbal communication: body posture and gesture

Body posture and gesture are both semiotic, in that they are aspects of human behaviour which are related to communication. Although neither of these features is strictly linguistic or verbal, however, they are often used in ways that interact with human speech. In Green (1968), it is claimed that in human communication only 30–35 per cent of the social meaning is conveyed through the use of language, and that our bodies communicate the rest. Certainly both gesture and the movement and placing of our bodies have communicative value: making eye contact in a discussion can encourage our interlocutor to speak; sitting with legs crossed and with the body oriented away from our interlocutor can be a sign – usually a subconscious one – that we are hostile to the other person or uninterested in what they are saying.

One aspect of this behaviour which, it is claimed, may be subject to cultural variation is *proxemics*, or the study of the flow and shift of distance between people. This would apply, if valid, both to people who are conversing and to those who simply happen to find themselves in the presence of others. Edward Hall (1959) offered the best-known account of proxemic behaviour, suggesting that distances between people could be classified as falling into four 'zones', which he categorized as follows:

1 Intimate (0–18 inches)
2 Personal (18 inches to 4 feet)
3 Social (4–12 feet)
4 Public (beyond 12 feet)

Hall contended, furthermore, that one could distinguish 'contact cultures' from 'noncontact cultures', the former including, for example, people from Arab countries, southern Europeans and Latin Americans, while the latter category embraced northern Europeans, Asians, North Americans and Indians. His observations suggested to him that people from contact cultures were likely to prefer shorter limits in the four zones listed above, while people from noncontact cultures preferred the longer distances. This classification would place Spaniards among the 'contact cultures', and English, Irish and North Americans, for example, in the 'noncontact' group. We would expect Spaniards, on this view, to tolerate greater physical proximity and, possibly, more bodily contact than, say, the English or the Irish. The study of such patterns of behaviour is difficult to carry out with rigour, although some of the work of Fernando Poyatos (1983), for instance, would suggest that at least some people who are familiar with both cultures are inclined to agree that the distinction is valid. It is worth bearing in mind, however, that many variables other than 'cultural difference' will have an effect on proxemic behaviour. Martin Remland and his colleagues, for instance, concluded that the influence of cultural norms has been greatly exaggerated. On the basis of their research into proxemic behaviour in people from the Netherlands, France and England (Remland et al. 1991: 229), they were able to maintain that 'proxemic and haptic behaviors are affected substantially more by an array of situational variables (e.g. relationship, conversational topic, emotional state, personality, etc.)'.

The use of *gesture*, on the other hand, is not only clearly related to the verbal dimension of communication, but is also culture-specific. Ian Gibson (1992: 172) says that 'Spaniards speak not only with their vocal cords but with the rest of their bodies' and he echoes the nineteenth-century traveller George Borrow, who insisted that English speakers of Spanish must learn to apply their hands to the 'indispensable office of gesticulation'. Others have pointed to the many details of difference between English hand and facial gestures and Spanish ones (e.g. Green 1968), while again suggesting that the inventory of English gestures and body postures is relatively poor compared with that of Spanish. Although the gestures accompanying Spanish speech are probably easy to interpret, their use requires both skill and practice, whether it be a question of the correct force with which to tap your face when saying *¡Qué cara!* or the timing of the exact moment in which to raise your hand to your forehead when saying *Estoy hasta aquí*, to let someone know that you've had enough!

FEATURE: SPATIAL EXPRESSION IN SPANISH AND ENGLISH

One area of contrast between Spanish and English, related to the issue of whether language can influence how we think, is the expression of spatial relationships. Examining how we talk about space may help us to uncover some of the facts about how language relates to general cognition, just as it can also reflect specific aspects of our different cultures.

Some interesting contrasts are revealed through the study of deictic reference in the two languages. The term 'deixis' is used to refer to the way in which various features of language and linguistic elements can only be properly understood if we are aware of the context in which they are being referred to. Thus, the locative particle 'here' (or *aquí*) cannot be fully meaningful for us unless we know enough about the linguistic context in which the word is uttered to be able to tell what location is being referred to by that word. Similarly, we cannot know which particular apple is being referred to by the demonstrative *esta* when someone uses an expression such as *esta manzana* unless we can actually see the person making a gesture or holding up the apple in question. Both locatives and demonstratives exhibit interesting contrasts between Spanish and English: for instance, in terms of the tripartite 'division of space' which is implicit in the sets *aquí–ahí–allí* and *este–ese–aquel*, compared with the binary division in the English pairs here–there and this–that. There are many subtleties, however, in the usage of such terms: for example, someone who is offering another person a choice between two apples which they are holding in either hand is likely to say, in Spanish: '¿Cuál prefieres, esta manzana o ésta?', while an English-speaker is more likely to say: 'Which do you prefer, this apple or that one?'

Deictic reference to movement also offers a variety of contrasts. For example, both *venir* and 'come' are considered by most speakers of Spanish and English to refer to movement towards the speaker; however, 'come' is frequently used to refer to movement towards a place that the speaker is not at ('Will you come to the party with me?'), whereas such usage is much less frequent in Spanish ('¿Quieres ir a la fiesta conmigo?').

There is some evidence that the particular language spoken may influence general cognition, including the way we think about spatial relationships (see Richardson 1998). In the picture below, for example, a ball drawn 'to the left of the sandals' can be positioned in either of the two locations (A) or (B), the first option indicating a deictic strategy for describing the location, the second indicating an 'absolute' strategy and dependent on the perspective of the viewer perceiving the scene.

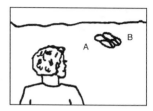

(Eng.)   Draw a ball to the left of the sandals.
(Span.)   Dibuja una pelota a la izquierda de las sandalias.
                              (adapted from Hill 1982)

When tested on groups of Spanish- and English-speaking students, respectively, the two groups showed significant differences with regard to their choice of strategy for this task, the English speakers preferring the deictic strategy and the Spanish speakers opting equally for the two strategies, (A) and (B). Results such as these offer broad support for the 'Whorfian' view which suggests that the particular language we speak influences the way we think.

READING: JOSÉ ANTONIO MARINA, 'LA COMICIDAD'

As the Spanish linguist José Antonio Marina demonstrates in the passage below (taken from his book *La selva del lenguaje*, 1998), language and culture come together in a special way in humour. Most jokes are linguistic in nature, even those that are not puns, in that their effectiveness will often depend on the effectiveness of the punchline, both in terms of its phrasing and (especially when the joke is relayed orally) in the quality of the delivery of the line: as we know, it's the way you tell it that counts. And frequently jokes are highly culture-specific.

Here, then, is one linguist's attempt at articulating the mystery of humour (with a few good jokes thrown in):

Voy a contarles un chiste:

Un judío ortodoxo recibe la noticia de que su hijo se ha hecho cristiano. Desolado, va a buscar consuelo en su amigo Isaac.

— Amigo Isaac, estoy angustiado. Mi hijo se ha convertido al cristianismo.

— ¡Qué me vas a decir a mí! — contesta Isaac —. El mío también. Y cristiano fervoroso.

Ambos deciden ir a buscar consuelo en su rabino.

— Rabino, estamos muy tristes porque nuestros hijos se han hecho cristianos.

Esperaban comprensión y apoyo, pero, lo que encontraron fue un rabino desesperado:

— ¡Qué me vais a decir a mí! — dijo —. Mi hijo también es cristiano. Y además se ha hecho cura. Lo único que podemos hacer es orar a Yahvé para que nos ayude en este trance.

Los tres judíos ortodoxos se postraron de rodillas y rezaron al Altísimo: '¡Oh, Yahvé! Estamos consternados porque nuestros hijos se han hecho cristianos.'

En ese momento se oyó una tremenda voz desde lo alto que decía:

— ¡Qué me vais a decir a mí!

Está claro que este chiste resulta incomprensible para quien no sepa nada de teología cristiana – que Cristo es hijo de Yahvé –, por lo que es un buen ejemplo de los requisitos de la comprensión. Pero he de confesar que he puesto este ejemplo con una doble intención. Me interesa mucho averiguar cómo comprendemos un chiste, porque me parece tarea de extremada dificultad. Decimos que hay personas sin sentido del humor, que no captan el significado de las ingeniosidades. ¿Qué les pasa?

Intentaré seguir el proceso de comprensión del humor estudiándolo en los niños pequeños. El chiste supone una violación de las expectativas, una irremediable sorpresa. El discurso no sigue la vía prevista, descarrila, organiza estropicios sin cuento.

La secuencia previsible se rompe, como en el caso siguiente.

Una niña dice:

—Mamá, ¿cuando sea mayor me casaré y tendré un marido como papá?

La mamá, sonriendo:

— Claro que sí, mi amor.

— ¿Y si no me caso, seré una solterona como la tía Ernestina?

— Sí, querida.

— ¡Ay, qué dura es la vida de las mujeres, mamá!

Este suceso puede comprenderse de manera realista, y entonces resulta trágico, no cómico. Es verdad que en la vida real puede darse la trágica alternativa entre la aspereza y la soledad. Por eso, para interpretar la afirmación de la niña como un suceso cómico hay que instalarse en la irrealidad, hay que sintonizar afectivamente con él. Françoise Bariaud (1983), autora del mejor estudio que conozco sobre la génesis del humor en el niño, explica que la comprensión del chiste tiene dos etapas: la percepción de lo inesperado y su evaluación. Hace después una finta interesante y lista. Antes de hablar de la comprensión, habla de la incomprensión. ¿Por qué una persona no entiende un chiste? Hay una incomprensión de origen cognitivo – como en el chiste sobre los judíos ortodoxos – que es fácil de explicar. El oyente no dispone de los conocimientos necesarios para saber de qué va la cosa. Se queda, pues, in albis. Más interesante es la incapacidad emocional. El sujeto que encuentra divertido un chiste tiene que percibir la incongruencia y, además, adherirse a ella. Tiene que entrar en el juego. Los niños nos instruyen adecuadamente sobre esto. La sorpresa sólo les resulta graciosa si la experimentan en un contexto afectivo de seguridad y juego. De lo contrario, puede resultarles turbadora.

Hace unos días presencié una escena curiosa en un aeropuerto. En una de las salas de espera había dos paseantes disparejos. Un niño de unos tres años muy divertido al separarse de su madre y un hombre de edad algo más que madura alto y obeso. Al encontrarse con el niño hizo un gesto cómico, a lo Frankenstein. El niño se rió, volvió junto a su madre, pero se separó enseguida. La escena se repitió, y el niño volvió al regazo de su madre y a separarse de él. Pero a la tercera vez, cuando se repitió la misma escena, o al menos eso es lo que yo vi, el niño de repente se echó a llorar y se refugió definitivamente en las faldas de su madre. ¿Qué había sucedido? Rothbart propone que en la percepción de lo cómico hay un juicio acerca de la seguridad de la situación. Alan Sroufe (1972), un conocido especialista en psicología infantil, indica que 'las cosas que hacen los progenitores que tienen más probabilidad de producir risa en el niño son las mismas cosas que casi seguramente le arrancarán lágrimas si las hace un extraño'. Bergson, un personaje de extremada perspicacia, advirtió que la comicidad exigía una cierta anestesia afectiva. Para considerar divertida la siguiente greguería: 'Al amputado de los dos brazos le han dejado en chaleco para toda la vida', hay que no ser el amputado ni prestar demasiada atención al amputado. Quien escucha un chiste sintiéndose afectado por su contenido lo interpretará de forma realista, o sea, no cómica. En una investigación llevada a cabo por Levine y Redlich (1960) sobre una población de adultos (enfermos y no enfermos), con la ayuda de estímulos humorísticos muy cargados de significación agresiva o sexual, resultó que, con un nivel de inteligencia equivalente, algunos adultos no comprendían el significado humorístico, que para los demás era muy claro. Se sentían agredidos por el argumento, y esta irritación bloqueaba cualquier otra interpretación.

No pretendo aclarar el misterioso fenómeno de la comicidad, sino poner un contundente ejemplo de la incapacidad de los paradigmas cognitivos para explicar la comprensión de un texto, de una situación, de una persona. Interpretamos las palabras desde nuestros conocimientos lingüísticos, y también desde nuestros prejuicios, y también – lo que supone una complicación añadida – desde nuestro estado afectivo. Sometida a tantas coacciones, barco zarandeado por tantas mareas, vientos, mares de fondo, oleajes, la comprensión resulta una actividad tan improbable como la buena navegación. Sólo los que sepan aprovechar las caprichosas bandadas de los vientos y las aguas mantendrán el rumbo. Zafándome de la metáfora: comprender es una tarea de inteligencia, astucia y tesón.

(Marina 1998: 159–62)

FURTHER READING

Asher, R. E., *The Encyclopaedia of Language and Linguistics* (London, Pergamon, 1993).
Volume 8 of this encyclopaedia contains useful articles on Spanish and on the language situation in Spain.
Batchelor, R. E. and Pountain, C. J., *Using Spanish: a guide to contemporary usage* (Cambridge, Cambridge University Press, 1992).
An excellent practical textbook on the uses of modern Spanish.
Ethnologue, *Spain*, http://www.sil.org/ethnologue/countries/Spai.html
A good starting point for information on Basque, Catalan, Castilian and Galician.
Mar-Molinero, C., *The Spanish-speaking World: a practical introduction to sociolinguistic issues* (London, Routledge, 1997).
Offers an account of sociolinguistic issues of relevance to Spain and other Spanish-speaking countries, including a discussion of minority languages.
Penny, Ralph, *A History of the Spanish Language* (Cambridge, Cambridge University Press, 1991).
The best guide to the historical development of Spanish.
Turell, M. Teresa, *Multilingualism in Spain: sociolinguistic and psycho-linguistic aspects of linguistic minority groups* (Clevedon, Multilingual Matters, 2001).
Chapter 1, 'Spain's multilingual make-up: beyond, within and across Babel' offers a good overview of Spanish multilingualism.

5

Icons and Archetypes: Who are their Heroes?

5.1 INTRODUCTION: ICONIC HUMAN FIGURES

Every culture has its own icons and archetypes – people, real or imaginary, who stand for qualities that are deemed significant for the culture concerned. Icons are defined by Horrocks (1995: 17) as 'key figures or exemplars, who have somehow lost their everyday reality and have become legendary figures, who seem to contain within themselves a whole résumé of emblematic meanings'. The most prominent such icon in the western world is probably Jesus Christ, but figures as diverse as Che Guevara, Princess Diana, Mahatma Gandhi, Diego Maradona or Christopher Columbus also fit the category, in that they are individuals who, in some sense, transcended the normal limits associated with a human life, and whose fame has grown so large that they have taken on a mythical status. They are admired by people from a wide range of cultures and backgrounds; on the one hand, people identify closely with them, and, on the other, they regard them as possessing qualities that set them apart from (and frequently above) the normal run of human existence, making them seem to stand outside time.

Icons are a highly visual phenomenon. Mention of William Shakespeare evokes an image based on the portraits of him with which we are most familiar. With an icon, we sense that we know what the person looks like, even if our image turns out to be a rather hazy one when we attempt to examine it. Miguel de Cervantes, the author of *Don Quixote de la Mancha* and Spain's 'equivalent' to Shakespeare, is himself iconic, in that most Spaniards would readily conjure up an image of the man when his name is mentioned. A similar thing would happen with many other figures, including, for instance, the dictator General Franco, the 1960s pop star Julio Iglesias, the popular post-war flamenco singer and actress Lola Flores or the Civil War heroine Dolores Ibárruri ('La Pasionaria'). Each of these people would evoke the era in which they lived, and figures such as these often serve, especially in the media, as a way of summing up a generation, a period of time or a particular sociocultural milieu. The degree of iconicity of any specific figure will vary subjectively from one observer to another, with factors such as age and level of education playing an important role: for many young Spaniards, Franco, Iglesias or Ibárruri may not be readily available as meaningful cultural icons, while the current heroes of sport and music may be much more significant. Despite this, there are always figures who persistently seem to hold special meanings, either within a particular culture or throughout many cultures, and the focus in this chapter is on Spanish examples of such figures.

The notion of an 'archetype' is related to the idea of the icon but is a more abstract concept. Some of the figures already mentioned would frequently be described as 'archetypal'. Gandhi, for instance, might be considered the archetypal pacifist, meaning that he encapsulates qualities which we think of as typical of a pacifist: he serves as a prototype or prime example, and is held up as a model to others who would be pacifists. The best-known Spanish

Figure 3: A Castilian Spanish icon? One famous depiction of the classic Castilian gentleman – often seen as an icon of 'Spanishness' – is this austere sixteenth-century portrait of a Spanish nobleman, Juan de Silva, who was Notary Mayor of Toledo. The picture is known by the title *El caballero de la mano en el pecho* ('The nobleman with his hand on his chest') and was painted by El Greco (1541–1614). (Museo del Prado).

archetypes are probably Don Quixote and Don Juan – the first an archetypal idealist fighting against the odds, the latter the archetypal seducer of women. As happens with any human figure (whether real or fictional), there is a temptation to oversimplify our description, to see the figure as a one-dimensional 'idealist' or 'seducer', while the character may be far more complex and, as an icon or archetype, is capable of carrying a variety of meanings.

The focus in this chapter is on human icons and archetypal figures, although it is worth bearing in mind that icons can be significant images of anything, including non-human animals and entities. A famous painting, for example, may attain iconic status: this is the case with El Greco's painting 'The nobleman with his hand on his chest' (see Fig. 3), which has often served as an icon of 'Spanishness'; and it is the case with Picasso's 'Guernica' (see Feature, Chapter 10), which has frequently served as an 'anti-war icon'. Other Spanish icons include such images as the flamenco dancer or the fighting bull, the Spanish fan or the Toledo sword. These are non-specific items, either objects or personality types, which are employed as a shorthand way of referring to certain qualities and characteristics. Frequently found in the context of tourist souvenirs, they are iconic in that they are used to evoke qualities deemed to be particularly 'Spanish', even if their use generally supports a false and simplistic interpretation of cultural specificity and risks reinforcing clichéd 'national' stereotypes.

The qualities we detect in icons and archetypes may be the conventional meanings associated with them, such as the impractical idealism of Don Quixote or the courage of the bullfighter, or they may be other qualities which are marginal to these or which subvert them. However they are used, these historical figures, fictional characters and cultural icons are 'given' elements of Spanish culture, and can thus be referred to, subverted, manipulated or otherwise employed, to assist in the process of cultural production. What they express will vary enormously from one situation to the next, and there will never be total agreement on the nuances of the meanings they convey.

However, they have been invoked repeatedly in a wide range of cultural productions, and have operated as powerful symbols within 'texts' which have something important to say about how people live their lives and interpret their existence. The texts in which they are thus used vary from written ones – novels, plays or poems – to advertising and film, to everyday conversation or popular cultural events such as the carnival or the Valencian *fallas*. In these contexts, what is said may range from the profound to the whimsical, from the melancholy to the satirical. However, if we think of the effect produced by a performance of Mozart's *Don Giovanni*, the centrality of Don Quixote to the spiritual quest of Miguel de Unamuno (see 9.5), or the powerful effect achieved through the use of the imagery of bullfighting by artists such as Goya or Picasso, we realize that icons and archetypes both operate at a fundamental level within particular cultures and also have universally applicable resonances of meaning.

5.2 'YO PIENSO, Y ES ASÍ VERDAD . . .': DON QUIXOTE DE LA MANCHA

One set of figures of major significance to Spanish people are archetypal characters from the history of Spanish culture. These are the protagonists of some of the major works of Spanish literature, who seem to embody certain characteristics specifically associated with Spanish sensibilities but also display qualities which people anywhere can identify with. Like Shakespeare's Hamlet or Melville's Captain Ahab, they are, on the one hand, culture-specific, since they emerge from a particular cultural context, but at the same time they are motivated by universal needs and desires, and they seek resolutions to human conflicts with which people from any culture can identify.

Probably the best-known such character, drawn from the most famous work of Spanish literature, is Don Quixote. The novel was published in two parts (in 1605 and 1615), and the principal intention of its author, Miguel de Cervantes (1547–1616), seems to have been to ridicule the popular stories of the time which featured fearless knights doing great deeds, slaying dragons and defeating their enemies. Cervantes' protagonist is an impoverished gentleman farmer who reads so many tales of chivalry that he ends up imagining he is a knight errant who must saddle up his horse, find a squire to accompany him, identify a maiden to whom he will dedicate his glorious deeds, and set off around the dusty roads of La Mancha in search of adventures.

A simplistic interpretation of this character would suggest that he be dismissed as an ageing fool who is out of touch with reality and who deserves only to be mocked. Cervantes' achievement, however, is to make this madness appealing, to represent it as signifying that undefinable dimension of human experience which is individualistic, rebellious and 'anti-establishment'. Even this, of course, is an oversimplification: there is a complex interplay throughout the book between the need to assert individual identity and the imperative to conform to the accepted standards of society. Cervantes was writing in the late sixteenth century, a time when Spanish society was becoming increasingly concerned with material possessions and outward appearances, and when there was enormous pressure to conform and to be seen to behave in a socially acceptable manner. Melveena McKendrick describes the Spain of the time in these terms:

> As the rich grew richer and the poor became destitute, Castilian society, seeking escape from a truth too hard to bear, became increasingly a society of outward display, of purchased honors and meaningless posturing, of hollow values with little relevance to reality. It was a society in which religious orthodoxy and intellectual containment marched hand in hand with social hypocrisy and laxity of manners; where self-delusion rubbed shoulders with insecurity, disillusion, fatalism, and cynicism; where, in the

face of a starving population, the cult of racial purity became the source of idleness and an excuse for inaction.

(McKendrick 1980: 182)

Apart from any simple burlesque based on a parody of tales of romantic chivalry, the book manages to comment, directly or obliquely, on the foibles and corruption of the Spain of the time and on the universal tensions between a particular individual's perspective on life and the desire to be appreciated by others. Major themes in the book include the relation between life and art, the nature of love, the corrupting influence of power and money and the inadequacies of systems of social justice.

Cervantes had had wide experience of life in general and Spanish life in particular by the time he started to write this book. In his early fifties when he composed it, he had already been a soldier in the Mediterranean; had worked as a servant of the Spanish Crown, gathering provisions for the ill-fated Armada expedition of 1588; and had more recently spent a rather fruitless and financially ruinous period attempting to collect taxes for the king. He had been taken captive by Muslim pirates and held hostage for five years in north Africa, and he had spent time in jail owing to his inability to handle his money affairs. This varied experience is distilled into a book wherein nothing is as it seems and where the consistent message is that the human imagination is unlikely to be satisfied with simple and obvious explanations. Irony and humour run deeply through the book: while the physical dimension of the comedy can be seen as slapstick, the action and the characters' comments on events cause us to pause and to reflect that there is something essentially human and very appealing about an individual's desire to transcend the limitations set on his or her experience by society.

The figure of Don Quixote can be read ultimately as a wry comment on conventionalism and a plea for faith and optimism. In this respect, Don Quixote's message could be seen as conforming with orthodox Catholic doctrine: faith is not achieved by reason but rather transcends it and requires of the believer a blind leap which ennobles his or her soul. In the contexts in which we witness this at work in Don Quixote's adventures, however, the effect is both comic and pathetic. Here he is, for instance, in an early part of the book (I. 4), accosting some merchants on their way from Toledo to Murcia to buy silks. Don Quixote believes they are knights and demands that they declare his mistress, Dulcinea del Toboso, superior in beauty to any other woman in the world: 'Todo el mundo se tenga, si todo el mundo no confiesa que no hay en el mundo todo doncella más hermosa que la emperatriz de la Mancha, la sin par Dulcinea del Toboso.' When the merchants protest that they cannot make such a declaration without having seen the woman, Don Quixote's reply is:

— Si os la mostrara ..., ¿qué hiciérades vosotros en confesar una verdad tan notoria? La importancia está en que sin verla lo habéis de creer, confesar, afirmar, jurar y defender; donde no, conmigo sois en batalla, gente descomunal y soberbia.

Blind faith is here presented as the highest virtue and, the implication is, the merely mundane logic of everyday affairs is insufficient to cater for the higher spiritual needs of the human soul; those who aspire to greatness and a superior quality of existence cannot have conventional limits set on their imagination. The conventional frames within which behaviour is meant to be contained are implicitly rejected by this anti-hero, and social constraints are perceived for what they are:

> Don Quixote, unable to understand that the chivalric ideal he still follows is out of date, is a fool, but his foolishness is also due to the falsity of his ideal ... [R]eading Cervantes, we are not subjugated by the majesty of an 'eternal' or rediscovered law, and we are not presupposing a law that also holds for ourselves. Simply, we criticize with Cervantes a set of cultural and intertextual frames.
>
> (Eco 1984: 8)

In the most famous incident in the book (in I. 8), Don Quixote sees windmills which he imagines are evil giants which he must attack and defeat. Having charged at the windmills with his lance, he falls to the ground, bruised and sore, after the lance gets caught in the sails. His squire, Sancho Panza, rebukes him for not listening to his earlier warnings that these were not giants but windmills, and that only a madman would believe otherwise. Don Quixote's reply, however, shows both how difficult it will be to rid his mind of the notions that he has and how firm is his faith in his own vision:

> — Calla, amigo Sancho — respondió don Quijote —; que las cosas de la guerra, más que otros, están sujetas a continua mudanza; cuanto más, que yo pienso, y es así verdad, que aquel sabio Frestón que me robó el aposento y los libros ha vuelto estos gigantes en molinos por quitarme la gloria de su vencimiento: tal es la enemistad que me tiene; mas al cabo al cabo, han de poder poco sus malas artes contra la bondad de mi espada.

Here, then, is the affirmation of an individualistic faith, asserted in the face of the rudest realities and the most violent evidence to the contrary: 'yo pienso, y es así verdad ...' ('I think, and it is really true ...'). What this comic figure embodies is the tension between an inner vision and an external reality which are felt to be at odds with each other. On one level, Quixote appears to have no sense at all of this tension – his single, crazy vision is imposed without hesitation on whatever situation he encounters; the reader, on the other hand, is acutely aware of the discrepancy between Quixote's vision of the universe and the more mundane conception of the world held by the characters with whom he interacts. One result of this is the slapstick effect of the humorous incidents that occur throughout the book. Another effect is more subtle, however, which is the way in which Cervantes allows Quixote's view to contaminate the world around him. Thus, in I. 3, the innkeeper who is mistaken for the lord of a castle by Quixote humours him by going through a ceremony in which he dubs Don Quixote a knight. In I. 7, Quixote's niece tells him that all his books have suddenly disappeared (the local barber and the priest had decreed that they should be burned because of their pernicious effects), and explains this by inventing a story about an enchanter who came to the room on a dragon and destroyed the books while Quixote was away.

Another illustration of how Quixote's view of the world infects those around him is offered in the progress made by his sidekick, his 'squire', Sancho Panza. As he begins his second expedition, Quixote persuades this local farm labourer to accompany him on his journey, suggesting that one of their adventures is likely to win him an island, of which he could become governor. Sancho is the alter ego of Quixote in many respects: down-to-earth, not a reader, he sees mundane realities for what they are but is overridden by Quixote's insistence on the reality of his fantasies. He is materialistic where Quixote is idealistic and altruistic; his motivation is focused on the island which he believes will be his to govern, while Quixote's is to counter evil and to put the world to rights in whatever way he can: 'Es gran servicio de Dios quitar tan mala simiente de la faz de la tierra', he declares.

Sancho can thus be seen as being more like our real selves, while Don Quixote represents an ideal to which we aspire. The Peruvian novelist Mario Vargas Llosa expresses the difference between the two characters in this way:

> Quixote is the prototype for those of us who believe in our own dreams and fantasies, those who feel we want to enrich our real lives with fiction and imagination, those who need an alternative world in order to be able to get by in the real one . . . Don Quixote is the hero, the vision, the flight of fancy; Sancho is the poor normal man, the person that we are every day of the week.
>
> (El País, April 1999; my translation)

What is attractive about Quixote's madness is that it offers an alternative to the ordinary and the humdrum: it is an imaginary excursion into a world of hope and fulfilment. Faith in a better world and the hope of attaining it are qualities that have been cited by numerous commentators on the book. In his comment on *Don Quixote*, the Russian novelist Fyodor Dostoevsky declared:

> In the whole world there is no deeper, no mightier literary work. This is, so far, the last and greatest expression of human thought; this is the bitterest irony which man was capable of conceiving. And if the world were to come to an end, and people were asked there, somewhere: 'Did you understand your life on earth, and what conclusion have you drawn from it?' – man could silently hand over Don Quixote: 'Such is my inference from life. – Can you condemn me for it?'
>
> (Dostoevsky 1984 [1876]: 260)

Quixote's faith, identified with an overwhelming passion for living, has often been reflected in the comments of Spanish writers and intellectuals who have discussed his character. For José Ferrater Mora (Ubieto et al. 1977: 407), *Don Quixote* represented the Baroque spirit of Spanish passion as against the 'European reason' which predominated in the seventeenth century; he opposed the *Quixote* to Descartes' *Discourse on Method*, dubbing the novel the *Discourse on the Lack of Method*. For Spanish intellectuals of the late nineteenth and early twentieth centuries, Quixote stood as an outstanding reminder of the past greatness of Spanish cultural achievements and as the expression of an idiosyncratic – and Spanish – view of the world. Among members of the '1898 Generation', which included writers such as Azorín, Antonio Machado and Miguel de Unamuno, Quixote was a constant theme, one to be reflected on as a means of better understanding their own identity.

5.3 OTHER CLASSIC SPANISH FIGURES

The famous Spanish figures presented below, along with Don Quixote, have all stood the test of time in terms of their ability to continue to fascinate people of different generations and to provoke debate about what they represent and the values they stand for. Any selection of this sort is necessarily subjective, although, in the case of those included, it would be difficult to omit them from the ranks of figures who seem to Spanish people to stand in an important way for certain qualities, even if there might not be universal agreement on what exactly those characteristics are. Both the real and the invented human figures discussed in this chapter are not only archetypal in that they embody a particular set of human qualities in themselves, they are also iconic in that they evoke a particular dimension of Spanish thinking or a certain epoch in Spanish history. Diverse as they are, they are also, therefore, figures that can be used as communicative elements – as signs – for the task of formulating a message or conveying an attitude. Whether they are employed for the enlightened purpose of showing others the path to a more fulfilled life or for the baser purpose of political and moral propaganda, these are figures whose personalities and biographies – genuine or imagined – are available, and have been available, to Spanish people, in the same way that the elements of the Spanish language itself are and have been available to them.

5.3.1 El Cid – hero and myth

Part legend, part historical fact, the myth of El Cid has become universally known throughout the world, having been woven into numerous stories, plays and films. The historical figure of Rodrigo Díaz de Vivar, known as *Mio Cid* – a half-Arabic, half-Castilian title meaning 'my lord' – lived the life of a highly successful frontiersman in the divided Spain of the eleventh century, fighting for both Christian and Moorish princes, as occasion demanded. This character then became the hero of an epic poem, the *Poema de mio Cid*, possibly composed as late as the thirteenth century, a time of military struggles between León and Castile, as well as between Christian and Moor. The poem glorifies the achievements of El Cid and idealizes his character, making him a worthy *Castilian* hero, depicting him as being, above all, loyal to the Castilian king of his day (Alfonso VI), and humane and compassionate in his treatment of family and friends, while also being a brave Christian warrior and a formidable foe.

The poem – almost 4000 lines long – tells the story of El Cid's struggle to counter the wrongs committed against him. Part 1 (the *Cantar del Destierro*) tells of his exile from Castile after he has been falsely accused of keeping taxes which he had collected for the king. After his sorrowful separation from his family, he and his men vanquish the Moors, and El Cid begins to regain the respect of Alfonso, to whom he has remained loyal despite his harsh treatment. In Part 2 (the *Cantar de las Bodas de las Hijas del Cid*), El Cid takes Valencia from the Moors, a feat which the historical Cid accomplished in 1094, and is increasingly successful in having his reputation restored. His success draws the attention of some young nobles, the *infantes* (or heirs) of Carrión. They persuade Alfonso to support their request to marry El Cid's two daughters, which they do at the end of this section – with the reluctant agreement of El Cid himself. In Part 3 (the *Cantar de la Afrenta de Corpes*), the *infantes* are shown to be cowardly in battle and display a similar lack of manliness when they run scared from a lion who comes into El Cid's quarters. Seeking revenge for being ridiculed, they take their wives, El Cid's daughters, to a remote place, where they whip them cruelly and leave them half-dead. King Alfonso then agrees to El Cid's request that he be allowed to seek justice for this offence by having his men challenge the *infantes* to a sword-fight. The *infantes* are defeated, and El Cid returns in triumph to Valencia.

The poem tells a dramatic story and is full of incident and adventure, while constantly insisting on the virtues of the hero, El Cid. This idealized figure is set against King Alfonso, who is seen to lack the abundant virtues of El Cid. The king's honour is tested continually by El Cid, and he is shown up as being unworthy of El Cid's respect, although, in fact, the latter never fails to treat him respectfully.

At one point, for example, El Cid sends the king a gift of fine horses. Since Alfonso has in effect disowned El Cid, honour demands that he should either not accept the gift (as El Cid is no longer his vassal), or else take the horses but readmit our hero to the ranks of those whom he favours. In his greed, he takes the horses but fails to recognize the warrior's worth. Similarly, El Cid's daughters marry the *infantes* of Carrión, but only at the insistence of King Alfonso and only after El Cid insists on turning the girls over to Alfonso and making him responsible for the decision to allow them to marry these men. As the king's wards, they should be defended by Alfonso, but the latter is shown again to lack honour, since it is El Cid who ensures that his daughters' mistreatment is avenged. The contrast between El Cid's noble virtue and

Alfonso's dishonourable behaviour is a major theme of the poem, a theme summarized in the following line, echoes of which are found throughout the three *cantares*: 'Dios, ¡qué buen vasallo, si oviesse buen señor!' ('Goodness, what a worthy vassal, if only he had as good a lord!') All the events recounted in the poem – whether real or imaginary – reinforce this idealized image of the hero.

What is known of the historical facts of El Cid's life is less flattering to his character. In the turbulent eleventh century, El Cid was indeed a fierce and brave fighter, but one who was willing to switch his allegiance if necessary from one king or prince to another (even fighting for the Muslims, if it suited him, which he did for the Muslim king of Granada). In the spirit of his times, he conquered territory ruthlessly and confiscated property from the innocent people who lived on it, dividing the spoils of war among his soldiers. He was reputed to be cruel in the treatment of his enemies: one of his first actions when he captured Valencia was to burn alive a Moorish prince in a public square. He ruled Valencia despotically, exacting steep tributes from its inhabitants, until his death in 1099 (Ubieto et al. 1977: 156–7).

The mythical Cid of the *Poema* is generous, fair, honest and loyal, traits which are taken by the poet to be essential Castilian qualities. El Cid is thus held up within the epic as an exemplar of nobility and virtue, a true Christian knight ever willing to take up his sword against the infidel. The myth thus generated centres on the glorification of military virtues, and has been invoked throughout Spanish history (notably during the Franco dictatorship) for the cause of reinforcing the image of Spain as essentially Christian and warriorlike. It has strengthened the perception of Spain as a country with a spiritual purpose, that of defeating the infidel, and has contributed to the myth of the Reconquest as a religious mission carried out by soldiers loyal to their king and to God.

5.3.2 Celestina – tragicomic anti-heroine

Celestina was one of the protagonists of a work published by Fernando de Rojas (d. 1541) in 1499 called the *Tragicomedia de Calisto y Melibea* (later referred to as *La Celestina*). A 'dramatized novel', it takes the form of 21 'scenes', or dialogues, which tell the story of the love between Calisto and Melibea and of the fateful events that occur as a result of their passionate affair. Calisto, a young aristocrat, falls in love with the beautiful Melibea, who initially rejects his advances on the basis that his intentions centre on the desire to satisfy his passion for her rather than on any matrimonial outcome. Calisto, through his servants, enlists the help of Celestina, described as 'a witch, shrewd in all manner of evil', asking her to use her guile and magic powers to get Melibea to reciprocate his love. Celestina's aims, however, are purely selfish: she wishes to take advantage of the two potential lovers, and she conspires with Calisto's servants to use their master's lovesickness to become rich.

Stating that 'virgins may appear cold on the outside but burn inside', she deploys both her clever tongue and the black arts in the task of getting Melibea for Calisto. We see her performing a magic ritual, invoking the devil, and calling on him to assist her in ensuring that Melibea falls in love with Calisto. She then dupes Melibea's mother into leaving her alone with the girl, who in turn is persuaded to meet Calisto, on the pretext that she will, by meeting him, help relieve the pain of an (invented) toothache.

For her success thus far, Celestina is well rewarded by Calisto. His servants, however, demand a share of the reward, and, when she greedily refuses, they kill her. They themselves are subsequently executed for her murder. Melibea eventually responds as expected to Calisto's advances, and they consummate their love. Hopelessly besotted with each other, they live only to be together, Melibea declaring that 'faltándome Calisto, me falta la vida' ('without Calisto, I am dead'). Their love does not last long, however, since, a month later, Calisto, after secretly visiting Melibea, falls from a ladder which he has used to scale the wall of her garden, and dies. Melibea's declaration of distress reveals both her devotion to Calisto and the carnal nature of the relationship: 'Oh la más de las tristes, triste! Tan poco tiempo poseído el placer, tan presto venido el dolor!' ('Ay me, of all others the most miserable! So short a time to possess my pleasure! So soon to see my sorrows come upon me!') (Rojas 1987: 382–3). Melibea subsequently goes to the top of a tower in her house, and explains to her father below that she and Calisto have been meeting in secret. She then throws herself from the tower and kills herself, causing enormous grief to her father, whose lament ends the story.

The work – a drama whose length makes it impossible to play on the stage without major adaptation – presents a world in which selfishness and greed predominate. Even the two lovers are seen to be obsessively concerned with fulfilling their own desires and ignoring the needs and feelings of others. For its time, it presented a relatively realistic story, compared with the tales of fantastic dragons and princes, lovelorn shepherds and fairy princesses, which were the standard fare for readers of the day. The ruling value is passion, whether it be the passion of love or the passionate pursuit of selfish desires and greed. As Francisco Ruiz Ramón suggests:

> In *La Celestina*, passion, the goddess of chaos, the real mistress of everyone's life, is raised to the status of destiny. Every character possesses the power to dominate and overcome, or to be dominated and conquered by their destiny . . . Passion and destiny are, in the end, a single tragic mask.
>
> (Ruiz Ramón 1984: 73; my translation)

Rojas' express purpose is to demonstrate the foolishness of being completely devoted to the object of your love; his young lovers' obsession with their feelings and with each other leads to grief for themselves and those around them. Nonetheless, the action focuses so much on that love that the work manages to be much more than merely a tale with a simple moral and a sad ending; there is a psychological depth to the depiction of the characters which encompasses many levels of meaning. More than anything, as Rojas suggests in his Prologue to the work, *La Celestina* portrays life as a struggle: 'Aun la mesma vida de los hombres si bien lo miramos, desde la primera edad hasta que blanquean las canas, es batalla' (Rojas 1987: Prólogo). Celestina is presented as an evil character, cunning and manipulative. She is an ex-prostitute who procures women for sexual purposes, and is unscrupulous and greedy, with a knowledge of black magic. Nonetheless, she is eloquent and astute in her dealings with those who use her services, and she is responsible for successfully bringing together the noble Calisto and the innocent Melibea.

Thus, the ambiguities in the work include the alacrity with which the young lovers discover the carnal pleasures of passionate love and the fact that the evil madam is the catalyst for the consummation of that love.

In the figure of Celestina are summarized qualities such as astuteness and avarice, an ability to manipulate, and a selfish worldly wisdom embodied in an old woman obsessively concerned with material values.

5.3.3 Teresa of Ávila – *la santa de la raza*

Variously treated through the centuries as a feminist heroine, a demure saint, a woman of genius or 'an independent theological thinker' (Williams 1991), St Teresa of Ávila or Santa Teresa de Jesús (1515–82) was undoubtedly a major figure of her time. She is also someone who has exerted a strong influence on generations of Spaniards, both as a religious leader and as a writer in Castilian.

She entered the Carmelite Order at the age of 20, an assiduous and saintly nun, determined to serve God for the rest of her life. However, her dissatisfaction with the relaxed lifestyle of the Carmelite nuns eventually led her to undertake a reform of the Order. She initiated this in 1560 and founded her first convent in 1562. She went on to establish some seventeen convents, all obeying the new and more austere rule which she laid down for the conduct of the nuns. Her reformed Order, the 'Discalced' Carmelites, devoted to a strict, ascetic way of life, formed part of the general movement of reform – known as the Counter-Reformation – which took place in the Catholic Church in the sixteenth century.

In her determination to develop the new style of religious life, Teresa was opposed by many both within and outside the Carmelites, and her courage and determination in following her goals became legendary. She was assisted in her work by another Spanish saint from Ávila, John of the Cross (1542–91), who reformed the male branch of the Carmelites and who was also a poet and mystic. Their combined efforts eventually brought about a reform, although the Carmelite Order suffered a split, in the process.

By the time she began the work of reforming the Order, Teresa had already had mystical experiences, through which she felt herself to be completely united with God, a 'bride of Christ'. Her principal writings are her *Life*, the *Moradas*, and the *Way of Perfection*. The main themes of these books are the need for virtue and obedience, the need for love of God, and the soul's approach to God through prayer and mystical experience. The latter is described particularly in the *Moradas* (or *Mansions*), where she sets out the seven stages the soul must go through to achieve union with God: the first four are aimed at detaching oneself from the material world through humility, self-knowledge and the experience of conversion, and the final three evoke the gradually increasing sense of union with God, described in terms of a 'mystical marriage'. The final mansion is the one where the soul senses complete and permanent identification with God's will:

> Digamos que sea la unión, como si dos velas de cera se juntasen tan en extremo, que toda la luz fuese una, ú que el pábilo y la luz y la cera es todo uno; mas después bien se puede apartar la una vela de la otra, y quedan en dos velas, ú el pábilo de la cera. Acá es como si cayendo agua, del cielo en un río ú fuente, á donde queda hecho todo agua, que no podrán ya dividir ni apartar cuál es el agua del río, ú lo que cayó del cielo.
>
> (Teresa de Jesús 1915, I: 483)

As Paul Julian Smith (1989) explains it, in the sublime mystical state experienced by Teresa, the imagination takes over from the intellect and the saint feels a pleasure without pain, where 'there is no suffering, only a pleasure which cannot be understood'. The experience cannot be expressed in words, but it dissolves differences and fuses opposites: the mind cannot be distinguished from the soul, or the self from the other; Teresa, in this exalted state, is 'at once rapt by communion with the Holy Spirit and shamed by an awareness of the physical incongruity of her position'; this mystic state is 'both internal and external, psychological and social' (Smith 1989: 25).

Teresa's longing for God was such that she expressed herself as being indifferent to whether she lived or died, even though she was obviously someone who lived life to the full. But death was welcome to her because it meant coming closer to God and achieving ultimate happiness. Without the reassurance of God's presence, she would despair, as she says in the following (from the *Exclamaciones o meditaciones del alma a su Dios*, written in 1559):

> ¡Oh! ¡vida! ¡vida! ¿Cómo puedes sustentarte estando ausente de tu Vida? En tanta soledad, ¿en qué te empleas? ¿Qué haces, pues todas tus obras son imperfectas y faltas? ¿Qué te consuela, oh ánima mía, en esta tempestuosa mar? ... pues no puede el entendimiento en tan grandes grandezas alcanzar quien es su Dios, y deséale gozar, y no vé cómo, puesta en cárcel tan penosa como esta mortalidad.
>
> (Teresa de Jesús 1915, I: 493)

It is essentially this same sentiment which she expresses in her most famous poem, the 'Verses born of the fire of her love for God'. In it, she says that being without God is more of a death than dying itself. She addresses her beloved God in these terms:

> Estando ausente de ti
> ¿qué vida puedo tener,
> sino muerte padecer
> la mayor que nunca vi?
> Lástima tengo de mí,
> por ser mi mal tan entero,
> *Que muero porque no muero.*
>
> (Navarro 1989: 76)

The truth is that Teresa was a complex character: she was a powerful, independent-minded and highly energetic woman, suffering the strain of being pulled between her sincere devotion to Christ and her ambitions for her Order. She wrote passionately, with an immediacy and a gift for vivid imagery which have captured the attention of readers ever since.

Teresa was canonized a saint in 1622. At that time she was already being treated by the Spanish civil and ecclesiastical authorities not simply as a strong woman and a saint, but as one who occupied a special position as essentially Spanish, a saint who represented the power and nobility of Spain itself. Teresa, it was claimed at the time, belonged to a family of *cristianos viejos*, i.e. a family whose line was not 'tainted' with the blood of Jews or Muslims. Hers was a wealthy and titled family, but the truth was that her father was of Jewish origin and, as a *converso*, or convert to Christianity, felt obliged to conceal his origins in order to gain acceptance in the society of his time. This fact was hidden or distorted over the succeeding centuries, in an attempt to ensure, at an official level, that Teresa could be invoked as a 'genuine' example of traditional Spanish strength and virtue.

Her status as *patrona de España* was confirmed and reinforced in the 1920s and again invoked during the Franco period. In the dictatorship, her image was used at a popular level to convey notions of demure piety and female selflessness, although, in the course of the Civil War, the traditional association of Teresa with strength and military virtues – including her reputation for 'manliness' – had been used as propaganda for the Nationalist side (di Febo 1988: 63ff.). She became patron saint of the Falangist *Sección Femenina* when it was set up in 1934 (see 6.4).

Franco was personally devoted to her and kept a relic of Teresa (her left hand, which had been severed from her body after her death) in the palace of El Pardo where he lived, from whence the hand was returned to the Carmelite Order in 1976. In a somewhat ghoulish fashion, parts of her body continue to hold strong iconic value today: the saint's left arm (without the hand) is kept on open display and venerated in a church in Alba de Tormes (Salamanca), the town where she died, and the sarcophagus containing her remains is located above the main altar of the same church.

5.3.4 Don Juan – archetypal seducer of women?

Don Juan is possibly even more 'universal' an archetype than Don Quixote; certainly he is more believable. Don Quixote lives in a world of his own invention and naively expects others to accept it as valid. In contrast, Don Juan knows well how other people see the world and derives pleasure from successfully manipulating them for one purpose: to achieve the transient pleasure of sexual conquest. All his efforts are focused on the immediate gratification of his personal desires. He unscrupulously pursues the aim of 'enjoying' whatever woman happens to attract his attention at any particular time and is determined to ignore the long-term consequences of his actions. He is charming, handsome and clever and has an enormous ability to flatter and deceive with pleasant words.

The character was first delineated in the play *El burlador de Sevilla y convidado de piedra*, generally attributed to a Spanish monk, Tirso de Molina (1571?–1648), in the early seventeenth century, although there may have been a legendary figure of this type who pre-dated the play. In Tirso's version, Don Juan attempts to seduce four women – two noblewomen and two peasants; within the terms of the strict code of 'honour' which operated in Spain at the time, such seductions are seen both as an affront to the women concerned and as impugning the good name (i.e. the social standing) of their husbands or fathers. Of the four women tricked by Don Juan, one – Doña Ana – is the fiancée of an old friend of his, the Marquis de la Mota. In that particular episode, Don Juan uses his friend's cloak to disguise himself in order to pretend to Doña Ana that he himself is de la Mota. As she is finally about to be seduced, Doña Ana discovers the trick that Don Juan is attempting to play on her and cries out for her father, Don Gonzalo, to help her. Don Gonzalo rushes to her assistance and challenges Don Juan, but, in the sword-fight which ensues, Don Gonzalo is killed. Don Juan flees, but, on his way, meets de la Mota and returns his cloak to him, so that, when de la Mota reaches the scene of the crime, he is mistakenly identified as the culprit and is arrested for the murder of Gonzalo.

As we would expect from a play written by a monk, there is a strong moral dimension to Tirso's version of the story. Don Juan is seen as unremittingly callous in his treatment of other people, but eventually he gets his come-uppance – supernaturally, at the hands of the murdered Don Gonzalo. Towards the end of the play, Don Juan addresses Gonzalo's statue, which has been erected over his tomb, and mockingly suggests that it should come to dinner with him that night. But the ghost of Don Gonzalo surprises Don Juan by accepting his invitation, turning up in the form of the stone statue, and, in turn, inviting Don Juan to be his guest the following night at his tomb. Don Juan accepts, and, despite warnings from his frightened servant Catalinón, goes the following night to keep his appointment to 'sup with the dead'. Here, too, the notion of honour is invoked, as Don Juan insists that as a gentleman he must keep his word and attend the feast of the dead, since, if he does not, 'the dead man will be able to call out my dishonour to the four winds'. After they have eaten, the statue takes Don Juan by the hand and drags him away; where exactly they go is a matter of some speculation. At the very least, Don Juan is taken into the realms of death, although traditionally it is held that he is taken off to Hell. Thus, the trickster, or *burlador*, is himself tricked, fulfilling the predictions made by other characters in the play, such as his father and his servant. The servant, Catalinón, had earlier warned him that he would pay for his deception of women with his death:

> . . . Los que fingís y engañáis
> las mujeres, de esa suerte
> lo pagaréis con la muerte.
>
> (Tirso de Molina 1967: 30)

Don Juan's reply to Catalinón was '¡Que largo me lo fiáis!' ('What a long credit you give me!'), and, as Austen (1939: 7) puts it, this expression runs through the entire play like a motto for the hero, emblematic of Don Juan's willingness to ignore the long-term consequences of his exploitative actions. When retribution is a long way off, it can be put to one side and forgotten; however, the point made by the playwright is, of course, that our actions do indeed have consequences. In the terms of sixteenth-century Spanish culture, the expected outcome is the flames of Hell which await the sinner, and Tirso's moral is that we must be aware of this fate, as we must also remember that we cannot be sure of having the opportunity to repent before we die. As the ghost of Don Gonzalo announces to Don Juan on taking his hand: 'quien tal hace, que tal pague' (ibid.: 92); at the feast, a song is heard which tells of future damnation for sinners:

> Adviertan los que de Dios
> juzgan los castigos grandes,
> que no hay plazo que no llegue
> ni deuda que no se pague.
>
> (ibid.: 91)

Since Tirso's time, thousands of versions of this story – with many variations on the character of Don Juan – have been created by authors around the world, including Molière, Hoffmann, Tolstoy, Rostand, Byron and Strauss, one of the best known being the opera *Don Giovanni*, written by the librettist Da Ponte and set to music by Mozart. The Spanish playwright José Zorrilla (1817–93) wrote a Romantic version of the play called *Don Juan Tenorio* (1844), which depicted the hero as a likeable adventurer, a nobly amorous suitor who eventually finds true love, being united with his beloved in death. Zorrilla's Don Juan is a more attractive rogue than Tirso's, a colourful and carefree character immersed in the swashbuckling action of an exciting adventure.

The fact that so many versions of Don Juan have been created attests to the fascination of this character and to the sense that in him are summarized a thirst for adventure, a delight in disguise and deceit, an outrageous ability to mock the notion of death and a propensity towards the conquest of the opposite sex, to produce a figure who is both a master of seduction and an emblem of childish recklessness. He is a mythic character, whose story is inextricably linked to the twin themes of love and death, and a figure that can be interpreted in many different ways.

In the 1920s, for instance, the psychoanalyst Otto Rank offered a Freudian explanation of the myth: Don Juan is an 'audacious blasphemer, who would deny conscience, guilt feelings, and anxiety' (Rank 1975: 87), and his seductions are a vain attempt to be reunited with an unattainable mother figure. For Rank, Don Juan's conflicts with other men represent his struggle to overcome the 'unconquerable father', although this too is futile, and in the end he is swallowed up in death by an avenging father-figure (the *convidado de piedra*, or 'stone guest').

The Hispanist Gerald Brenan (1970: 217) saw Don Juan as merely a figure deriving from adolescent male fantasies, and certainly not a 'Spanish type' representative of how Spanish men behave. For Brenan, Spain was not a country in which men could easily achieve serial seduction, for the simple reason that Spanish women would not allow them to, since the latter, in Brenan's view, were more interested in family and having children than in sexual love *per se*.

Within the story, there are male–female conflicts, fights between rival males, and the struggle between life and death embodied, above all, in a dead man's act of revenge; but perhaps more than anything, Don Juan symbolizes simply the perennial conflicting human desires of love and domination.

FEATURE: CHRISTOPHER COLUMBUS – MORE FAMOUS THAN JESUS CHRIST?

Christopher Columbus (1451–1506) is possibly the best-known name in the world. The scholar Felipe Fernández-Armesto, author of a biography of Columbus (1996), reported on a street poll in Hong Kong which showed the explorer to be more famous than Jesus Christ, Alexander the Great, John F. Kennedy or John Lennon (*New York Times*, January 1992). His case is one more instance of a figure in whom history and legend meet: there are many unknown aspects to his life (including the precise date of his birth and exactly when he left Genoa, the Italian city where he was born), but his achievement in leading the first successful voyage of discovery across the Atlantic is unquestioned, as is the fact that the members of that expedition sighted land, five weeks after leaving the Canary Islands, on 12 October 1492.

Columbus' status is variously seen as that of a hero or a villain. He depicted himself in his writings as a struggling outsider who managed to accomplish his goal in spite of the misfortunes which befell him and despite the frequent lack of support from other people. He probably exaggerated his situation, although there is no doubt that he spent at least six or seven years seeking the resources he needed for the Atlantic voyage he wished to undertake. He was about 40 years old when he succeeded in getting that support, and at that stage in his life he had already undertaken numerous voyages around the Mediterranean and the eastern Atlantic. By then he had developed not just his enormous enthusiasm for a major Atlantic journey but also a thorough practical knowledge of navigation and cartography. He had also read widely on world geography, including speculations about the lands which, it was generally believed, could be found in the 'Ocean Sea' (i.e., the Atlantic).

Columbus was not alone in his conviction that it would be possible to reach the Orient by crossing the Atlantic, though there was widespread fear that that ocean was so huge that it was not humanly possible to cross it. Columbus' crews – in the *Niña*, the *Pinta* and the *Santa María*, the three caravels that he took on his first Atlantic crossing – also feared being lost in the vast unknown expanse of water, and came close to mutiny on more than one occasion, although this nervousness finally yielded to a sensation of enormous relief when they sighted land. On returning from that journey, Columbus assured the Catholic Monarchs in Spain that he had achieved his goal of reaching Asia: he never really understood that he had in reality found his way to a vast new continent, despite the fact that, by the end of his life, he had carried out a total of four transatlantic journeys, exploring much of the Caribbean and reaching the northern coast of South America.

Columbus was essentially a seafarer and an explorer, and displayed little talent for administering the land that he claimed for the Spanish Crown. He appears not to have been either an archetypal conquistador (he preferred exploration to warfare) or a ruthless schemer (since he died isolated and poor) although he has often been portrayed as both. He was courageous and determined, supremely skilled in navigation, highly intelligent and largely self-educated. He is linked in our minds with the 'discovery' of the New World, and is irrevocably associated with the ambivalent values we so often perceive in the first Europeans to explore that continent: on the one hand, a pioneering sense of adventure and, on the other, a very human susceptibility to the attractions of status and material gain.

READING: MIGUEL DE CERVANTES, *DON QUIXOTE DE LA MANCHA*

The following extracts from *Don Quixote de la Mancha* are taken from Part I, Chapters 1 and 8, respectively. In the first set of extracts (from Chapter 1), Cervantes presents to us the gentleman farmer who devotes too much of his time to reading and thus ends up demented, and the preparations he makes to undertake his adventures as a knight errant. In Chapter 8, he narrates the episode of the windmills, which has become the most famous incident from the book.

Chapter 1

En un lugar de la Mancha, de cuyo nombre no quiero acordarme, no ha mucho tiempo que vivía un hidalgo de los de lanza en astillero, adarga antigua, rocín flaco y galgo corredor. Una olla de algo más vaca que carnero, salpicón las más noches, duelos y quebrantos los sábados, lentejas los viernes, algún palomino de añadidura los domingos, consumían las tres partes de su hacienda. El resto della concluían sayo de velarte, calzas de velludo para las fiestas, con sus pantuflos de lo mesmo, y los días de entresemana se honraba con su vellorí de lo más fino. Tenía en su casa una ama que pasaba de los cuarenta, y una sobrina que no llegaba a los veinte, y un mozo de campo y plaza, que así ensillaba el rocín como tomaba la podadera. Frisaba la edad de nuestro hidalgo con los cincuenta años; era de complexión recia, seco de carnes, enjuto de rostro, gran madrugador y amigo de la caza. Quieren decir que tenía el sobrenombre de Quijada, o Quesada, que en esto hay alguna diferencia en los autores que deste caso escriben; aunque por conjeturas verosímiles se deja entender que se llamaba Quejana. Pero esto importa poco a nuestro cuento; basta que en la narración dél no se salga un punto de la verdad.

Es, pues, de saber, que este sobredicho hidalgo, los ratos que estaba ocioso (que eran los más del año), se daba a leer libros de caballerías con tanta afición y gusto, que olvidó casi de todo punto el ejercicio de la caza, y aun la administración de su hacienda; y llegó a tanto su curiosidad y desatino en esto, que vendió muchas hanegas de tierra de sembradura para comprar libros de caballerías en que leer . . . .

En resolución, él se enfrascó tanto en su lectura, que se le pasaban las noches leyendo de claro en claro y los días de turbio en turbio; y así, del poco dormir y del mucho leer se le secó el cerebro de manera que vino a perder el juicio. Llenósele la fantasía de todo aquello que leía en los libros, así de encantamientos como de pendencias, batallas, desafíos, heridas, requiebros, amores, tormentas y disparates imposibles; y asentósele de tal modo en la imaginación que era verdad toda aquella máquina de aquellas soñadas invenciones que leía, que para él no había otra historia más cierta en el mundo. . . .

En efecto, rematado ya su juicio, vino a dar en el más extraño pensamiento que jamás dio loco en el mundo, y fue que le pareció convenible y necesario, así para el aumento de su honra como para el servicio de su república, hacerse caballero andante y irse por todo el mundo con sus armas y caballo a buscar las aventuras y a ejercitarse en todo aquello que él había leído que los caballeros andantes se ejercitaban, deshaciendo todo género de agravio y poniéndose en ocasiones y peligros donde, acabándolos, cobrase eterno nombre y fama. Imaginábase el pobre ya coronado por el valor de su brazo, por lo menos, del imperio de Trapisonda; y así, con estos tan agradables pensamientos, llevado del extraño gusto que en ellos sentía, se dio priesa a poner en efecto lo que deseaba. Y lo primero que hizo fue limpiar unas armas que habían sido de sus bisabuelos, que, tomadas de orín y llenas de moho, luengos siglos había que estaban puestas y olvidadas en un rincón. . . .

Fue luego a ver a su rocín, y aunque tenía más cuartos que un real y más tachas que el caballo de Gonela, que *tantum pellis et ossa fuit*, le pareció que ni el Bucéfalo de Alejandro ni Babieca el del Cid con él se igualaban. Cuatro días se le pasaron en imaginar qué nombre le pondría: porque (según decía él a sí mesmo) no era razón que caballo de caballero tan famoso, y tan bueno él por sí, estuviese sin nombre conocido; ansí, procuraba acomodársele de manera que declarase quién había sido antes que fuese caballero andante, y lo que era entonces; pues estaba muy puesto en razón que, mudando su señor estado, mudase él también el nombre, y le cobrase famoso y de estruendo, como convenía a la nueva orden y al nuevo ejercicio que ya profesaba; y así, después de muchos nombres que formó, borró y quitó, añadió, deshizo y tornó a hacer en su memoria e imaginación, al fin le vino a llamar Rocinante, nombre, a sus parecer, alto, sonoro y significativo de lo que había sido cuando fue rocín, antes de lo que ahora era, que era antes y primero de todos los rocines del mundo.

Puesto nombre, y tan a su gusto, a su caballo, quiso ponérsele a sí mismo, y en este pensamiento duró otros ocho días, y al cabo se vino a llamar don Quijote, de donde, como queda dicho, tomaron ocasión los autores desta tan verdadera historia que, sin duda, se debía de llamar Quijada, y no Quesada, como otros quisieron decir. Pero, acordándose que el valeroso Amadís no sólo se había contentado con llamarse Amadís a secas, sino que añadió el nombre de su reino y patria, por hacerla famosa, y se llamó Amadís de Gaula, así quiso, como buen caballero, añadir al suyo el nombre de la suya y llamarse don Quijote de la Mancha, con que, a su parecer, declaraba muy al vivo su linaje y patria, y la honraba con tomar el sobrenombre della.

Limpias, pues, sus armas, hecho el morrión celada, puesto nombre a su rocín y confirmándose a sí mismo, se dió a entender que no le faltaba otra cosa sino buscar una dama de quien enamorarse: porque el caballero andante sin amores era árbol sin hojas y sin fruto y cuerpo sin alma. Decíase él: 'Si yo, por malos de mis pecados, o por mi buena suerte, me encuentro por ahí con algún gigante, como de ordinario les acontece a los caballeros andantes, y le derribo de un encuentro, o le parto por mitad del cuerpo, o, finalmente, le venzo y le rindo, ¿no será bien tener a quien enviarle presentado, y que entre y se hinque de rodillas ante mi dulce señora, y diga con voz humilde y rendida: 'Yo, señora, soy el gigante Caraculiambro, señor de la ínsula Malindrania, a quien venció en singular batalla el jamás como se debe alabado caballero don Quijote de la Mancha, el cual me mandó que me presentase ante la vuestra merced, para que la vuestra grandeza disponga de mí a su talante"?' ¡Oh, cómo se holgó nuestro buen caballero cuando hubo hecho este discurso, y más cuando halló a quien dar nombre de su dama! Y fue, a lo que se cree, que en un lugar cerca del suyo había una moza labradora de muy buen parecer, de quien él un tiempo anduvo enamorado, aunque, según se entiende, ella jamás lo supo ni se dio cata dello. Llamábase Aldonza Lorenzo, y a ésta le pareció ser bien darle título de señora de sus pensamientos; y, buscándole nombre que no se desdijese mucho del suyo y que tirase y se encaminase al de princesa y gran señora, vino a llamarla Dulcinea del Toboso, porque era natural del Toboso: nombre, a su parecer, músico y peregrino y significativo, como todos los demás que a él y a sus cosas había puesto.

Chapter 8

En esto, descubrieron treinta o cuarenta molinos de viento que hay en aquel campo, y así como don Quijote los vio, dijo a su escudero:

— La ventura va guiando nuestras cosas mejor de lo que acertáramos a desear; porque ves allí, amigo Sancho Panza, dónde se descubren treinta, o pocos más, desaforados gigantes, con quien pienso hacer batalla y quitarles a todos las vidas, con cuyos despojos comenzaremos a enriquecer, que ésta es buena guerra, y es gran servicio de Dios quitar tan mala simiente de sobre la faz de la tierra.

— ¿Qué gigantes? — dijo Sancho Panza.

— Aquellos que allí ves — respondió su amo — de los brazos largos, que los suelen tener algunos de casi dos leguas.

— Mire vuestra merced — respondió Sancho — que aquellos que allí se parecen no son gigantes, sino molinos de viento, y lo que en ellos parecen brazos son las aspas, que, volteadas del viento, hacen andar la piedra del molino.

— Bien parece — respondió don Quijote — que no estás cursado en esto de las aventuras: ellos son gigantes; y si tienes miedo, quítate de ahí, y ponte en oración en el espacio que yo voy a entrar con ellos en fiera y desigual batalla.

Y diciendo esto, dio de espuelas a su caballo Rocinante, sin atender a las voces que su escudero Sancho le daba, advirtiéndole que, sin duda alguna, eran molinos de viento y no gigantes aquellos que iba a acometer. Pero él iba tan puesto en que eran gigantes, que ni oía las voces de su escudero Sancho, ni echaba de ver, aunque estaba ya bien cerca, lo que eran; antes iba diciendo, en voces altas:

— Non fuyades, cobardes y viles criaturas; que un solo caballero es el que os acomete.

Levantóse en esto un poco de viento, y las grandes aspas comenzaron a moverse, lo cual visto por don Quijote, dijo:

— Pues aunque mováis más brazos que los del gigante Briareo, me lo habéis de pagar.

Y diciendo esto, y encomendándose de todo corazón a su señora Dulcinea, pidiéndole que en tal trance le socorriese, bien cubierto de su rodela, con la lanza en el ristre, arremetió a todo galope de Rocinante y embistió con el primero molino que estaba delante; y dándole una lanzada en el aspa, la volvió el viento con tanta furia, que hizo la lanza pedazos, llevándose tras sí al caballo y al caballero, que fue rodando muy maltrecho por el campo. Acudió Sancho Panza a socorrerle, a todo el correr de su asno, y cuando llegó halló que no se podía menear: tal fue el golpe que dio con él Rocinante.

— ¡Válgame Dios! — dijo Sancho —. ¿No le dije yo a vuestra merced que mirase bien lo que hacía, que no eran sino molinos de viento, y no lo podía ignorar sino quien llevase otros tales en la cabeza?

— Calla, amigo Sancho — respondió don Quijote —; que las cosas de la guerra, más que otras, están sujetas a continua mudanza; cuanto más, que yo pienso, y es así verdad, que aquel sabio Frestón que me robó el aposento y los libros ha vuelto estos gigantes en molinos, por quitarme la gloria de su vencimiento: tal es la enemistad que me tiene; mas al cabo al cabo, han de poder poco sus malas artes contra la bondad de mi espada.

— Dios lo haga como puede — respondió Sancho Panza.

FURTHER READING

Berkeley Digital Library SunSITE, *The lay of the Cid*, http://sunsite. Berkeley.EDU/OMACL/Cid/
  An online translation of the *Poema de mio Cid*.
Cervantes, M. de, trans. J. M. Cohen, *Don Quixote* (Harmondsworth, Penguin, 1950).
  A good translation of *Don Quixote*.
Du Boulay, Shirley, *Teresa of Avila* (London, Hodder & Stoughton, 1991).
  An excellent biography of St Teresa.
Rojas, Fernando de (ed. D. S. Severin) *Celestina* (Warminster, Aris & Phillips, 1987).
  A bilingual edition of the *Celestina*.

6

Love: How do they Love?

6.1 INTRODUCTION: LOVE, SEX AND GENDER

The degree to which love is an area of fundamental importance, relevant to all cultures everywhere, is indicated by the extent to which it is a universal theme in literature, art, philosophy and sociology. Furthermore, every society builds a cultural edifice that relates sex to love and romance, to kinship and marriage, and, by extension, to a wide range of political, legal, social and religious customs, and to some of the pinnacles of human cultural achievement in art and literature. That sex entails a wide range of culturally significant phenomena is a generally recognized fact. Robert Padgud expresses the idea in the following terms:

> [B]iological sexuality is only a precondition, a set of potentialities, which is never unmediated by human reality, and which becomes transformed in qualitatively new ways in human society. The rich and ever-varying nature of such concepts and institutions as marriage, kinship, 'love', 'eroticism' in a variety of physical senses and as a component of fantasy and religious, social, and even economic reality, and the general human ability to extend the range of sexuality far beyond the physical body, all bear witness to this transformation.
>
> (Padgud 1998: 19)

Legal distinctions in the area of love and sexuality are now minimal in western society. The principle of monogamy, the equal legal status of men and women, the free availability of contraception, access to divorce, restricted availability of abortion, relative tolerance of pornography, children's rights to care and protection, etc., are some of the points on which there is increasing (or even complete) agreement in Europe. It is EU policy to increase the degree of harmonization in the legal context, so that any remaining differences, within the EU countries at least, seem set to diminish further in the future.

For certain EU countries, including Spain, but also Portugal and Ireland, accommodation to the European norm in certain areas has been fairly recent. For instance, in Spain, the adoption of relatively 'liberal' legislation on contraception, divorce and abortion has happened relatively recently: contraception was legalized in 1978, divorce was introduced in 1981 and the law allowing abortion under certain circumstances was passed in 1985. This kind of assimilation towards European practice can be seen as having both an internal and an external dynamic. For many Spaniards, the modernization of their country seemed to imply the need for such liberalization. At the same time, gradual integration into the structures of the EC was itself a factor towards more progressive legislation in these areas. Thus, both the need for liberal legislation, associated with a vision of a more 'enlightened' social situation for Spaniards, along with the more practical ambition of integration into EU institutions, encouraged a loosening of traditional social restrictions.

The sociologist Inés Alberdi has articulated this double motivation in the following terms:

> An ideology of modernization has exercised an enormous influence on Spanish society and has been one of the cornerstones of social change in recent decades. Admiration for Europe, combined with a desire to get closer to it, has functioned as an ongoing ambition, bringing about a change in attitudes well ahead of any changes in behaviour.
>
> (Alberdi 1999: 265; my translation)

In terms of the public or social dimension of sexuality, perhaps the most dramatic legislative change to be introduced in Spain was the lifting of censorship on publications and the media in 1976, in the wake of which Spanish society appeared at times to be obsessively concerned with nudity, eroticism, pornography and the public display of sexuality. This phenomenon, the so-called *desmadre sexual* of the late 1970s, is probably best explained as an understandable reaction against the tight restrictions imposed by a combination of church and state forces during the Franco dictatorship.

With respect to the individual, or private, dimension, this has at least two elements: sexual roles and gender identity. A person's sexual role refers to their expected behaviour and sexual orientation, and derives from the implicit assumption in early childhood that there is an absolute distinction between men and women, that one is either male or female and that one cannot be both. Therefore, sexual role is, for example, the area implicated in the usual discussions of private sexual morality: whether to use contraception or not, whether sex outside marriage is right or wrong, etc. Gender identity, on the other hand, is constructed by each individual as he or she grows up. It includes the above elements of the sexual role (though it may conflict with socially acceptable sexual orientations), but also involves the appropriation of behaviour associated with one particular gender or the other; we learn, through a cultural process, to behave in ways that are appropriate to either men or women, internalizing a self-identification and developing a public persona that conforms to cultural norms. Gender identity, then, is a cultural accretion which relates in an important way to the sex of the growing child, but is not determined biologically.

The process of developing gender identity takes place within a particular cultural context, and will necessarily be influenced by the characteristics of that context. In other words, if men, for example, behave in a more *machista* fashion in one culture than in another, it is unlikely that this is the result of any particular genetic differences between the two groups of males concerned. The difference is rather the outcome of differentiated cultural practices in the two societies, different forms of behaviour which are transmitted to the children growing up in the two cultures.

The mention of machismo at this point is not intended as a way of pre-empting the discussion of gender issues offered below (6.4). The stereotypical image of the swaggering, domineering male and the dutifully submissive female is a cliché with little relevance to the Spain of today. Yet differentiated roles for men and women are an obvious reality for western societies generally, and certain features of male and female behaviour distinguish Spain from other countries. And, again, a close examination reveals that gender roles in one part of Spain may differ subtly from those that predominate in another part of the country.

Given the complexity of the issues involved, however, and working on the principle that, as with the other themes we address, there is an intimate, private dimension to our current topic, as well as a sociological aspect, the following sections explore, respectively, the behaviour of contemporary Spaniards in relation to love and sexuality (6.2), some of the ways in which feelings of love and sexual desire are articulated within Spanish poetry (6.3), and the changes taking place in modern Spain around gender issues (6.4).

6.2 'EL AMOR VERDADERO LO PUEDE TODO'

The behaviour of men and women in relation to love and sex entails both a public dimension relating to legal constraints, religious prescriptions and social customs (including marriage), and a private dimension revolving around the individual's assertion of his or her own gender identity, and relations between couples and within families. While certain aspects of these appear to develop universally in cultures around the world (e.g. every society has a prohibition on incest), different cultures will emphasize the various elements to a different degree, and there will often be subtle differences between cultures as regards the precise forms which these behaviours take. In relation to love and sex, there still remain noticeable behavioural differences between the various European cultures, differences which may appear trivial to an outside observer but which may be of major importance for, say, a partner in an intercultural relationship.

In general, love survives well as a valid concept in modern, advanced societies, despite the cynicism which may exist alongside it. This includes Spaniards – both male and female – who maintain a belief in love; in one recent survey (CIS 1995a: 1), only one in seven Spanish adults disagreed with the statement 'El amor verdadero lo puede todo' ('Love conquers all').

If this appears to be an argument for the view that the average Spaniard is a romantic individual, the romantic love that Spaniards believe in is a love based generally on fairly sensible foundations. This can be seen from evidence that the most important factors influencing the initiation of love relationships are deemed to be the other person's character and commitment to sexual fidelity, followed by the importance of a person's beliefs and values, with physical attractiveness coming in fourth place (CIS 1995a: 7). Most people, in the survey mentioned, reported that they had got to know their partners only gradually, while the 'love at first sight' phenomenon was confined to just under 23 per cent of those surveyed (who used the phrase *fue un flechazo* to describe the initiation of their relationship) (CIS 1995a: 6). Once their interest has been aroused, the strategies people employ to attract another person also seem sensible enough, and include showing an interest in knowing about the other person and telling them what they want to hear. 'Playing hard to get' is not a favoured technique and is employed by less than 14 per cent of Spaniards, according to themselves; even less popular, however, is its opposite, 'mostrarse fácil de conseguir' – only 3.4 per cent of Spaniards said they do this. All of this points to an emphasis on long-term, stable relationships, and this appears to be what most Spaniards are interested in when they think about sexual love.

Short-term relationships are also possible, of course, and are deemed acceptable behaviour by many. When people get involved in such relationships, looks are likely to play a more important part, although the personal qualities of the prospective short-term partner are not insignificant: these two factors were considered important for 53.7 per cent and 45.8 per cent of respondents, respectively, with regard to short-term relationships in the 1995 survey (1995a: 22). Indeed, sex without love was considered acceptable to more than half the Spaniards surveyed: only 45 per cent disagreed with the statement: 'It is possible to have sexual relations with someone without being in love with them'. We can only speculate on the sex and age profile of the people making up the group which approves of this behaviour. Since the respondents were divided more or less equally between males and females, we cannot be sure – although we might reasonably conjecture that more males than females and more young people than old would be inclined towards this view.

Whatever the case, media representations of sexuality and the confident flaunting of sexual attractiveness are certainly features of modern Spanish society. The combination of the media dimension and sex appeal are neatly encapsulated in a poem by Ana Rosetti, published in 1985, called 'Chico Wrangler', which describes an instance of love – or at least of sexual arousal – at first sight of a particularly attractive young man:

Dulce corazón mío de súbito asaltado.
Todo por adorar más de lo permisible.
Todo porque el cigarro se asienta en una boca
y en sus jugosas sedas se humedece.

> Porque una camiseta incitante señala,
> de su pecho, el escudo durísimo
> y un vigoroso brazo de la mínima manga sobresale.
> Todo porque unas piernas, unas perfectas piernas,
> dentro del más ceñido pantalón, frente a mí se separan.
> Se separan.
>
> (Rosetti 1985: 165)

The contrast between this uninhibited expression of sexuality and the mores of the 1950s is obvious enough. In the 1950s, social norms and the Catholic Church's strictures ensured that there was a silence around the expression of sexual desire and a strongly clandestine quality to much sexual activity. Men had impulses that simply needed curbing; women, if they were respectable, never thought about sex, and resisted – ideally to the death – any attempt by a man to rob them of their virtue. Any other behaviour by a woman caused her to be branded a 'tart'. 'Making love', in that period, referred not to physical intimacy but to the process whereby a man set about conquering the object of his affection, in a spirit of abnegation and utter dedication. One of Spain's foremost women writers, Carmen Martín Gaite (b. 1925), describes how this was envisaged as a kind of military campaign, a siege on the beloved: ' "Hacer el amor" … significaba iniciar un asedio, a veces descrito en términos de estrategia militar, para convencer a la elegida del interés especial que despertaba su persona' (Martín Gaite 1987: 106). And she quotes from a textbook of the time which depicted courtship in those terms; the authors clearly saw the man's role as being to undertake the attack: 'Siempre deben ser ellos los que inician el cerco, los que sostienen el sitio y los que se deciden a avanzar en regla hasta el absoluto sometimiento de la posición deseada' (ibid.). Whether this is an accurate reflection of how boys and girls interacted at the time or not is open to question. We can imagine that there was quite a gap between the 'official' version of courtship and the reality – although conservative opinion resisted any relaxation of behaviour for as long as possible. Here, for example, is the lament of one reactionary bishop of the time on the changes that were occurring in the 1960s:

> It is deplorable to see the habit of couples touching each others' arms and necks and backs, and carrying on outrageously on public benches, in a way never seen before in Spain, other than in the hiding-places which conceal such sordid goings-on.
>
> (quoted in Roca i Girona 1996: 197)

Certainly, nowadays, it is generally accepted that a young person's relationship with a member of the opposite sex is much more likely to be a natural development from a friendship struck up in the context of normal social activities among boys and girls, one usually initiated in school, college or the person's neighbourhood. Liberal parents place few enough restrictions on casual meetings between the sexes, and frequent and intense socializing often complements a busy weekly schedule of study or work. At all times of the year, young Spaniards find time and opportunities to meet, often in large numbers, and frequently in the vicinity of noisy, crowded bars. *La marcha* continues all year round, and apparently around the clock: at least at weekends, the favoured haunts – the bars and discos where the mating game is played out – often stay open until the first light of dawn, as Spaniards accustom their bodies and minds from an early age to a routine of marathon nocturnal socializing.

This takes place with parents' knowledge and approval, however, and it is in this respect, more than in any other, that young Spaniards' sexual behaviour differs from that of their grandparents. And when love relationships blossom, they invariably do so in a context of acceptance by the family and friends of the couple concerned: the process of becoming a part of the important (extended) family begins early, with visits to the family home and invitations to family meals. The strength of this family tie, and the facility for incorporating the love relationship into the family, are borne out by the results of the CIS survey mentioned earlier, where 73.6 per cent of respondents stated that their love relationship entailed no loss of contact with their family (CIS 1995a: 9).

Marriage is high on the agenda of most couples, a great majority of Spaniards still considering it an important institution. In 1997, for example, a survey showed that almost two-thirds of Spaniards felt that marriage was, in general, a 'fairly or very important institution' (CIS 1997b: 10). Certainly, most Spaniards look to a potential partner out of a need to find someone to share their lives with: this was the single most important motivating factor for those involved in relationships in the 1995 CIS survey (CIS 1995a: 21). Other factors alluded to included, in order of importance, 'looking for a meaning in life', 'the desire to form a family and have children', and 'the fear of finding myself alone in the future'.

Once they have formed a stable love relationship, Spaniards are inclined to be faithful to their partners and not to seek other relationships. Of the 1949 people surveyed by the CIS in 1995 (all of whom were adults between 18 and 64), almost half (46.5 per cent) had had sexual relations with just one person during their lives, notwithstanding the fact of flirtatious behaviour: about half those surveyed said they did at least a little flirting with people they found attractive, whether they were involved in a love relationship or not. The overall trend is definitely towards establishing one stable relationship: 64.4 per cent of respondents said they did not like at all the idea of having a series of brief relationships with different people.

More often than not, therefore, a stable relationship implies marriage for a Spaniard, and marriage usually implies a church wedding and having children. Even if the couple live together for some time before getting married – a trend which appears to be on the increase – there is still a tendency to have the wedding blessed by the Church. This is a strong general preference among Spanish adults: 90 per cent of the married people who were interviewed for the

Figure 4: The cartoonist Juan Ballesta regularly contributes wry commentaries on the social and sexual mores of contemporary Spain, such as this cartoon which appeared in *Cambio16* in May 1988.

1995 survey had married in church. Perhaps more surprising is the finding that the preference for a religious ceremony is also very marked among young people. In a 1997 survey of 15–29-year-olds (CIS 1997b), only 17.6 per cent wished to live together without getting married and 59.6 per cent preferred a church wedding, 23.9 per cent feeling that the best course of action was to live together first and then to get married *por la Iglesia*. Only 16.4 per cent stated a preference for a civil wedding over a church wedding.

Marriage, for most Spaniards, is closely related to having children. Although they are relatively permissive about the idea of having a sexual relationship during the *noviazgo*, there is still a strong degree of support for the notion that marriage and children go together. It is true that there is a relatively high level of acceptance that one's son or daughter might have a child outside marriage – only 38 per cent of people felt it would be a problem for them if their daughter had a child while single (CIS 1992: 20) – but, of the factors influencing young people in the direction of marriage, the strongest are 'family pressures' and 'having children' (CIS 1997b: 11). It is unusual for children to be born outside marriage in Spain: the rate in 1996, for example, was just 11.7 per cent of live births (Eurostat 1999a). This was the third lowest rate in the EU (after Greece and Italy) and 12.7 per cent below the EU average. In the same year, the rate in France was 38.9 per cent, and in the UK, 35.5 per cent, while the highest rate in Europe was the Danish one, at 46.3 per cent.

Even within the context of marriage, however, most Spaniards would like to have more children than they do. The birth rate is one of the lowest in the world: in 1999, the rate was just 0.94 per cent (*El País*, January 2000); but many people (36 per cent of the adult population) would like to have two children, and 30 per cent would prefer to have three (CIS 1994: 9). If they have fewer children than they would like to, the explanation has to do with money: 'cuesta mucho criar bien un hijo' was the reason most frequently cited in a 1994 CIS survey (ibid.: 10).

Current family sizes offer a stark contrast with the traditional Spanish Catholic preference for large families. Before the general availability of contraception, and with generally lower levels of education, large families (of six and more children) were not unusual in Spain. In the 1950s, V. S. Pritchett could write of Spanish women that '[t]hey are passionate lovers of children: there is marriage and eight children in their eyes' (Pritchett 1984 [1954]: 74); now, however, less than 2 per cent of Spaniards would prefer to have more than four children (CIS 1994: 10).

People look to their relationship with their partner to provide love, happiness and, eventually, children. The new-found confidence of more prosperous Spaniards – especially women – appears to have led to higher expectations with regard to happiness and fulfilment. Each partner in the new Spanish relationship is likely to value and respect himself and herself, and couples seem now to be more likely to achieve a fair balance between the concerns and priorities of the man and those of the woman. Without a doubt, the other traditional Spanish bogeyman, the neighbour's wagging tongue (*el qué dirán*), is much less significant now than it used to be, either in terms of influence on the selection of a mate or in terms of how the couple choose to live their lives. Spaniards generally feel reasonably satisfied with their relationship with their partners. In the 1995 CIS survey, respondents were asked: 'How satisfied are you with your relationship?', and 91 per cent answered 'a lot' or 'sufficiently' (CIS 1995a: 13). When they were then asked about factors contributing to the success of their relationships, the principal factors cited were as follows (in order of importance):

1 mutual affection
2 children
3 shared experiences
4 good communication

Bottom of the list of the 11 causes were *el qué dirán* and financial advantage.

This generally optimistic picture of Spanish love relationships is supported by a French lifestyle survey (reported in *El Mundo* in January 1993) which concluded that, of all Europeans, Spaniards were the ones most satisfied with their love life: they scored 8 out of 10, compared with the European average of 7.5.

Not all relationships run smoothly all the time, however. The divorce rate in Spain is currently rising (although the level is still low compared with other European countries); selfish behaviour, unreasonable expectations and general incompatibility hinder Spanish relationships, as they do in other cultures, even if there appears to be a relatively high degree of successful partnering in the case of Spain.

Although non-conventional forms of living together – including homosexual partnerships – are readily accepted by a majority of Spaniards, the general trend appears to be towards the maintenance of fairly conventional forms of *convivencia* and a continued respect for marriage, with the inclusion of children, so that, in Spain at least, the family remains strong.

6.3 THE POETRY OF LOVE

Spanish poetry, like the poetry of other cultures, abounds with exquisite verses in which poets have articulated the joy and the pain, the ecstasy and the agony, of love. The powerful emotions generated by being in love can induce poetic expression, and the textures and rhythms of poetry seem to be especially suited to capturing those feelings.

This very transformational effect of love is itself articulated in, for example, the classic Spanish text *El Libro de Buen Amor*, a long poem by Juan Ruiz, Arcipreste de Hita, which recounts a series of love stories parodying popular medieval tales warning of the dangers of excessive love. Here is one account (in fourteenth-century Spanish) of what happens when love strikes:

> El amor faz sotil   al omne que es rudo,
> fázele fabrar fermoso   al que antes es mudo,
> al omne que es covarde   fázelo muy atrevudo,
> al perezoso faze   ser presto e agudo.
>
> Al mançebo mantiene   mucho en mançebez
> e al viejo faz perder   mucho la vejez . . .
>
> (Arcipreste de Hita 1976: 20)

Certainly men – and presumably, though less visibly, women too – have been led to *hablar hermoso* under the real or imagined influence of love. Much of the beautiful language they have used has been employed to express the beauty of the beloved. The 'Fábula de Polifemo y Galatea', by Luis de Góngora (1561–1627), tells the classic story of the love between Acis and Galatea, ruined by the jealousy of the giant Polyphemus, who kills Acis with a stone. Although Góngora's language can be hard to decipher, since he alters normal word order and makes liberal use of metaphors, his verses are often highly effective, as in the following famous lines on the surpassing beauty of Galatea:

> Ninfa, de Doris hija, la más bella,
> adora, que vio el reino de la espuma.
> Galatea es su nombre, y dulce en ella
> el terno Venus de sus Gracias suma . . .
>
> Purpúreas rosas sobre Galatea
> la Alba entre lilios cándidos deshoja:
> duda el Amor cuál más su color sea,
> o púrpura nevada, o nieve roja.
> De su frente la perla es, eritrea,
> émula vana. El ciego dios se enoja,
> y, condenado su esplendor, la deja
> pender en oro al nácar de su oreja.

Góngora's message is that the sea (and just about everything and everyone else) adores Galatea, the beautiful nymph, daughter of Doris, in whom Venus has 'summed up all the beauty of the three Graces'. Her complexion is an ineffable pink, between rose-red and lily-white: the poet cannot decide whether it is best described as a snowy purpura (a purple shell formerly used to extract red dye) or as reddish snow. The pearls from the Red Sea are only a poor imitation of her beautiful forehead, and the pearl's presumption, in daring to try to imitate her, angers Cupid, the god of love, to such an extent that he condemns the pearl to hang – as an earring, from Galatea's ear.

This poem, like most of the best-known love poetry, is written from a male point of view. Women, disadvantaged with respect to men over the centuries, have written less, and, to compound the injustice, those who have written have often been ignored or excluded from anthologies. Janet Pérez has suggested that '[u]nawareness of past or present Spanish women writers, poets or otherwise, constitutes the norm rather than the exception' (Pérez 1996: xxv). Some examples of poetry by women have been included here, although inevitably the chief emphasis is on poetry by men.

One particular concern of men's has been to encourage young women to 'seize the day', to make the most of their youthful beauty by enjoying the delights of love (presumably in the company of the male in question), before time catches up on them and their beauty fades. There is an ancient tradition of such poetry, going back to classical antiquity – the theme is normally given the Latin name *carpe diem* ('seize the day') – and it was frequently the theme of choice for poets wishing to demonstrate their verbal ingenuity, if not their actual love, for a member of the opposite sex. This was a particular obsession of the Golden Age poets. One example is this well-known sonnet by the poet and soldier Garcilaso de la Vega (1501–36), who, like Góngora, was steeped in the Classical Renaissance tradition of his time, and much of whose poetry is inspired by the works of ancient Latin and Greek authors:

> En tanto que de rosa y azucena
> se muestra la color en vuestro gesto,
> y que vuestro mirar ardiente, honesto,
> enciende al corazón y lo refrena;
> y en tanto que el cabello, que en la vena
> del oro se escogió, con vuelo presto,
> por el hermoso cuello blanco, enhiesto,
> el viento mueve, esparce y desordena;
> coged de vuestra alegre primavera
> el dulce fruto, antes que el tiempo airado
> cubra de nieve la hermosa cumbre.
> Marchitará la rosa el viento helado,
> todo lo mudará la edad ligera,
> por no hacer mudanza en su costumbre.
>
> (Garcilaso de la Vega 1970: 225)

In the octave the poet lingers on the beautiful features of the beloved: her face and complexion – a mixture, again, of red and white – the frank, honest innocence of the look in her eyes, her hair flowing down her beautiful white neck; and in the sestet, he invokes the elements of nature and the notion of the inexorability of time, with a view to urging her to soften her attitude (to him?) and to pluck the 'fruit of her happy spring' before time 'cubra de nieve la hermosa cumbre', or turns her beautiful hair white.

Sensuality can be expressed with much less technical complexity, of course. On a more popular level – the level of the street – the following lines (by J. Cano) are written on a water-fountain, the *Fuente de la Amapola*, in a street in the Sacromonte neighbourhood of Granada:

> Cuánto me gustaría ser
> la fuente de mi barrio,
> pa' cuando pases y bebas
> sentir muy cerca tus labios.

The sensuality of the lines is accentuated by their being found on a street-corner, written on an old fountain; Spanish culture seems to have a higher tolerance of sensuality and the public expression of sexuality than many others. It is not unusual to find couples kissing openly in public, and there seems to be less embarrassment attached to this than in Anglo-Saxon culture. But what is beyond question is the emotional impact of such a frank expression of sensuality, and this can be universally appreciated.

It may be debatable whether 'el amor no es más que la sexualidad magnificada', as Pedro Mata once claimed, but certainly love and sex have been interlinked in Spanish poetry since the earliest times. An emphasis on this connection may or may not be a specifically male obsession, but even in traditional ballads, the male point of view predominates, and women's desire – as articulated by men – can often appear pernicious, debilitating and disruptive. The depiction of women as evil temptresses, intent on having their way with men, and whose advances lead to the man's downfall, is a common theme in much medieval literature. In the lines below we witness one medieval man's lament at not being able to resist the allure of a woman's charms:

> ¡Maldita sea la Fortuna, que así me quiere tratar!
> Nunca me da bien cumplido ni menos mal sin afán,
> por una hora de placer cien mil años de pesar.
> Yo amaba una señora que en el mundo no hay su par.
> (quoted in Castro Lingl 1998: 142)

Damnation in Hell is the plight of the one who falls to the temptations of sexual pleasure, presumably sexual acts carried out beyond the bounds of the married state to which, at least in terms of the conventions of the time, they should have been confined.

This poetry is misogynistic: it suggests that women are a corrupting influence, weak, venal and dangerous, disrupting social normality and likely to lead the honest man astray unless he takes due precautions. But misogyny is not confined to popular literature: many of the learned authors of the medieval and Golden Age periods betray such prejudice against women in their poetry. The satirical poetry of Francisco de Quevedo (1580–1645) contains plenty of evidence of such attitudes. One of his best-known poems is a satire on money called 'Don Dinero'. In this poem, a young woman expresses her love for Don Dinero, and sings his praises over the course of ten stanzas. What the stanzas describe, however, is the talent this gentleman has to corrupt judges, make people believe he is noble, and exercise influence over the great of his day. On one level, the poem is an attack on the power of money. The suitor is described, for example, as being 'gallant and like gold':

> Es galán y es como un oro,
> tiene quebrado el color,
> persona de gran valor,
> tan cristiano como moro.
> Pues que da y quita el decoro
> y quebranta cualquier fuero,
> *poderoso caballero*
> *es don Dinero.*

On another level, however, it implies the venality of the young woman, who is depicted as being more than willing to submit to this 'powerful gentleman':

Madre, yo al oro me humillo.
El es mi amante y mi amado,
pues de puro enamorado
anda de contino amarillo:
que, pues, doblón o sencillo,
hace todo cuanto quiero,
poderoso caballero
es don Dinero.

Quevedo generalizes this sentiment until it becomes a blanket condemnation of the supposedly mercenary qualities of all women:

Nunca vi damas ingratas
a su gusto y afición:
que a las caras de un doblón
hacen sus caras baratas . . .

Although such misogynistic sentiments are rarely expressed today in the poetry of the educated middle classes, both the notion of women's venality and negative comments on women's sexuality are to be found in abundance in certain areas of popular culture. This is the case, for instance, of some of the *coplas* composed during carnival time in Córdoba, when the verses written to mock 'respectable behaviour' and social normality become, among other things, a vehicle for expressing crude anti-female sentiments. One such *copla*, for example, recounts how a barber gets the better of a polite young woman who ends up 'jumping for joy' when he uses his 'brush' on her:

Una niña de elevada distinción
Fue a cortarse las melenas
A lo garzón.
El barbero 'mu' tunante y diligente
Se la puso en postura diferente.
Vaya salero:
La peló y la afeitó con esmero
y la niña de gusto bailaba,
Cuando le pasaba
La brocha el barbero.

(quoted in Gilmore 1998: 40)

The barber is clever and devious, but the woman is depicted as putting on a respectable front while, deep down, she wants the sex that the barber gives her. As David Gilmore (1998: 41) puts it, 'what is high is lowered, fastidiousness is circumvented, and the modesty of woman is exposed as fraudulent'. While the woman is portrayed as hypocritical, the male viewpoint is reinforced by the depiction of the man as being the one in charge: it is he who has 'agency', who is in control of events.

This is an example of carnivalesque parody, of street-songs composed in a context where the aim is to ridicule everyone and anyone, but especially the polite middle classes and the rich and powerful. In the spirit of the carnival, degradation is permitted, and the implication is that, if you object to such treatment, you should go elsewhere.

Women, of course, are also very capable of suggesting to men that they go elsewhere. The contemporary poet Amalia Bautista expresses her impatience with the feeble advances of some of the men she knows in her poem 'Juego sucio', published in the collection *Cárcel de amor* (1988):

> El juego de los hombres es odioso
> Porque sus intenciones son tan dobles
> Como la caja negra que usa el mago
> En sus mejores trucos. Ya no quiero
> Que me inviten a ver exposiciones
> Que me aburren; tampoco me divierte
> El amigo de siempre que declara
> Morir por mí y, con todo, resignarse;
> No quiero que me llame inteligente
> Quien desliza su mano sudorosa
> Para tocar mis muslos; me repugna
> Que una voz impostada me pregunte
> Si tengo algo que hacer ese domingo.
> Dejadme ser la puta de los héroes
> Y nunca habrá una mácula en mi honra.

Implicit in this poem is an allusion to another long-standing tradition in European literature: that of the 'unrequited lover', the man who burns with a pure love for his beloved, but whose overtures are rebuffed. Some of the Golden Age poets already mentioned offer examples of the pain of unrequited love, as, for instance, in the case of the shepherd Salicio's love for Galatea in Garcilaso's 'First Eclogue', where the poor man's situation is expressed thus:

> ¡Oh más dura que mármol a mis quejas,
> y al encendido fuego en que me quemo,
> más helada que nieve, Galatea!
> Estoy muriendo, y aún la vida temo;
> témola con razón, pues tú me dejas . . .
>
> (Garcilaso de la Vega 1970: 5)

Love can hurt for a variety of reasons, of course, not the least of which may be the cultural differences between the lovers. In the traditional ballad called 'Por los caños de Carmona' (quoted in Smith 1964: 152–3), dating from about the thirteenth century, the Christian man and Muslim woman are deeply in love, but the man is feeling guilty about this relationship which crosses religious boundaries, all the more so since he has not attended mass for seven years and, contrary to his religion, he eats meat on Fridays:

'comemos la carne en viernes
lo que mi ley defendía.
Siete años había, siete,
que yo misa no oía;
si el emperador lo sabe
la vida me costaría.'

His beloved suspects that he may be upset because he has a lover in France, or because he fears repercussions from the Muslims on account of his relationship with her. But he reassures her:

'No tengo miedo a los moros
ni en Francia tengo amiga;
mas vos, mora, y yo cristiano
hacemos muy mala vida.'

Whatever the dangers, they will be true to one another, across the cultural divide. They pledge their love, and each of them is even willing to adopt the other's religion if necessary, in order to maintain their relationship:

'Por tus amores, Valdovinos,
cristiana me tornaría.'
'Yo, señora, por los vuestros,
moro de la morería.'

6.4 GENDER ISSUES IN SPAIN

Gender is based around a core biological difference between the sexes; but gender refers mainly to the respective roles that men and women play in society, and to the sense of maleness or femaleness that each person has in relation to their own identity. There is a general consensus that gender identity is an aspect of learned behaviour, and that, in that sense, it is cultural. To what extent there may or may not be some hereditary transmission of tendencies (to think or behave in certain ways) is not clear. Whatever the case, there are certainly significant ways in which gender roles alter over time and vary from one culture to another.

Both female and male gender roles have changed enormously in Spain in recent decades. Contemporary young Spanish men and women generally accept without question the principle of equality, the need for a fairer distribution of responsibilities within the home and in the family, and the rights of both men and women to seek fulfilment through their careers.

These views are radically different from the attitudes which prevailed in the

Spain of the Franco dictatorship. Then, Spaniards were taught that a woman's place was in the home, and that she should look after her children and give support to her husband. The husband's power over his wife was not only a social reality but was also written into law. He was the legal owner of the home itself and of any property in it, and could dispose of either without his wife's consent. The wife could not sell any such belongings without her husband's consent, nor could she officially travel away from home or even open a bank account without her husband's permission. If a husband and wife separated, the wife could lose the matrimonial home, and an adulterous husband was entitled to far more lenient treatment under the law than an adulterous wife. Although many of these legal provisions were applied only sparingly in Spanish courts, they reflected a mentality which favoured male dominance – and they reinforced that mentality.

During the Franco dictatorship, male dominance was also taken for granted within the *Sección Femenina* (SF), the women's section of the National Movement (Franco's Falangist political organization). The SF combined commitment to the Franco regime with a very particular type of educational zeal. It organized programmes for women at the local level in regional crafts, domestic and rural economy, literacy, dance, singing, etc. It was founded in 1934 by Pilar Primo de Rivera, sister of José Antonio Primo de Rivera, the founder of the *Falange Española*. The approach adopted by the SF is neatly summarized in this extract from a speech by Pilar Primo de Rivera in 1939:

> The only patriotic mission which has been allocated to women is the home . . . Let us teach women to look after their home . . . Let us teach this way of life that José Antonio wanted for all Spaniards, so that Spanish women, when they have children, will raise them to love God and to believe in the Falange's way of life.
>
> (quoted in Riera and Valenciano 1991: 38; my translation)

The role of a man, according to this view, was to focus on achievement outside the home and to provide for his family. A woman's principal role in life was to become a mother and housewife, look after the home, care for her husband and children, and not concern herself with the public sphere.

Notwithstanding its conservative ethos, the SF was among those who put pressure on the Franco government to bring in legislation to improve the legal position of Spanish women. This was done, not in a spirit of sexual equality, and much less out of any feminist conviction, but because the SF and the government recognized that women were choosing to work outside the home, and they saw the growing need for cheap unskilled labour in the late 1950s and early 1960s. They also recognized that many of the laws regulating women's lives were simply not practicable. A new Act, on *Los Derechos Políticos, Profesionales y de Trabajo de la Mujer*, introduced in 1961, abolished many of the regulations mentioned above, and, for the first time since 1942, gave women the right to work after they married (although only if their husbands agreed to this). Its effectiveness was very limited: up to 1975, for example, a woman's husband could still claim legal entitlement to her wages!

As already mentioned, with the economic changes of the 1960s came a demand for more workers, which in turn had an effect on the rate at which women took up employment. As Brooksbank Jones (1997: 78) suggests, the developmentalism of that period had two phases, in the first of which there was a rapid increase in male employment (with a rise of 400 000 jobs between 1964 and 1969), but, in the second phase, i.e. between 1969 and 1974, male employment actually fell, while there was an increase of 870 000 jobs for women. Many of these new jobs were in the service sector, especially tourism, although a large number of women also took up jobs in factories.

It was also in 1961 that the general principle of equal pay for equal work was introduced. Nonetheless, there was very little enforcement of this, particularly in the private sector, and discrimination persisted for years after the new law was passed. Nowadays, although there is complete equality before the law, women's income is still lower in practice than that of men; in 1998, average pay for men was over 208 000 pesetas per month, while the average for women was 159 000 pesetas (Instituto de la Mujer 2000). Despite the fact that, for example, women make up about 48 per cent of the workforce in the professional and technical sectors and some 42 per cent of public service employees, only some 5 per cent of company directors in Spain are women.

Both the *desmadre sexual* of the late 1970s – the apparently obsessive concern with sexual matters in the wake of the abolition of censorship – and the *revolución reproductiva* – which led to the legalization of contraception in 1978 and the introduction of abortion in 1985 – were influential factors in changing Spanish perceptions of how men and women could, and should, live their lives. They reinforced the trend away from the old *machista* society of the early Franco period, as well as reducing the influence of the Catholic Church, and were a sign of the recognition on the part of both men and women that their bodies were not there to be appropriated by others.

Although Spanish women have been cautious about adopting the more radical versions of feminism, they have been very aware in recent decades of the need to improve women's actual situation in society, as opposed to merely the legal position. The *Instituto de la Mujer* was set up by the PSOE government in 1983 and has taken a lead in pushing the equality agenda in Spain since then, with significant levels of success. The Institute's brief has extended to all areas of Spanish society, including education and work, and it has devoted a great deal of energy to conducting research into gender discrimination and gender differences generally, as well as suggesting changes in many areas of Spanish society.

In education, major changes have occurred also. Under Franco, separate curricula were devised for boys' and girls' education, and most of the resources were channelled into the education of boys. Although both boys and girls generally had access to primary education during the 1940s and 1950s, secondary education was an elitist, male-dominated area. For example, on average during the period 1940–45, females represented only some 35 per cent of those studying for the *Bachillerato* (the state examination held at the end of secondary-level schooling). Again, significant changes began to take place in the 1960s, so that, by the academic year 1968–69, 45 per cent of *Bachillerato* students were female (Campo 1993, I: 241). During most of the dictatorship, universities were also reserved for a privileged minority, and male students predominated; however, in the academic year 1976–77, female students outnumbered male students for the first time, a pattern which has tended to be repeated since. Nowadays, as Garrido (1993: 155) puts it, 'young women study harder than their male counterparts': in 1991, approximately 36 per cent of women aged between 20 and 24 were studying, while only some 28 per cent of men in that age group were students (Garrido 1993: 265). Although girls are more likely to study, and more likely to be successful at their studies, than boys, there is much evidence of gender stereotyping in terms of subject and career choice. For instance, at the highest level of secondary education (COU – *Curso de Orientación Universitaria*), girls constitute 54–58 per cent of health, social sciences, humanities and languages students, but only about 35 per cent of science and technology students (Brooksbank Jones 1997: 65).

The points mentioned so far are some of the more salient sociological and legal facts about changing roles in Spain. There are many other aspects of male and female behaviour which are worthy of comment. Many of these are intimate aspects of people's everyday lives, realities which are difficult to explain and almost impossible to capture in statistics. They are, nonetheless, important facets of the different gender identities of Spanish men and women. Some of the latter centre on (1) the use of place and space by men and women; (2) attitudes to church and school; and (3) domestic chores.

6.4.1 Use of place and space

The distinction between the domestic and public spheres mentioned above has its counterpart in everyday life in terms of a distinction between *casa* and *calle*. The traditional roles played by Spanish men and women, respectively, implied that women were meant to confine their activities to the home, and to a limited number of places, identifiable as 'female spaces' (including, for instance, the market-place). This has now largely broken down, especially in urban areas. But it is still the case that, in certain parts of Spain at least, the 'geography of sex' persists. The ethnographer David Gilmore (1998: 129) insists that, at least in Andalusia, 'sexual quarantine is an unambiguous empirical reality' and is 'a fragment of life as it is personally experienced'. He describes how, in some parts of rural Andalusia, women are generally confined to interior or enclosed spaces; when they are out in public places, their bodies and their voices take on a muted quality. The women he observed would never enter a bar unaccompanied, or, if they did, they would be perceived as morally suspect, and their sexual modesty would be thrown into question. Normally, women would not even accompany their menfolk into bars, just as it would be highly unusual for men to shop at the market-place, for instance. While the situation he is referring to may be exceptional, in terms of the degree of segregation he describes, it is still a fact that, even in Spanish towns and cities, most shoppers – especially in food-markets – are women, the people one sees in bars tend to be men, and, certainly, it is unusual for women to drink alone in bars.

There still appear to be stigmas attaching to these behaviours in Spain – the woman in the bar being seen as 'fair game', and the man shopping in the market being classed as a *marica* – stigmas which are less accentuated in other western cultures. Related to this is the distinction between the assertive role played by men in public, compared with the more passive role they would traditionally adopt in the home. Out of doors, Spanish men still seem reluctant to be seen to allow their wives to make decisions about where to go or what to do; in the home, on the other hand, the woman is more likely to assert her authority. These patterns may be changing, and certainly at an intellectual level Spanish men are adopting more egalitarian attitudes, but even the new Spanish man often comes across as being uncomfortable with the notion of being seen as passive, complaisant or lacking in assertiveness.

6.4.2. Women in church and school

Church and school are also places where women predominate. Daily attendance at mass and participation in church-related activities are associated far more with women than with men. Men, and in particular younger men, are rarely seen in church, except on special occasions such as weddings, funerals or baptisms, or at Sunday mass if they are accompanied by their wives and children. This is despite their participation in the processions, typically during Holy Week, when Brotherhoods organize the processing of favoured images of Christ, the Virgin Mary or a patron saint (see 9.4). Again, involvement in run-of-the-mill church activities and everyday presence in church seem to be associated with the private, family sphere, whereas participation in the processions is at least as much about asserting public status as it is about faith or piety, so that it seems possible to extend the distinction between 'home focus' and 'public focus' to this area, just as it was seen to be relevant to the areas of shopping and visiting bars.

A similar point could be made in relation to school, since education also is an area closely associated with the intimacy of home and family. Apart from issues such as gender stereotyping in class activities and subject choice, the area of children's schooling is one where mothers, rather more than fathers, tend to make decisions. While fathers may have an input, and while it is probable that with younger couples the decisions are shared more evenly between the partners, it is frequently the case that the mother decides both which school the children will attend and what they will study when they get there. Children's progress is more likely to be monitored by mothers than fathers, to the extent that parent–teacher meetings, or *reuniones de padres*, are often jokingly referred to in many schools as *reuniones de madres*, since the attendance of fathers is minimal.

6.4.3 Domestic chores

Perhaps the area where the *casa/calle* distinction is most clearly seen, and where we witness the most obvious difference between theoretical and practical egalitarianism, is the area of domestic work. Although in Inner (1988) it is reported that only 46.2 per cent of Spanish men agree with the statement 'Housework is women's work', the facts suggest that, in practice, men are still not inclined to take on their share of domestic chores. Spanish boys do far less housework than girls, a pattern which is repeated among adult men and women. Few chores are done predominantly by men, and there are many which men rarely or never touch (Inner 1988: 30). Prime among the latter are chores related to clothes: 9 out of 10 Spanish men never do any ironing, and about 8 of every 10 men never wash clothes, while almost all those men who do, do it only occasionally. The domestic areas favoured by men concern DIY and rubbish: only 14.3 per cent of men never do any DIY, and only 17.2 per cent never take out the rubbish!

The spectacular – and very valuable – improvements made in the status of women in Spain have brought important gains for both sexes, although a difficult period of adjustment is clearly being experienced at the moment. Men, in particular, often have real difficulties readjusting their value systems: as the former Director of the National Library, Carmen Lacambra, put it: 'All that is necessary for women to have total independence is that men should accept the idea' (*El País*, August 1994). Such readjustment of male values is not easy, but is clearly required in order to ensure that men live out the principles of equality that they are increasingly espousing in theory.

FEATURE: FLAMENCO DANCE

'Cuando bailo, lo que intento es enamorar. Soy una mujer que va a enamorar a un hombre, ese hombre que está ahí, bailando conmigo.' This is Cristina Hoyos' statement on the meaning of the art-form for which she has become famous: flamenco dancing. Seeing her passionate dance, with her sensuous arm and hand movements and intricate footwork, the validity of her summary of flamenco dancing is beyond doubt. Although it is about much more than love – it is often, very importantly, about sadness and grief – flamenco dance is centrally concerned with the nature of the visceral attraction between men and women.

Too often dismissed as an irrelevant cliché, flamenco music and dance is a complex and highly sophisticated form of artistic expression, and an element of Spanish culture that millions of Spaniards identify with. It is particularly significant within the culture of Andalusia, for example, while it is only of very limited relevance in much of the north of Spain, but, like bullfighting, it has come to occupy a special place as an icon of Spanish culture, and the figure of the female flamenco dancer, dressed in a brightly-coloured ruffled dress (the *batas de colas*), is frequently used as an image of 'Spanishness', often within the context of tourism. Debased versions of flamenco, with poor-quality music and dance, have frequently been offered as entertainment to foreign tourists who are deemed to know no better, and have had the effect of depressing the general standard of performance. In recent decades, however, there has been a renewal of interest in flamenco, with the result that it has gained in status both within Spain and internationally. The male flamenco dancer Joaquín Cortés is perhaps the best-known exponent of this new wave of interest in the art-form, which has also led to the production of important films based around flamenco by directors such as Carlos Saura and Antonio Gades.

Although the origins of flamenco are obscure, it is most closely associated with the gypsies of southern Spain, in whose communities it flourished from the early eighteenth century. Spanish gypsies were essentially nomadic, and had their own culture, including their own customs and traditions and their own language (*Caló*), which is still spoken today. They now occupy an ambiguous status within Spanish society. On the one hand, their association with flamenco places them at the centre of what we might think of as being essentially Spanish; on the other hand, their socio-economic status tends to be low, with the result that they are often associated in the minds of *payos* (non-gypsies) with poverty and marginalization, and the social anathema felt towards them by the majority of Spaniards makes them outsiders within the dominant Spanish community.

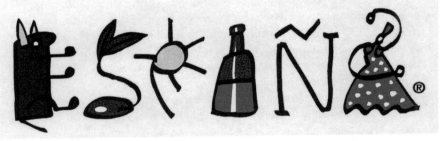

Figure 5: Toying with clichéd images of Spain, this postcard manages to suggest both celebration and mockery of some of the typical Spanish stereotypes, including bullfighting and flamenco. Mikel Urmeneta © Kukuxumusu.

READING: MANUEL VICENT, 'UNA HISTORIA DE AMOR'

Manuel Vicent (b. 1936) has written many stories of modern Spain which have been published in Spanish newspapers and magazines. His stories reflect the everyday concerns of Spanish people, and the social background of the stories is often that of modest or underprivileged urban-dwellers. In 'Una historia de amor', he tells how a young couple dream of buying their own flat, as a prelude to getting married and settling down. The young man, Julián, is tempted into crime as a way of obtaining the money for the flat, however, and his attempts at robbery land him in jail. It is in the sordid surroundings of the jail's 'nido de amor', where prisoners' conjugal visits take place, that the relationship between himself and his *novia* is eventually consummated. In the extract below, we see how he finally gets permission to meet his girlfriend on intimate terms: the flat they had both earlier dreamed about has become a rather grotty room in Carabanchel Prison . . .

De una forma casi diabólica, las ardientes cartas de aquella chica llegaban a la cárcel con besos de carmín, y el recluso Julián Requejo Gómez ya no se metía ningún hierro. El funcionario mantenía la promesa en pie. Si seguía siendo un buen muchacho, un día no muy lejano podría estar a solas con su novia en el cuarto. ¡Ese día había llegado! Tuvo que formalizar todos los requisitos, firmar volantes y esperar tres meses. Finalmente, un papel sellado por la junta del establecimiento, a modo de pasaje para embarcar, cayó en sus manos. El galán podía presentar ante el tribunal un cuerpo troceado por el amor. Varios costurones le cruzaban la tripa y en la garganta le brillaba una cicatriz de traqueotomía con una tonalidad azul. Mientras se acercaba el momento de palpar sólidamente la esfumada silueta de aquella mujer, él cumplía con ahínco la penitencia diaria sonriendo. Barría la celda con la humildad de un fraile motilón, soldaba cañerías, se comía el rancho dejando la cuchara aparte, saludaba a los carceleros con un 'buenos días nos dé Dios', asistía a misa y ponía paz en las reyertas de la galería. Luego, en el patio, se sentaba en un rincón para soñar. Veía pasar aviones y palomas torcaces por el cuadrilátero del cielo y pensaba en aquellas excursiones de domingo a Chinchón o al Jarama con ella. Aún sentía en la palma el suave volumen de unos senos bajo la blusa estampada y recordaba aquellos pelillos dorados como el vello del melocotón que la brisa hacía irisar en los muslos de la chica. Esa felicidad campestre se había ido al demonio por culpa de un maldito piso en Alcorcón. La chica se resistía a entregarse fuera del matrimonio y él tuvo que coger una escopeta para cazar unos millones.

El primer jueves de visita se lo dijo en el locutorio. Ella le traía el salchichón y las noticias de los amigos, iba a contarle la película de Paul Newman, y entonces a través del plástico arañado se lo soltó gritando de golpe.

— ¡He conseguido el permiso!
— ¿Para qué?
— El sábado podré estar contigo una hora.
— ¿Dónde?
— Aquí dentro. En un cuarto. Los dos solos. Hay una tabla.
— ¿Y qué vamos a hacer?
— No seas bruta.

La chica había excitado la memoria de su amante encarcelado durante años con unas cartas ardientes. Y ahora dudaba. Simplemente sentía miedo. Podría creerse que su escrúpulo era demasiado cruel, pero la chica tenía motivos para recelar de esos guardianes de mirada lasciva, de unas rejas oxidadas, de un ambiente miserable con aspecto de basurero e incluso de la pasión de aquel hombre que en un instante de furia amoroso tanto tiempo reprimida sería capaz de estrangularla en un zarpazo. Ella todavía pensaba para su amor en un piso de lámparas rosas, en una almohada con iniciales conyugales bordadas por sí misma; pero el recluso Julián Requejo luchó a muerte por el derecho a la comunicación que establece la Constitución democrática, lloró, suplicó de rodillas, se mordió los puños, tampoco se introdujo esta vez ningún hierro por la boca, y después de unas semanas de zozobra la novia transigió, y aquella tarde de sábado cruzó la reja como una gacela asustada.

Previamente él se había ofrecido voluntario para limpiar el nido. Con una fregona y un cubo de agua con zotal frotó el suelo, las paredes y la tabla de pino. Pasó un trapo por la bombilla y puso una mata de geranio en la cabecera del banco. Compró refrescos de naranja del economato y extendió una sábana sobre la madera de la operación. Ahora el hedor a besugo podrido se había mezclado con una veta de desinfectante mortal.

Llegado el momento, el funcionario hizo pasar a la doncella hacia una zona social donde la esperaba el galán de las cicatrices. Allí la cogió de la mano, ambos penetraron en el cuarto y el guardián quedó en el pasillo cronometrando la hora. No tenían nada que decirse. La novia se sentó temblando como un pájaro en el filo de la tabla y, primero, se bajó el borde de la falda con dos tironcillos nerviosos sonriendo con la cara fija en la pared. El le pellizcó suavemente un brazo. Y murmuró:

— Por favor.
— ¿Qué vas a hacer?
— Querías un piso. ¿Te acuerdas?
— Sí.
— Esto es un piso.

Entonces la chica comenzó a acariciarle el pecho por dentro de la camisa y con la yema de los dedos recorrió los dientes de sierra de unos costurones mal cosidos que su amante tenía repartidos por el tronco. Después de un suave forcejeo ella abandonó el cuerpo y entonces él acudió en una galopada de caballo a tomar posesión de su heredad. Fuera, un celador leía un periódico, a veces miraba el reloj y ponía la oreja en la puerta del nido. Y no lograba oír nada.

(Vicent 1984: 124–6)

FURTHER READING

Alberdi, Inés, *La nueva familia española* (Madrid, Taurus, 1999).
Contemporary Spanish attitudes towards love relationships and divorce are discussed in Chapters 4 and 6, respectively.

Brooksbank Jones, Anny, *Women in Contemporary Spain* (Manchester, Manchester University Press, 1997).
Offers an account of feminism and of a wide range of issues relating to women generally in modern Spain.

Inner, *Los hombres españoles* (Madrid, Ministerio de Asuntos Sociales, Instituto de la Mujer, 1988).
An account of Spanish men's views in the late twentieth century.

Keefe Ugalde, Sharon, *Conversaciones y poemas: la nueva poesía femenina española en castellano* (Barcelona, Siglo XXI, 1991).
Examples of poetry by contemporary Spanish women poets.

7

Money: Food and Shelter, Wealth and Power

7.1 MONEY, GOODS AND MEANINGS

At a fundamental level, the concept of money relates to the ways in which we satisfy basic human requirements: the need for food and shelter, the need to clothe ourselves and look after our young. But consumption is more than the mere satisfaction of material needs. Much of our spending is concerned with acquiring non-essential items, and the particular items we choose to purchase are determined to a great extent by cultural factors: why else, for example, would Spaniards have a level of consumption of fish and shellfish four times the average for the rest of the world?

How we actually use our money – how we shop, or the process of consumption – relates to our wants at least as much as it does to our needs. Thus, money lies in the realm of values, of questions about what we believe to be important. And values will necessarily vary from culture to culture. Not only are spending and consumption value-laden, but the very acquisition of money – becoming, to a greater or lesser extent, wealthy – is similarly intimately related to what we view as our priorities. The degree to which we commit ourselves to obtaining wealth and, further, the extent to which we are prepared to use foul means or fair to obtain wealth can tell us about the values we hold dear.

Money is, therefore, more than just a common denominator for economic activity. Economic activity, and the institutions relating to it, do not exist apart from the rest of our human reality but are, in the words of Thomas Eriksen, 'an integrated part of a social and cultural totality' (Eriksen 1995: 162). Hence, a discussion of money matters raises issues of personal values, of ethics, of (self-) esteem, of social class and of the manipulation of power for personal gain.

Money is a basic means of rendering different goods and services comparable by measuring their value on a shared scale, but, of course, not everything can be bought and sold. Although certain things of major human importance – love or friendship, for example – cannot be exchanged for money, money and goods are also factors in the establishment and maintenance of human relationships. In this sense, money relates to essential human meanings, and the relationship between money and meaning is characteristically communicated through the use of goods.

Human rituals – whether of eating, of travelling, or of socializing – are conventional ways in which we convey meanings, and such rituals entail the use of money and goods. As Douglas and Isherwood (1979) suggest:

> Rituals are conventions that set up visible public definitions . . . . [M]ore effective rituals use material things, and the more costly the ritual trappings, the stronger we can assume the intention to fix the meanings to be. Goods, in this perspective, are ritual adjuncts; consumption is a ritual process whose primary function is to make sense of the inchoate flux of events.
>
> (Douglas and Isherwood 1979: 44)

This illustrates some of the key factors of relevance to the notion of 'money' being examined here: the relation of money to personal values and priorities; the uses made of money for asserting uniqueness of identity or cultural difference; its connection with socially acquired cultural preferences; its relation to issues of wealth and power, of esteem and social standing; its position straddling both the public and the private spheres, i.e. on the one hand, the economy is a publicly owned social system, just as consumption is a socially shared reality, and, on the other hand, our spending choices reflect aspects of our private vision of the world.

In this chapter, I address the issue of money in the Spanish context from a broad cultural perspective. This entails not only engaging with issues of materialism, power, corruption and the acquisition of wealth and goods, but also reviewing the economic system which has evolved in Spain and which is concerned to manage and regulate the processes of consumption and production.

Looked at from an economic perspective, Spain is a prosperous country, but its prosperity is a recent development following a long period of relative poverty. Industrialization and modernization have progressed rapidly since the 1950s, and the economic transformation has been accompanied by a major political transition from dictatorship to democracy. The shift is bound up with that tension between what Geertz (1993: 240) calls 'essentialism' and 'epochalism', i.e. the need to reconcile the desire to continue an indigenous way of life – the need to be true to one's own sense of identity – and the need to be in tune with the times, to capture the 'spirit of the age', to be modern. Most Spanish commentators would probably argue that, if there has been a winner in this conflict, it has been the latter, since Spain has devoted its energy over the last few decades to the process of modernizing, Europeanizing and globalizing.

Certain features of Spanish society and culture can serve as a backdrop to the discussion which follows, since they are money-related features which are frequently taken as key qualities of Spain and Spaniards. These are:

- the historical tradition (now well outmoded) of a strong class division between a powerful elite and an impoverished popular class;
- the sense of an 'opportunity lost' in squandering the wealth which poured into the country in the wake of Spain's entry into the New World in the sixteenth and seventeenth centuries;
- the persistent disparities within Spain between relatively wealthy and relatively poor parts of the country;
- the predominance in recent years – at least up to the mid-1990s – of the *cultura del pelotazo*, i.e. the obsession with acquiring easy money, especially through shady dealing and corrupt practices;
- the devotion of Spaniards to games of chance – lotteries, gaming machines, casinos and other forms of gambling; Spaniards spend well over 3.2 billion pesetas per annum on this (Tamames 1996: 573);
- the persistence, despite the widespread prosperity, of a significant number of poor and marginalized people in Spanish society;
- the very high rate of unemployment: 15.1 per cent in January 2000 – the highest rate in the EU (Eurostat 2000).

According to a recent UN report, Spain occupies eleventh place (out of 174 countries) in a league table of development in the world, ahead of countries such as Germany, Austria and the UK (*El País*, August 1998). The reasons for this are factors such as high life expectancy (77.7 years; the European average is 74.3 years), excellent literacy rates (97.1 per cent), and high rates of participation in education (90 per cent). The expression *vivir bien* normally refers to the concept of luxury living and to high levels of consumption; in reality, the Spanish art of living may well depend less on such material values and more on knowing how to prioritize those aspects of life that make it genuinely fulfilling.

7.2 THE SPANISH ECONOMY

Spain has one of the most advanced economies and one of the highest average per capita incomes in the world. The current economic wealth of the country is generally associated with two major strategic events that have taken place in Spain since the 1950s: the shift in economic policy during the latter part of the Franco dictatorship, which led to the economic boom of the 1960s, and the incorporation of Spain into the EU (then the EEC) in 1986.

The boom experienced by Spain in the *años de desarrollo* was a consequence of the new economic policies brought in by the Spanish government in the late 1950s and the favourable international economic climate of the 1960s. In 1959, the Franco government introduced a Stabilization Plan aimed at cutting inflation, reducing public expenditure and fomenting foreign investment in Spanish industry. The tough measures taken, combined with a protective tariff regime designed to help Spanish products to compete against imported goods, led to rapid growth during the following decade which continued unabated until the oil crisis of 1973–74.

Between 1960 and the mid-1970s, Spanish people experienced a degree of affluence previously unknown in the country. Relatively suddenly, creature comforts and consumer goods came within the reach of the ordinary Spaniard. For example, the rate of car ownership rose from 1 per cent of households in 1960 to 10 per cent in 1974; the number of Spanish homes with refrigerators rose from 4 per cent to 66 per cent; whereas less than half of Spanish households had a bathroom or shower in 1960, 86 per cent of them had one by 1974 (Hooper 1987: 26).

The Spain that was so rapidly being left behind at this stage was the closed and socially repressed Spain of the post-war period, a time when economic growth had stagnated and when it sometimes seemed as though little had changed since the Middle Ages. Spain had not experienced an industrial revolution comparable to that of Britain or other western countries. It thus reached 1960 in a state of 'semi-industrialization', with many remnants of the old, traditional Spain still in place. Agriculture still occupied nearly 40 per cent of the active workforce, with only 21.7 per cent of Spaniards employed in industry (Campo 1993, I: 380). Traditionally, wealth and power were the preserve of a small minority of upper-class Spaniards, whose interests had been defended over the centuries by the most significant institutions in the country, including politicians, the armed forces and the Catholic Church. However, some measure of industrialization did take place during the dictatorship, and in the 1950s, Spaniards began to move in ever-increasing numbers to the industrial centres, especially Madrid and Barcelona, drawn by the promise of work in factories. Not all of these found the better life they were looking for, and many, especially those who were forced to live in the shanty towns on the outskirts of the cities, ended up living in conditions which were not much better than those they had left behind in the country.

The period 1960–75, however, brought about major changes in the Spanish way of life. By 1970, the number of people working in agriculture had already dropped to 24.9 per cent (ibid.), with a majority of the country's wealth now being generated in manufacturing, construction and services (especially tourism, which was rapidly becoming Spain's major industry). Economic growth during the period averaged 6.8 per cent per annum (ibid., I: 55), an increase higher than that of almost any other economy in the world. Partly, the explanation for the high rate of growth is the fact that the starting point was so low. But the effect of this growth was to make Spain resemble more closely the economies of its advanced European neighbours, and the optimism generated by increased affluence fuelled the growing belief in modernization. Spaniards had a strong sense of the need to 'catch up' with other, more prosperous countries, and developed a conviction that such 'catching up' was feasible. This was reflected in the various applications made by Spain during this time to join the EEC, a process which would culminate in the country's eventually becoming a member in 1986. This sense of a need to modernize and to be on a par with countries like France, Germany and Britain was also a motivating factor in the achievement of the political transition from dictatorship to democracy in the 1970s.

At the time of Franco's death in November 1975, there was much uncertainty about what the future held for Spain. Once Adolfo Suárez took over as Prime Minister in July 1976, however, and began to establish his leadership, much of the doubt dissipated. Suárez moved at lightning speed to dismantle the structures of the old dictatorship and put a new democratic order in place (see 2.4). Naturally, the emphasis at this stage was on political rather than economic matters, with the result that the government followed loose economic policies, which allowed wages to rise significantly ahead of inflation. In late 1977, however, an attempt was made to bring the economic situation under control through the formulation of the Moncloa Pacts. These were a series of agreements drawn up between government, opposition, employers and trade unions which aimed to protect the economy with measures such as controlling the money supply, limiting government expenditure and minimizing wage increases. In succeeding years, wage increases were kept low but, partly due to the second oil crisis of 1979, the rate of inflation in Spain continued to be high, running at between 15.2 per cent and 8.1 per cent in the period 1980–85 (Salmon 1995: 9).

By the mid-1980s, Spain was once again experiencing rapid growth, fuelled by the optimism surrounding its entry into the EC and, from 1987 onwards, underpinned by substantial amounts from the European Structural Funds. At this time, under a nominally Socialist government, Spain was following liberal economic policies which fostered enterprise while emphasizing profitability and competitiveness. Much of Spanish industry was still run on traditional lines, with endemic problems of overstaffing and low productivity. In the more open market of the enlarged EC, many firms could not survive the pressure of competition and were either closed down or restructured. At the same time, state-owned companies were increasingly being privatized.

This shakeout was causing many job losses, even as the economy as a whole was doing well and leading business people, bankers and politicians were leading lives of conspicuous affluence. The get-rich-quick mentality of the time was captured in the statement made by the then Minister for Finance, Miguel Boyer, to the effect that 'Spain is the country in which it is easiest to get rich in the shortest possible time'. *Cambio16* dubbed the country 'La España de Isabel y Don Felipe', a label which neatly encapsulated both the iconic status of Isabel Preysler, a leading socialite and close friend of Minister Boyer's, and the new-found elegance and sophisticated style of Felipe González, the 'Socialist' Prime Minister.

In the wake of the 1992 *fiesta*, with the untrammelled optimism surrounding the events of that year, came what Spaniards termed the *resaca* of

1993, as many public authorities found that they had run out of money. In Andalusia, the *Junta* (Andalusian autonomous government) was unable to pay teachers and civil servants for several months. In an international climate which was tending towards recession, Spain in the mid-1990s was still attempting to streamline old industries and modernize her economy. The country ended the decade with a slowly improving economy, thanks again to prudent economic policies and transfers from the EU. She managed to reduce her balance of payments deficit sufficiently to meet the criteria for entry into the EMU (Economic and Monetary Union) in 1998, and joining the group of *euro* countries has meant that the process of modernization and integration into Europe has continued apace. While the economy is now in relatively good shape, problems and challenges remain, including relatively high unemployment levels, a costly public administration, and significant inequalities in wealth between the various regions of Spain.

The picture presented by the Spanish economy at the turn of the century, then, could hardly be less like the predominantly rural economy of the 1950s. Most employment in Spain is now found in the services sector (61 per cent), with industry and construction between them accounting for some 30 per cent and agriculture employing a mere 10.8 per cent (Campo 1993, I: 381). Given the EU context, it is necessarily an open economy, with high levels of inward investment from other, especially member countries, although the level of international trade has some way to go before it reaches general European levels.

7.3 MONEY AND THE SPANIARD

Most Spaniards in the prosperous 1990s seemed to be devoting their time to the business of improving their material welfare, where possible, to the point of affluence. However, there were some who took pains to remind their compatriots that other values were important, too. In 1992, for instance, the novelist Rosa Montero listed the negatives in Spanish society as: amnesia; lack of solidarity; an obsession with money; an ethical vacuum; and corruption. The amnesia she spoke of referred to her perception that Spaniards were forgetting their past, forgetting what were often humble origins, and that they were too ready to think and act as if affluence were always the norm. Forgetting poverty – and ignoring the poor – meant failing to come to terms with a past that had seen at least as many hard times as good times.

The new Spain that worried such commentators was characterized by the pursuit of riches and the attainment of powerful positions which would be the envy of one's friends and acquaintances. The sociologist Amando de Miguel summarized this attitude succinctly in his book *Los españoles*: 'These days, being someone means earning a lot of money in a job which many others covet' (De Miguel 1990: 209).

7.3.1 Traditional Castilian attitudes to work and money

In his book, de Miguel reminds us of the more traditional account of the Spaniard's relationship to money, quoting, for example, Ramón Menéndez Pidal's description of the Spaniard as someone whose character is marked by 'indifference towards material things' (ibid.: 211). Menéndez Pidal, of course, was writing at the beginning of the twentieth century, with a scholar's fascination with the Spanish, and especially the Castilian, past. It was out of that Castilian past that the image of the noble, spiritually inclined, non-materialistic Spaniard had emerged.

In this vision of the Spaniard, money was something to be treated with disdain, or at least it was beneath the dignity of a gentleman to be preoccupied with making it. Wealth was simply there as part of what one was born into, and, if you had not been born into it, it was important to disguise that fact and act as if you had. Certainly, the virtues of honest toil for financial reward were not given any special prominence in this version of the Spaniard.

Such attitudes were often interpreted by outsiders as reflecting laziness and vanity, which were seen as the natural companions of pride and egotism. Thus the English traveller Francis Willughby, who visited Spain in 1664, attributed the poverty of Spanish agriculture to 'the wretched laziness of the people . . . walking slowly, and always cumbered with a great cloak and long sword' (quoted in Shaw 1997: 106). Earlier still, the Florentine ambassador to the Spanish Court in 1513 had written in the same vein:

> the country is very poor, not from lack of natural resources but from the laziness of the people. The men are proud, and think that no other nation compares with theirs. They speak with extreme deliberation and try to appear of more consequence than they are.
>
> (quoted in Sedgwick 1925: 153)

The legacy of Castilian history can be seen in such attitudes, and they are marked by the whole process of reconquering land from the Moors. This is because the practice of distributing large tracts of reconquered territories to military leaders meant that wealth was seen as something acquired through the exercise of military virtues, something to be conquered through force of arms rather than created through hard work and enterprise.

The availability of such methods of acquiring wealth did not help to instil values that prioritized economic activity. If you were physically strong and brave and displayed loyalty to your superiors (whether sincere or feigned), you were likely to be rewarded with riches and power.

Associated with such attitudes is the famed self-centredness of Spaniards. Both Spanish and foreign commentators have often made reference to an apparent lack of solidarity and of a sense of 'civic spirit' among Spaniards. Ian Gibson contrasts Spaniards and Germans in this respect, seeing the latter as people who appreciate the need to conform to the rules of how to behave in public – almost to the point of excess. Spanish people, on the other hand, often seem not to appreciate how their actions may impinge on others (with the exception, perhaps, of their own family members), and therefore frequently ignore, for instance, the possible consequences of not obeying parking regulations or of dumping rubbish in the countryside.

7.3.2 'La cultura del pelotazo'

In recent times, much media attention in Spain has been directed at the widespread and ruthless pursuit of selfish interests and the prevalence of greed. Reference has already been made to some of the condemnation of this attitude voiced by Spaniards themselves, and the media have provided plenty of cases for us to criticize. Scandals and instances of corruption have been numerous; among the most notorious cases are those of Juan Guerra, Luis Roldán and Filesa.

A bothersome brother – Juan Guerra

This was the first big political scandal of the 1990s, though it was far from being the most serious case to emerge in a decade when numerous instances of corruption were revealed in the Spanish media. Juan is the brother of Alfonso Guerra, who was deputy Prime Minister in the Spanish government and assistant secretary-general of the PSOE while it was in power in the 1980s. It emerged in 1990 that Juan Guerra had been occupying a government office in the centre of Seville, from which, it was alleged, he was conducting extensive private business. Although the courts eventually judged that the office had not been used illegally, Spaniards were more than a little suspicious about what Guerra had been doing and about the uses he might have been making of his family connections. Their suspicions became more acute when they learned that he had gone from the 'rags' of being unemployed to rather spectacular riches in the space of a few short years in the late 1980s. His brother had been the architect, with Felipe González, of the PSOE's electoral success during that decade. In the wake of this scandal, however, Alfonso was forced to resign from his position. The Guerra case is also deemed to have been responsible for the introduction of a new crime into the Spanish Penal Code, viz., the crime of *tráfico de influencias*. Although Juan Guerra was ultimately found not guilty of most of the accusations brought against him, he became something of a legendary figure in the Spain of the early 1990s, an icon representing the corrupt connections between business and politics, the epitome of *enchufe* ('being well connected') and *amiguismo* ('having friends in the right places'). He was celebrated in sardonic carnival songs in Cádiz, and in a collection of *sevillanas*, from which the following verse is taken (cited in Martín de Pozuelo et al. 1994: 126):

Ay Juanito de mi alma
La que has liao.
Hace poco en el paro
Y ahora forrao.

Gamekeeper turns poacher – Luis Roldán

From 1986 to 1993, Luis Roldán was head of the Civil Guard, a police force with something of a reputation for toughness. He started his career in public life as a PSOE activist and was elected on to Zaragoza City Council in 1979. He came from a very modest background and had only a basic level of education, although he liked to pass himself off as a graduate in both Engineering and Business Studies. He rose to become the first civilian head of the Civil Guard. The most astonishing aspect of his career, however, was that, by 1993, he had amassed a fortune worth over 3000 million pesetas, with residences in Madrid, Paris and the Caribbean Islands. After *Diario16* published reports of his spectacular wealth in November 1993, many questions were raised about how this money had been acquired, and a government commission was set up to investigate his activities. Roldán, however, had already fled the country. The former head of a prestigious police force had now become Spain's 'most wanted man'. Roldán was eventually arrested and put on trial in Madrid. After a lengthy court case, he was convicted of an array of financial misdemeanours. These included misappropriating for his personal use 600 million pesetas from the 'Reserved Funds' of the Civil Guard which was meant to be used to make secret payments to informers and special agents; extracting some 800 million pesetas from four construction firms as bribes for the award of building contracts, and obtaining 85 million pesetas from two companies for special protection (which turned out to be non-existent) from the terrorist group ETA (*El País*, 26 February 1998). When the scandal broke in 1994, it caused the downfall of José Luis Corcuera, Minister for the Interior, who was forced to give up his seat in parliament.

20-20 Vision – Filesa

Financing modern election campaigns is expensive, and since, in theory, Spanish political parties can only be funded from the public purse, they have been finding it increasingly difficult to meet election expenses since the first democratic elections in 1977. Major parties have been known to resort to illegal means of funding. To finance their 1989 and 1993 general election campaigns, the PSOE used funds given to them by 'Grupo 20-20', a group of companies set up with this express purpose and linked circuitously to other PSOE-related firms, notably Malesa, Time Export and Filesa. These existed mainly on paper rather than in terms of actual business practice: their operations largely being confined to providing 'consultancy reports' to large corporations, including major banks such as BBV and Banco Central. For these reports – which consisted sometimes of simple collections of newspaper articles – such companies paid up to 244 million pesetas each. One company, Banco Hispanoamericano, paid 204 million pesetas for a study entitled 'Banking mergers in the run-up to Spanish integration into the EC' – the most fascinating aspect of this report was that the study was received in 1989, i.e. three years after Spain's entry into the EC!

The story of these activities began to emerge in 1991 when a disgruntled Filesa accountant, Carlos von Schouwen, took the company to court for an indemnity payment after he had been made redundant. This action triggered a series of enquiries which lasted for several years and which almost forced the Socialist government to set up a special parliamentary investigation into the matter. Instead, the PSOE broadened the remit of the investigation to cover all payments made to all political parties since 1977.

The Supreme Court judge in charge of the investigation, Marino Barbero, called the operation an example of extortion, since the party was using its position in power to extort money from large corporations, an activity he compared to the extraction of the *impuesto revolucionario* by ETA.

These cases appear to bear out the contention by many commentators that the concern with money reached the point of obsession in the Spain of the late 1980s and 1990s. As Joan Barril put it:

> Earning money has ceased to be merely a functional necessity and has become a whole way of life. And it is no longer just bankers who are devoted to this philosophy. Now it is selfless arts graduates, heroic employees in the social welfare system, poets in their attics and post-psychiatric patients – all have abandoned their pasts and have taken with gusto to this new culture which revolves around one thing: making money.
>
> (*El País*, September 1998; my translation)

While Spaniards naturally express disgust at the behaviour of corrupt politicians and business people, they are not entirely surprised that those who are well connected (who have *enchufe*) use their connections to look after themselves and those close to them. As Ian Gibson says: 'Spaniards have traditionally assumed that anyone in public office uses his or her position to engage in *la picaresca*' (*Sunday Times*, January 1992). It is to the book which gave rise to the term *picaresca* that we shall now turn our attention.

7.4 'GETTING ON': THE PICARESQUE NOVEL *LAZARILLO DE TORMES*

The word *picaresca* refers to the notion of craftiness or guile, and suggests an ability to slyly look after one's own interests, with a fairly comprehensive disregard for moral scruples. Spaniards have a strong concept of *la picaresca*, and the *pícaro, or 'rogue'*, is a recognized personality-type in the Spanish cultural tradition. The literary genre of the 'picaresque novel' originated in Spain, and it went on to become common in many European countries.

One of the earliest and best known examples of the picaresque genre is *La vida de Lazarillo de Tormes*, an anonymous work which was probably written in the 1530s, although the earliest known editions of it date from 1554. The hero of the book, Lazarillo (or 'Lázaro'), tells the story of his life, of his *fortunas y adversidades*, concentrating mainly on the events of his early years, but bringing his story up to his mid-twenties. The book depicts poverty, deprivation, social exclusion and rank hypocrisy in sixteenth-century Spanish society in a relatively realistic manner, and does so with a great deal of irony and sheer fun.

We sympathize with Lázaro as he proceeds through his hard life, starting with his impoverished background and going on to make his way in the world in the service of a series of generally harsh and miserly masters. The most memorable of the book's seven chapters are probably the first three, which recount Lázaro's experiences with his first three masters, the blind man, the priest and the squire. Here Lázaro is taking the first steps on his independent journey through life, learning to survive by his wits and suffering the hardships and deprivations of a street-beggar in sixteenth-century Spain. Food, or the lack of it, is a constant theme, as is the preoccupation with surviving and 'getting on' in society.

Lázaro's first master, the blind man, assures him that, although he will not be able to provide him with gold and silver, he will teach him how to survive in the rough-and-tumble world of the streets of Salamanca: 'Yo oro ni plata no te lo puedo dar, mas avisos para vivir muchos te mostraré' (Jones 1963: 7; all quotations are from this edition). He starts with a very crude lesson, by getting Lázaro to put his ear to a stone figure of a bull on the old Roman bridge in Salamanca, promising the little boy that he will be able to hear 'gran ruido dentro dél'. The blind man then lifts his hand and smashes Lázaro's head against the stone bull, laughs at the boy's innocence, and warns him that he must know more than the devil himself: 'Necio, aprende que el mozo del ciego un punto ha de saber más que el diablo' (p. 7). Lázaro quickly begins to learn to be streetwise, and makes the acquisition of such skills the guiding philosophy for his life. He states that the very purpose of his telling the story of his adventures is to demonstrate the importance of this principle: looking after your own interests is what life is all about, and the greatest virtue consists in achieving material success. The nobleman to whom the book is supposedly addressed is told that Lázaro has decided to recount the story of his life 'para mostrar cuánta virtud sea saber los hombres subir siendo bajos' (p. 8).

Lázaro's first role-model is very competent at making money. He is a master of cunning and deceit, with an unscrupulous ability to fake sincerity when praying, claiming he knows prayers to cure all ills and prescribing cures using plants and roots to rid people of their pain. But, for all the money he gathers from this activity, he treats Lázaro stingily: '[C]on todo lo que adquiría y tenía, jamás tan avariento ni mezquino hombre no vi, tanto que me mataba a mí de hambre' (p. 8).

The little boy thus adopts the moral stance of those around him, and pits his wits against his master in order to ensure his survival, undoing the seam of the blind man's bag in order to get at the food inside it and then sewing it up again, or making a little hole in the bottom of the wine jug so that he can drink the wine which the blind man refuses to share with him. In each case, the blind man ends up outwitting Lázaro, realizing what is going on and getting his revenge – the wine jug, for instance, is eventually used to hit Lázaro over the head and thus repay him for his deceit. In the end, however, Lázaro has the last laugh by getting the blind man to leap headlong into a stone post, when he thinks he is about to jump across a stream.

Lázaro abandons his first master and, in the second chapter, comes across a clergyman in Maqueda who asks Lázaro to help him serve mass. The action revolves around the chest in which the selfish priest stores his loaves of bread and to which Lázaro is forced to gain access in order to mitigate his hunger, because, as he says, he has fallen out of the frying pan only to end up in the fire: 'Escapé del trueno y di en el relámpago . . . . No digo más sino que toda la laceria del mundo estaba encerrada en éste' (p. 17). Lázaro gets a locksmith to make him a duplicate key which allows him to filch bread from the chest behind the priest's back. The latter notes the loss and attributes it to mice entering the old chest through some of the holes in the wood. He attempts to solve the problem by placing a mousetrap in the chest, but Lázaro then not only removes the bread when he opens the chest but also takes the piece of cheese used as bait in the trap. When the priest's neighbours suggest that perhaps a snake is responsible for the disappearance of the food, he takes to staying awake at night to catch the snake. Lázaro, meanwhile, to hide the key from the priest, keeps it in his mouth while he sleeps. Unfortunately for him, however, the key causes him to make a whistling sound while he sleeps, which the priest interprets as the hissing of the snake. The climax of this episode occurs when the priest raises a bludgeon and unleashes a mighty blow at the 'snake', thus leaving Lázaro unconscious for some three days. The priest dismisses Lázaro from his service, enjoining him to find another master and to go with God, since he has no need of such a 'diligent servant'! 'Lázaro, de hoy más eres tuyo y no mío. Busca amo y vete con Dios, que yo no quiero en mi compañía tan diligente servidor' (p. 27).

Lázaro's third master is a much more sympathetic character than either the callous blind man or the greedy priest. This master – the squire, who has a typical *hidalgo*'s obsession with appearance and 'honour' – is merely made to look shallow and ridiculous. He has no money and no way of making any, although he is determined to give the appearance of being wealthy. He wears his only suit of fine clothing when he is out in public, and even picks imaginary food from between his teeth when walking the streets of Toledo, in order to reinforce this impression. Lázaro is at first taken in by appearances, believing he has at last found a prosperous master, but quickly realizes that the only food that will enter the squire's house will be whatever he himself can beg. The squire makes much of the virtues of not over-indulging in food, informing Lázaro that the less he eats, the longer he will live: 'Vivirás más y más sano . . . porque . . . no hay tal cosa en el mundo para vivir mucho que comer poco.' To this, Lázaro's ironic inward comment is that, if that is the case, he is likely to live forever, as he has always been obliged to observe that rule: 'Si por esa vía es ... nunca yo moriré, que siempre he guardado esa regla por fuerza, y aun espero en mi desdicha tenella toda mi vida' (p. 32).

The squire is not harsh or cruel, and Lázaro quickly develops an affection for him, thinking that he is simply to be pitied for his poverty: 'es pobre y nadie da lo que no tiene' (p. 37). As readers, however, we can still see what Lázaro, having adapted early on to the material values of those around him, appears not to be able to see, i.e. that the squire's values are shallow and worthless. Lázaro pities the squire because he is poor and therefore cannot genuinely justify the self-important image he projects to the outside world, but it is the lack of resources that Lázaro fixes on and not the values underlying it. Here are Lázaro's reflections on the idiocy of being obsessed with appearances when one does not have the wherewithal to back it up:

> ¡Grandes secretos son, Señor, los que vos hacéis y las gentes ignoran! ¿A quién no engañara aquella buena disposición y razonable capa y sayo, y quién pensara que aquel gentil hombre se pasó ayer todo el día sin comer, con aquel mendrugo de pan que su criado Lázaro trujo un día y una noche en el arca de su seno?
>
> (p. 33)

> (Your ways are mighty mysterious, Lord, and people don't understand them! With that refined way he acts and that nice-looking cape and coat he'd fool anyone. And who would believe that that gracious man got by all day yesterday on a piece of bread that his servant Lazaro had carried all day and night inside his shirt for safekeeping.)
>
> (Rudder 1995)

Over the course of the book, Lázaro learns to compromise his principles for the sake of getting on in the world, and, at the end of the story, he is married and has risen to the position of town-crier, depicting himself as having achieved a high level of success. With the anonymous author's ironic eye, we see the success as partial and as an indication that Lázaro has sold out completely on any moral principle.

In the brief final chapter of the novel, he concludes that he could not ask for more: 'Pues en este tiempo estaba en mi prosperidad y en la cumbre de toda buena fortuna' (p. 55). He has achieved the social success which he has been taught to crave by everyone he has met throughout his life, and the hypocrisy and duplicity he is obliged to indulge in to maintain it he considers a small price to pay.

This novel stands as an ironic account of attitudes to money and material success in sixteenth-century Spain. No doubt the account is partial – there must have been another, more prosperous world in the Spain of the time, despite the poor way in which the Spanish authorities managed the country's economy, and in particular, the way in which the resources flowing from the New World were squandered on making war in Europe. But the poverty which is depicted was a reality too. And it is also a universal in human culture, at least as much as wealth and prosperity are.

7.5 MONEY AND POWER: BUSINESS CULTURE AND POLITICAL CULTURE

Money and power – business, economics and politics – are aspects of life which can reflect cultural differences. Both within Spain, and between Spain and other countries, we perceive differences of behaviour which we can attribute to cultural factors. Business relations are never divorced from relations of a more general type: doing business with Andalusians means first relating to Andalusians in the way that one would, no matter what the nature of the relationship was; being political in Madrid means taking account of the Castilian nature of the city and its people. The stereotypes which must be avoided are therefore both the stereotypes about 'Spaniards' in general, as distinct from Germans, Americans, Finns, etc., and the stereotypes about how Andalusians differ from Galicians, Catalans from Basques, and so on (see 3.2).

This is not to deny, however, that it is possible to compare one region with another or one country with another. Sensible general comparisons can carry a certain validity, and careful study of practices and attitudes can reveal genuine differences. Where we need to be cautious is in the interpretation of such studies, bearing in mind the danger of essentialism, and opting for explanations which take social and historical factors into account, rather than attributing differences to putative 'character traits'.

Some studies of this type which yield interesting results and which bear on Spanish business and political culture are reviewed here.

7.5.1 Cultural differences in organizations: the Hofstede survey

The sociologist Geert Hofstede (1991) coordinated an extensive survey among IBM employees from 53 different countries, with a view to examining cultural differences in the behaviour of the various groups. While acknowledging the immense difficulties associated with attempts to offer general profiles of people's behaviour, Hofstede posits four major parameters along which he believes such behaviour can be described. The four dimensions he identifies are: power distance; collectivism v. individualism; femininity v. masculinity; and uncertainty avoidance. These dimensions yield a typology for the Spanish case which can be broadly described as follows:

(a) A relatively high level of authoritarianism
This relates to the 'power-distance' dimension, in other words, 'the extent to which less powerful members of institutions and organizations within a

country expect and accept that power is distributed unequally' (Hofstede 1991: 28). Spain occupies 31st position in the ranking of 53 countries (Britain comes in at around 43rd), which suggests that, in Spain, authoritarian attitudes are not extremely strong, although, according to these results, they would be stronger than in Britain. This implies that, unlike in small power-distance countries, people working in business in Spain, for example, would expect a more autocratic style of decision-making on the part of their bosses; similarly, in the area of family life, Spaniards would expect children to be obedient to their parents, while senior members of families would be treated with a higher level of deference than younger family members. Those who know Spain well might baulk at describing Spanish children as obedient, although it is true that, in the educational sphere at least, teachers and lecturers are often accorded a degree of deference which is greater than, say, in Britain or Ireland.

(b) A 'collectivist' approach to social and business relations
The spirit of 'collectivism' is much stronger in Spain than in, for example, the USA (which occupies first position in the 'individualism' ranking) or in Britain (in third place). This suggests that Spanish people tend to identify closely with strong, cohesive in-groups, which offer protection and support throughout a person's lifetime. The first core group to which a person belongs is the family, and family loyalty often appears to be stronger in Spain than in many other European countries. Loyalty is extended, however, to groups outside the family, but, in these also, the sense of group identity may be stronger than in other cultures. In return for the protection it offers, the group will often demand strong loyalty and subordination of the individual's interests to those of the group. Latin America and certain oriental countries also demonstrate these qualities, at times to a much greater extent than Spain (Guatemala, for instance, comes last on the list of 53 countries for 'individualism'). This factor may be of relevance in relation to the widespread use of *enchufe* and *amiguismo* in Spain, and with hiring practices, often based on personal contacts, which might strike outside observers as nepotistic.

(c) A moderately 'masculine' culture
The third dimension examined by Hofstede is the one he called masculinity–femininity. The entire sample of IBM employees surveyed by Hofstede showed distinct differences between men and women in the emphasis they placed on different work objectives. Men tended to stress goals such as high earnings and advancing to higher-level jobs; women, on the other hand, stressed such factors as a good working relationship with one's direct superior and working with people who cooperate well with one another. These different preferences, while encountered consistently in the data, reflect learned social roles: there is no suggestion that such roles are 'biologically determined', but rather they are acquired through the socializing process that takes place as a child grows within a particular society.

The score for Spanish employees (42 per cent) placed Spain among what could be called the 'moderately masculine' group of countries (putting Spain in joint 37th place out of the 53 countries). While we must enter the usual caveats about possible differences between individuals and among the different regions of Spain, we might recognize the picture that these results suggest of a culture where social contact is valued highly and where material ambition is normally balanced with the need for cooperation and sharing. By way of contrast, countries with a relatively high masculinity index included Ireland, with an index of 68 per cent (in joint seventh place), and Britain with an index of 66 per cent (in joint ninth place); Japan topped the masculinity index, with a score of 95 per cent.

(d) A culture that avoids uncertainty

Hofstede's 'Uncertainty Avoidance Index' (UAI) is a measure of the degree to which people can tolerate unpredictability, and Spain's relatively high score (86) places it among the top 20 per cent of countries studied (in joint tenth place). This suggests that Spaniards are more likely to experience stress at work (feeling insecure about their position in an organization), are more inclined to believe that company rules should not be broken, and tend to remain with a particular employer on a long-term basis. In contrast, the scores for Great Britain and Ireland put those countries in joint 47th place.

Hofstede validly stresses the distinction between such statistics, which refer to general tendencies among members of a society, and the reality of anxiety and insecurity as experienced by particular individuals within that society. While these figures suggest a greater likelihood that certain behaviours will manifest themselves in the members of a group, the whole range of possible behaviours is still possible within any one individual. In the light of these statistics, Hofstede suggests that 'the *culture* of a country ... is, among other things, a set of likely reactions of citizens with a common mental programming', *not* a combination of properties of the 'average citizen', nor a 'modal personality' (Hofstede 1991: 112).

7.5.2 Political corruption and cultural difference

One of the major factors in any discussion of a country's 'political culture' is the extent of corruption and illicit dealing in that country. We have seen that this issue has been prominent in recent years in the Spanish case, and we might wonder whether there is evidence of a cultural tendency towards such practices.

One comparative study of people's perceptions of corruption in a range of countries is the Corruption Perceptions Index. This is a measure of the perceptions of the degree of corruption in some 85 different countries as seen by business people, risk analysts and the general public. In the 1998 Index, for example, the least corrupt country – and the only one to score a full 10 on the Index – was considered to be Denmark. In 85th place, the most corrupt country was judged to be Cameroon. On this scale, Spain occupied joint 23rd place with Botswana, which contrasts with the UK in joint eleventh place, Ireland in 14th place and the USA in joint 17th place. The EU country occupying the lowest place on this Index was Italy, in 39th place, with Greece in 36th (Transparency International 1998).

We need to be cautious in attempting to draw conclusions from this Index, since, as the authors make clear, this is not an 'index of corruption' (which would be impossible to compile) but an index of perceptions of corruption. We may note that developing countries tend to occupy lower positions on the Index than more developed (particularly western) countries. If we bear in mind that the Index originates in the west, we might wonder if the perceptions being measured are predominantly western. It would be wrong, therefore, to interpret these results as necessarily offering solid evidence about cultural differences, although the advantage of the Index is that it clearly can help to draw attention to corrupt practices, especially in countries which achieve a low score. Presumably, the relevant Spanish authorities will hope that Spain's score will improve from its current position of 23rd place, which may translate into less corrupt practices in business and politics.

Many comparative social and political studies have been prompted by the frequency with which stories of political scandal have broken in Latin Europe in recent years. There has even been an attempt to formulate a hypothesis about a 'southern syndrome' which would separate Mediterranean countries from others, especially the countries of northern Europe. As we have seen, political corruption in Spain has often taken the form of illicit funding of political parties, with funds being channelled from a legitimate business source through one or more 'fictional' companies, and into the coffers of legitimate political parties.

There is a particular problem relating to Spain in that the multi-party democratic system has only been revived relatively recently (since the 1970s) and the parties involved emerged in a context where public financing of parties was already in place. But, given that the level of involvement of the Spanish general public in political activity has historically been relatively low, party income from membership dues is among the lowest in Europe. And with the long hold on power of the PSOE in the 1980s and early 1990s, the temptation to combine political influence and party-funding activities seems to have been irresistible to many. Furthermore, when we recall the corrupt nature of the Francoist system that preceded the transition, we may conclude that the new political elite of democratic Spain was, in certain respects, merely building corrupt practices on an existing structure which encouraged such behaviour. From this evidence, Pujas and Rhodes (1998), for example, conclude that the proliferation of political corruption in this region stems from a combination of particular developmental patterns and political opportunity structures.

This would suggest that historical factors which lead to the existence of opportunities for corruption are at least as much to blame for the existence of corrupt practices, as any putative features of the 'Latin' character or personality.

FEATURE: TOURISM IN SPAIN

Tourism accounts for over 10 per cent of Spain's Gross Domestic Product and provides employment directly to about 1.5 million people, while indirectly supporting the employment of millions of others.

The most spectacular dimension of Spanish tourism is the influx of over forty million foreign tourists into Spain every year. The factors that make Spain a desirable destination include natural resources such as climate and long stretches of fine beaches, as well as the long tradition of Spanish friendliness and hospitality.

Since the 1960s, Spanish tourism has been dominated by a *turismo de masas* in the Mediterranean region, and resorts catering to this trade have proliferated along the Andalusian, Valencian and Catalonian coasts, as well as on the coasts of the Balearic and Canary Islands. What were once quiet fishing villages have in many cases been transformed into cosmopolitan urban centres with lines of shops, bars and discos surrounded by rows of high-rise hotels and apartment blocks, catering for visitors arriving from other countries (especially the countries of the EU) for their package holidays in the sun.

The typical Mediterranean apartment block or hotel, with swimming pool and adjacent bars, shops and nightlife, offers the foreign tourist an easy and familiar style of relaxation in comfortable circumstances. Visitors to these resorts find their needs catered for in ways that rarely expose them to the challenge of encountering cultural or even linguistic difference. The 'real Spain' of the hinterland remains largely hidden from view.

There are, however, other types of tourism in Spain. Historical and cultural sites all over the country draw millions of overseas visitors every year. Spain's north coast, with its cooler Atlantic climate, also attracts large numbers, although this is a destination particularly favoured by Spaniards themselves. Easter-week festivities and *ferias* also attract large numbers of people from Spain and outside to locations all over the country at certain times of the year.

Spanish culture is embodied for the mass tourist in bottles of San Miguel beer, in *sangría* and *sombreros*, and in souvenirs which utilize the iconography of bullfighting and flamenco dancing. Spanishness is therefore packaged for millions of foreign visitors as a debased Andalusian stereotype with connotations of passion and exoticism, at once both reassuringly familiar (since these are universally available images), and hinting at a colourful 'otherness' which promises an intensity and vividness transcending normal human emotions. Such reductionist imagery, and the industry which purveys it, can evoke both ridicule and resentment on the part of Spaniards themselves, along with an explicit or implicit dismissal of the tourist as a cultural 'other' whom it is best to ignore, since it often appears impossible to enlighten them as to the true nature of the country they are visiting.

READING: MIGUEL DELIBES, *LOS SANTOS INOCENTES*

Miguel Delibes (b. 1920) is one of Spain's major living novelists. He has won the Nadal, the Príncipe de Asturias and the Cervantes Literary Prizes as well as the Nacional de las Letras and the Nacional de Narrativa for his writings. Some of his best-known works are *El camino* (1950), *Cinco horas con Mario* (1966) and *El disputado voto del señor Cayo* (1978).

His novel *Los santos inocentes* (1981) depicts life on a country estate in Spain during the Franco dictatorship. Conditions for farm labourers are abysmal and the distinction between them and the *señores* who are the proprietors of the estate is reminiscent of feudal times. The living conditions depicted in this book are exceptional and this situation was not typical of rural workers in Spain generally in the mid-twentieth century; however, in certain parts of Castile and Andalusia, the gap between the haves and the have-nots on the land continued to be enormous until recently. It is still possible to find owners of large estates with little interest in developing their land: in September 1981, *Cambio16* reported on a number of cases where people whose families had lived and worked on land for generations were making desperate attempts to persuade absentee landlords to allow them to buy that land.

The first chapter of this experimental novel focuses on the uneducated and simple-minded farmhand, Azarías, whose tenderness towards a hunting hawk contrasts with the indifference shown by his own master towards him.

This is how the book begins:

A su hermana, la Régula, le contrariaba la actitud del Azarías, y le regañaba y él, entonces, regresaba a la Jara, donde el señorito, que a su hermana, la Régula, le contrariaba la actitud del Azarías porque ella aspiraba a que los muchachos se ilustrasen, cosa que a su hermano, se le antojaba un error, que,

luego no te sirven ni para finos ni para bastos,

pontificaba con su tono de voz brumoso, levemente nasal,

y, por contra, en la Jara, donde el señorito, nadie se preocupaba de si éste o el otro sabían leer o escribir, de si eran letrados o iletrados, o de si el Azarías vagaba de un lado a otro, los remendados pantalones de pana por las corvas, la bragueta sin botones, rutando y con los pies descalzos e, incluso, si, repentinamente, marchaba donde su hermana y el señorito preguntaba por él y le respondían,

anda donde su hermana, señorito,

el señorito tan terne, no se alteraba, si es caso levantaba imperceptiblemente un hombro, el izquierdo, pero no indagaba más, ni comentaba la nueva, y, cuando regresaba, tal cual,

el Azarías ya está de vuelta, señorito,

y el señorito esbozaba una media sonrisa y en paz, que al señorito sólo le exasperaba que el Azarías afirmase que tenía un año más que el señorito, porque, en realidad, el Azarías ya era mozo cuando el señorito nació, pero el Azarías ni se recordaba de esto y, si, en ocasiones, afirmaba que tenía un año más que el señorito era porque Dacio, el Porquero, se lo dijo así una Nochevieja que andaba un poco bebido y a él, al Azarías, se le quedó grabado en la sesera, y tantas veces le preguntaban,

¿qué tiempo te tienes tú, Azarías?

otras tantas respondía,

cabalmente un año más que el señorito,

pero no era por mala voluntad, ni por el gusto de mentir, sino por pura niñez, que el señorito hacía mal en renegarse por eso y llamarle zascandil, ni era justo tampoco, ya que el Azarías, a cambio de andar por el cortijo todo el día de Dios rutando y como masticando la nada, mirándose atentamente las uñas de la mano derecha, lustraba el automóvil del señorito con una bayeta amarilla, y desenroscaba los tapones de las válvulas a los automóviles de los amigos del señorito para que al señorito no le faltaran el día que las cosas vinieran mal dadas y escaseasen . . .

y, conforme caía la noche, ya se sabía, Azarías, aculado en el tajuelo, junto a la lumbre, en el desolado zaguán, desplumaba las perdices, o las pitorras, o las tórtolas, o las gangas, cobradas por el señorito durante la jornada y, con frecuencia, si las piezas abundaban, el Azarías reservaba una para la *milana*, de forma que el búho, cada vez que le veía aparecer, le envolvía en su redonda mirada amarilla, y castañeteaba con el pico, como si retozara, todo por espontáneo afecto, que a los demás, el señorito incluido, les bufaba como un gato y les sacaba las uñas, mientras que a él, le distinguía, pues rara era la noche que no le obsequiaba, a falta de bocado más exquisito, con una picaza, o una ratera, o media docena de gorriones atrapados con liga en la charca, donde las carpas, o vaya usted a saber, pero, en cualquier caso, Azarías le decía al Gran Duque, cada vez que se arrimaba a él, aterciopelando la voz,

milana bonita, milana bonita,

y le rascaba el entrecejo, y le sonreía con las encías deshuesadas y, si era el caso de amarrarle en lo alto del cancho para que el señorito o la señorita o los amigos del señorito o las amigas de la señorita se entretuviesen, disparando a las águilas o a las cornejas por la tronera, ocultos en el tollo, Azarías le enrollaba en la pata derecha un pedazo de franela roja para que la cadena no le lastimase y, en tanto el señorito o la señorita o los amigos del señorito o las amigas de la señorita permanecían dentro del tollo, él aguardaba, acuclillado en la greñura, bajo la copa de la atalaya, vigilándolo, temblando como un tallo verde, y, aunque estaba un poco duro de oído, oía los estampidos secos de las detonaciones y, a cada una, se estremecía y cerraba los ojos y, al abrirlos de nuevo, miraba hacia el búho y, al verle indemne, erguido y desafiante, haciendo el escudo, sobre la piedra, se sentía orgulloso de él y se decía conmovido para entre sí,

milana bonita . . .

(Delibes 1981: 9–13)

FURTHER READING

Anuario El País (Madrid, El País).
   Published yearly, this contains commentaries and statistical summaries relating to contemporary Spanish society, including the economy, education and the arts.
INE (Instituto Nacional de Estadística, Spanish Statistical Institute), http://www.ine.es
   Access to a broad range of statistical information on Spain.
Lawlor, Teresa and Rigby, Mike, *Contemporary Spain: essays and texts on politics, economics, education and employment, and society* (London, Addison Wesley Longman, 1998).
   Parts II and III offer a broad view of the context of the economy, education and employment in Spain.
Project Gutenberg, *The Life of Lazarillo of Tormes: his fortunes and misfortunes as told by himself*, available from http://promo.net/pg/
   An English translation of the *Lazarillo* is available from this site.
Ross, Christopher, *Contemporary Spain: a handbook* (London, Edward Arnold, 1997).
   Chapter 5 gives a handy general overview of the modern Spanish economy.

8

Home and School: Learning to Be a Spaniard

8.1 INTRODUCTION: THE FORMATIVE INFLUENCE OF HOME AND SCHOOL

The individual is born with certain innate abilities and predispositions, including, for example, the feeding reflex and, it would seem, the ability to learn a language. But to become a fully realized human being, the individual must accumulate a corpus of knowledge. A significant amount of this knowledge consists of the skills required in order to know how to move around in the world and become a functioning member of human society. As Clifford Geertz suggests: '[W]hat sets [man] off most graphically from nonmen is less his sheer ability to learn (great as that is) than how much and what particular sorts of things he *has* to learn before he is able to function at all' (Geertz 1993: 46).

The disposition towards social interaction is presumably an innate biological quality of human beings. The particular form which that social interaction takes, however, is a cultural phenomenon and, as such, will vary with the circumstances in which the learning process is carried on. The forms of socialization learned in one geographical location will not be exactly the same as those that prevail in another. But these circumstances will also vary over time; historical progression will thus affect the nature of the learning context, so that a child born in 1990 will have a different formation from one born in 1970.

It is worth adding, however, that not only is this process of socialization bound to vary according to the cultural context in which it takes place, but the process itself is sufficiently important for it to actually constitute culture. In other words, a large part of culture consists of the particular patterns and habits that are established during this formation of the individual. Furthermore, the very plasticity and malleability of the young human being – associated with the child's predisposition to learn – means that what is acquired is learned at a deep level: the early years of childhood are particularly significant in forming our identity. Edward Hall articulates the significance of learning, and especially of early learning, in the following terms:

> Everything man is and does is modified by learning and is therefore malleable. But once learned, these behavior patterns, these habitual responses, these ways of interacting gradually sink below the surface of the mind and, like the admiral of a submerged submarine fleet, control from the depths.
>
> (Hall 1976: 37)

It would be difficult to overstate the importance of early learning in establishing patterns of behaviour, and, without doubt, the learning of particular patterns is culturally ordained. To say this is to suggest that there are powerful ways in which the specific culture in which a child is reared will influence him or her towards certain habits of thinking and acting and away from others. On the other hand, it decidedly is not to suggest that there are simplistic ways in which each individual can be associated with one particular national, regional or ethnic cultural context.

The primary formative influences which are the concern of this chapter, namely family and education, are available – in forms which vary from place to place – to the young person growing up in almost any part of the world today. But if we are to reflect on the formation of Spanish people, we cannot do so without taking into consideration both the heterogeneous nature of the 40 million people we refer to as 'Spanish' and the fact that Spanish people are linked, as much as any others in the developed world, to a wider global culture associated with commercialism, the media and international communications. The process of formation through the influence of family and formal education is, therefore, as much the process of formation of young Basques, young Andalusians or young Castilians as it is the formation of 'young Spaniards'. By the same token, it is no less a process of forming simply 'a young person in the modern world', who will share cultural characteristics with Coke-sipping, Internet-using, TV-watching counterparts in other countries around the globe. It is dangerous, therefore, to attempt to articulate the characteristics of the formation received by 'Spaniards', because, by doing so, we run the risk of appearing to suggest that the notion of national identity can be accepted uncritically, and that, in some essentialist way, we can present a homogeneous portrayal of a culture-specific formation of the individual which is different from the formation of individuals in 'other' cultures. A four-year-old child watching *Los Teletubbies* or *Pokémon* in a high-rise flat in Barcelona may well be said to have more in common culturally with a similar urban child in Britain or Ireland than with a retired farm labourer in Galicia, and such distinctions are ignored at our peril. It seems clear that the cultural significance of the global dimension is set to strengthen in the years to come, with important consequences for traditionally defined 'national' cultures. But, at least for the present, the idea of national identity has certainly not lost its validity, and, although it is fraught with particular difficulties in the Spanish case, the concept of a characteristic formation for 'Spanish people' appears to have genuine merit.

As societies progress and become more advanced, the amount and complexity of what is deemed necessary for the young person to know increase, with the result that human societies devote very significant resources to establishing and maintaining educational systems. The structures and institutions which are put in place are 'public' in the sense that they operate in the public sphere, beyond the private confines of individuals or families. This secondary educator – the system of schooling in the public sphere – also appears to be both a universal of human culture and a phenomenon that takes on culture-specific characteristics. The institutions of learning established by any society will necessarily be imbued with the cultural values of that society. In this sense, the educational system will reflect the kind of society in which it exists. The system prevailing in a particular society will not be immune to the political complexion of that society, to its economic and industrial characteristics, to the beliefs and patterns of social behaviour that predominate, and to prejudices and cultural preferences.

In Spain, the areas of family and education have undergone a major transformation in recent decades. The extent of these changes is perhaps an indication of the degree of importance which the new Spain attaches to these two aspects of life. In general, the family and the educational system in Spain reflect the processes of democratization and modernization which have taken place in the country since the 1950s. And, in the other direction, changes in family relationships and morphologies and reforms in the educational system have contributed to an accelerated process of transformation of Spanish society as a whole.

8.2 THE FAMILY IN SPAIN

The principal function of the family in everyday life is probably that of the socialization of the young person. Given that the socializing role is so important, it is not surprising that family forms can vary so much across cultures. Depending on what the particular societies' priorities are, families will reflect those priorities and vary the degree of emphasis they place on different aspects of the family. Thus, in certain societies, family relationships may be given a high priority, while other societies will place less emphasis on them; some societies may insist on members rigidly conforming to strict patterns of family life and behaviour, while others will accept or encourage a multiplicity of forms, or a variety of types of relationships between family members.

Most Spaniards live within a nuclear family environment, i.e. one where both parents live with their children. The point is not as trivial as it may appear: in fact, Spain has the highest proportion of people living in nuclear families in the EU. On the one hand, this reflects the importance which Spaniards generally attach to the family: a 1997 survey, for example, showed that Spaniards considered the family to be the single most important aspect of life, more important than work or friends and much more important than politics or religion (CIS 1997a: 4). On the other hand, the strength of the nuclear family unit is indicative of the degree to which traditional family forms persist, despite the relative acceptability of unconventional forms.

The child who grows up within a 'new Spanish family', therefore, is not only taught to regard family itself as being extremely important, but is also being sent a message about the persistence of 'traditional' family priorities within a context of ongoing sociocultural change. Inés Alberdi (1999) asserts that the fundamental change which has taken place in the family hinges on the attenuation of authoritarian attitudes and a strengthening of democratic values. She goes on to claim that the principal characteristics of the modern Spanish family are as follows:

- families generally have an increased level of prosperity and live in greater comfort than before;
- the forms which families take are more varied than before, and there is a high level of tolerance for unconventional family forms, including the idea of children being born outside marriage;
- families are more democratic and more egalitarian, with a reduction in the level of authority of the father;
- the woman's role is no longer exclusively identified with life within the home, and women increasingly work outside the home;
- Spanish people generally marry late and have fewer children than before, although the children they have then become the focus of the family;
- the Spanish family is 'long and narrow' in shape, with increased life expectancy for grandparents and with fewer children than before.

The Spanish family still displays certain quite 'traditional' characteristics, however, the first being the sheer importance of the family itself and the level of solidarity and support that Spaniards find in it. It is still an important source of assistance to the individual, whether this takes the form of helping to set the children up by finding work for them through personal contacts, or whether it is the support given by grandparents to a working couple who need help with childminding. An indication of the frequent contact between parents and their adult children is that 74 per cent of Spanish women see their parents at least once a week (Campo 1993, I: 155).

The most striking feature of parental support for Spanish children, however, is the extent to which children continue to live with their parents until well into their twenties or even thirties. This phenomenon (dubbed the *familia colchón* in Spain) is widespread, and statistics indicate that the percentage of 15–29-year-olds who live with their parents is higher in Spain than in any other European country (CIS 1997b: 1). Most young Spaniards consider it normal to live with their parents until well into their twenties, and they do not expect to be able to move out of their parents' home at an early age, although the majority would also recognize that it is not considered normal in most other countries. One result of this is the most crowded households in Europe: the average rate of occupation in Spain is 3.2 people per household, compared with an overall average rate of 2.6 for the EU generally (Eurostat 1999a).

Economic factors are those most often cited as the explanation for this pattern: Spain has the highest rate of youth unemployment in the EU; the price of houses and apartments is high, so that most young people, even if they have a job, find it difficult to set up home separately. A further factor is the emotional closeness that tends to exist between parents and children in Spain: levels of communication between the generations tend to be good, and this reinforces the trend towards the children continuing to live at home. Relatively protective Spanish parents are not inclined to encourage their children to leave the nest; relatively cosseted Spanish children take the easy option and continue to enjoy the cleanliness and comfort of their parents' home well into their adult years. Striking out on your own, short of marriage or finding employment away from home, is still unusual in Spain, and is particularly so in the case of young women. Such a statement of independence may well be interpreted as an act of rebellion, or at least as a signal of discontent.

While this family support continues a long-standing Spanish tradition, it still marks a change from the classic pattern of family living, especially with respect to the position of members of the extended family. As mentioned above, the typical pattern of family life in Spain now is for people to live in nuclear families. In the 1950s or 1960s, however, it would not have been unusual for other family members to be living in the home, including elderly aunts, uncles or grandparents.

These family members are now more likely to live independently, a pattern reinforced by factors such as greater longevity and an improved level of health for older people. Thus, elderly Spaniards will nowadays be more likely to make a positive contribution to the standard of living of their young relatives than to be a burden on them, as happened in the past. The predominance of the nuclear family is also an indication of the degree of acceptance among Spaniards of conventional forms of marriage and of the traditional options for raising children. As we saw in Chapter 6, although they tend to marry relatively late, Spaniards are still inclined to conform to the convention of wedlock in preparation for having children, and the level of births outside marriage is still among the lowest in Europe.

The high level of commitment to the family and the persistence of relatively traditional family forms do not signify that the family is always a happy place to be, or that the situation is totally unproblematic. Spanish families are not immune to the problems that beset families in other parts of the developed world, so that questions such as changing gender roles for men and women, domestic violence, the ambivalent and at times pernicious influence of the mass media, drug abuse and the strong role played by schools in the formation of young people are issues of relevance to the Spanish case also. The fact remains, however, that one of the most notable features of Spanish culture (and indeed of Hispanic culture generally) is still the central importance of the family.

8.3 MODERN SPANISH EDUCATION

The systematic education of the young is not just about the task of dispensing knowledge and skills; as suggested earlier, it is also about the business of socialization, of learning to become a member of a community. This process entails the acquisition of a culture, so that the educational system transmits values, principles and prejudices even as its visible curriculum focuses on the more tangible subject areas of mathematics, history, science or languages. The aspect of education which is least amenable to description is probably in one sense the most obvious: this is the fact that the characteristic ethos of any educational institution is one which prioritizes a concern with the promotion of human development. The mission of any school or college is to help people to advance. This is what underpins all its activities and what differentiates it from commercial and administrative institutions. This does not imply that there will be uniformity across educational establishments: different schools and colleges will prioritize different values, and there will be conflicts – often serious ones – between the different priorities and emphases that coexist within any one such institution. But it is difficult to conceive of any place of learning as operating without a profound sense that it is linked into the fundamental human desire to advance and improve.

While many educators will identify with this underlying idea of an ongoing project on a relatively idealistic level, the Spanish parent encouraging his or her child to succeed at school is likely to think of the project in more material terms. Education has been of major importance in Spain in recent times, not least because it is seen as the most efficacious way of improving one's socio-economic position. Most young people in Spain are passionately encouraged to acquire a qualification as a passport to a job, and, in line with this, student numbers both at upper secondary and tertiary levels have grown enormously in recent decades.

This is reflected, for instance, in the 1996 OECD statistics for completion of upper secondary education: in the year in question, 45 per cent of Spaniards aged 25–34 had completed upper secondary education, while only 16 per cent of those aged 45–54 had done so (OECD 1996). The huge increase reflects the low starting point, i.e. the relatively low level of participation in education in mid-century; compared with other industrialized countries, the general educational level in Spain is still relatively low, presumably because of the low educational attainment of older generations of Spaniards: of the 15 EU countries, for example, Spain has the lowest percentage of 25–59-year-olds to have completed upper secondary education, with the exception of Portugal (Eurostat 1998: 4).

The Spanish educational system has undergone a number of major reforms in recent times. Significant changes were undertaken even during the later years of the Franco regime. The technocratic turn taken by the regime in the 1960s led to an increased emphasis on education, with a greater commitment to the provision of basic education for all. Numbers of pupils in primary education rose by 60 per cent in the period 1960–80, while the number of secondary school pupils (at *Bachillerato* level) rose by no less than 753 per cent in the same period (Boyd-Barrett and O'Malley 1995: 7). The new provision, particularly at secondary level, represented not only a quantitative increase but also a qualitative change, since the vast majority of the new schools being established were (secular) state schools rather than those run by the Church. Thus, while, in 1970, 72 per cent of primary pupils were attending private schools (the majority of which would have been run by the Church) this figure had fallen to just 35 per cent by 1987 (ibid.: 7). The *Ley General de Educación*, passed in 1970, established compulsory education up to the age of 14 and set out two major routes for secondary education after that age, an academic stream called the *Bachillerato Unificado Polivalente* (BUP) and a 'non-academic' (and less prestigious) stream called *Formación Profesional* (FP).

During the 1980s, PSOE governments introduced two general educational reforms. The first of these, the *Ley Orgánica del Derecho a la Educación* (LODE), was passed in 1984 and introduced a strong element of democratization into the educational system, providing for the participation of parents, teachers and pupils in governing bodies in schools, universities and other centres of education. These provisions applied not just to secular state schools but also to religious-run schools and any other grant-aided private schools. Funding for private schools increased dramatically during the 1980s, and has continued to rise since then, but, in return, central government exercises more control over the content of the curriculum and forms of governance. The most recent major reform, the *Ley de Ordenación General del Sistema Educativo*, or LOGSE, passed in 1990, stipulates further curriculum reform (with a special emphasis on improving the quality of FP), strengthens the provision of early (pre-school) education in an attempt to redress the disadvantage suffered by children from poorer socio-economic backgrounds, and raises the minimum school-leaving age to 16.

As is clear from the above, much of the effort that has gone into Spanish educational reform in recent decades has been aimed at combating the traditional elitism of the system, associated with the privileges and power of the upper classes and supported over a long period of time by both state and Church.

A liberal and reformist approach to education had been adopted by the state authorities during the period of the Second Republic in the 1930s, but this was rapidly dismantled by the Franco regime in the wake of the Civil War. Authoritarian values and attitudes were favoured and actively encouraged during the dictatorship, with the state deliberately taking a subsidiary role to the Church in the early years of the regime. *Libertad de enseñanza* was then deemed pernicious by the right-wing authorities (Maravall 1995: 45), since it implied the availability of a 'godless' system of education which would undermine the moral values of young Spaniards. The Ripalda Catechism, which was in use in schools during the dictatorship, had this to say on the subject of freedom of education:

> Are there any other dangerous freedoms?
> Yes, sir: the freedom of education, the freedom of propaganda and the freedom of association.
> Why are these freedoms dangerous?
> Because they are used to teach falsehoods and to propagate bad habits.
> (quoted in Brassloff 1986: 42)

Ironically, in resisting the educational reforms of the PSOE, the Catholic Right has been vociferous in more recent years in its defence of educational freedom, since this is now taken to imply the continued existence of denominational, i.e. Catholic, education.

Education is no longer viewed as a privilege in Spain but as a right, and as an area of life which is of major importance to everyone. Perhaps the most obvious manifestation of this is the developments that have taken place in higher-level education. Participation at this level has grown enormously. Universities and individual faculties have grown to sometimes prodigious sizes in an attempt to cater for the growing demand. The sheer growth in numbers was not matched, however, by a similar increase in financial resources, with the result that there have been major problems of *masificación* (overcrowding) in many faculties. Demographic changes (in particular, the falling birth rate) are changing this, but despite the recent signs that the increase is slowing down – numbers entering university actually dropped in 1996–97 for the first time in 56 years – there are still many overcrowded classrooms, especially in the more popular faculties such as Law and Medicine, and the prevailing atmosphere is often characterized by students as being aggressive and overly competitive.

Huge numbers of university graduates fail to find relevant employment, with the result that the state-organized examinations for entry into the professions (*oposiciones*) have become the principal means for them to obtain positions in areas such as law, medicine, education, local authorities or the civil service. There is nothing quite like the system of *oposiciones* in the English-speaking world. Thousands – in some cases, hundreds of thousands – of young people take the examinations each year, and offers of employment are then made to a limited number. The number of offers varies, and depends on the level of need for the relevant professionals in any particular year, but most of those who sit the examinations are disappointed. Many people repeat the process and undergo the strain of the examination year after year, being continually disappointed, since no advantage is given to those who have previously applied. The result can be a continuous period of stressful effort on the part of young hopefuls, who suffer the demoralizing effect of failing to ' enter their chosen career.

8.4 EDUCATION AS UNIVERSALIZATION: *EL VALOR DE EDUCAR*

Education is about helping others to achieve their potential. It requires leadership and entails creativity and vision: the Latin *ex-ducare* means 'leading out', taking people beyond the current limits of their world and showing them something new. In cultural terms, this suggests the need to explore what is beyond the limits of our cultural awareness, the need to explore 'otherness'. Recognizing the reality of otherness, as we have been suggesting throughout this book, means not just seeing how 'different' another person is – a person from another country, another culture – but having a real awareness of the otherness within ourselves. The recognition of a common humanity in all the individuals we come across goes hand in hand with a recognition of the potential for difference that all of us, as individuals, carry within.

Just such an expansion of our horizons – education as universalization – is the main theme of the book *El valor de educar* (1997) by the Spanish philosopher Fernando Savater (b. 1947). Savater advocates a vision of education as enabling people to become fully human: a person has to grow into a state of being fully a person. This does not just happen spontaneously, but requires effort, planning and dedication. Savater's is a liberal, humanist vision: the human race is involved in a project of improvement and development, striving for a fuller and better life for each new generation. Education is at the heart of that struggle; it is concerned with every aspect of life and living, and rests on a necessary sense of hope and optimism about what can be done in the future and about the quality of life that can be achieved. The better the education offered, the more it will focus on meanings; ultimately, what is being learned – at all levels of education, but especially in the elementary stages – is how to be human in the world, with all that that entails in terms of appreciating human meanings and learning how to interact with other people. Things in the world are never just things, but have human meanings attached:

> La vida humana consiste en habitar un mundo en el que las cosas no sólo son lo que son sino que también significan; pero lo más humano de todo es comprender que, si bien lo que sea la realidad no depende de nosotros, lo que la realidad significa sí resulta competencia, problema y en cierta medida opción nuestra.

> (Savater 1997: 31)

Education, then, is about the child entering the world and society and about knowing how to appropriate the reality of the world in the most fully human way possible. The family plays a central role in teaching the child how this is done – not by oppressively dictating the child's behaviour but by conveying to the child what is important and what is not: in positive terms, this means teaching principles of behaviour; on the negative side, it means conveying prejudices. But the parents of the child must not (as Savater suggests many actually do) relinquish their responsibility for exercising authority. Parents who only wish to play the role of 'friend' to their children forget that they have experience and knowledge of the world which are superior to those of their children and which necessarily set them apart from them. The inability to provide a structure of authority for the child is ultimately damaging; this 'eclipsing' of the family is something Savater laments, and the aspect which is most lamentable, according to him, is the confusion that exists about the role of the father: rejecting despotic authority of the traditional sort – the sort which they witnessed in their own families as they grew up – modern fathers are unsure about their role, the challenge to them being to know how to combine a reasonable level of control and authority with the capacity to express tenderness and care.

Some degree of compulsion, some 'forcing', is an essential element of education – not the compulsion typical of the times of the Franco dictatorship, with indoctrination in 'national Catholicism' and the instilling of military virtues – but a discipline which allows growth to take place, a discipline which enables the child to grow into freedom. But, for the child to learn, a model must be presented; there is no model 'within the child': 'El maestro no estudia en el niño el modelo de madurez de éste, sino que es el niño quien ha de estudiar orientado por un ejemplo de excelencia que el maestro conoce y le transmite' (ibid.: 96). The model presented should be neither rigid nor incapable of being altered and adapted; and the teacher, in turn, has an obligation to understand the pupil as well as possible, the better to know how the pupil may progress effectively. However, the teacher's approach, according to Savater, should not be based on what the child is now but on that which the child can reach in the future. And a necessary element of the vision which the teacher has to offer the child is the society in which both teacher and child live. What the teacher transmits to the child is not merely a simplistic, singular vision of the world; rather, the effective teacher gives the child a good grasp of the set of cultures and values that are in conflict within the group to which that child belongs.

From these principles flow a set of practical implications which can have an effect on what is taught and how it is taught. For instance, the fact that the child is being educated for a future which is different – and hopefully better – than the present implies an emphasis on creativity and innovation; hence, whatever the practical technological needs of Spanish society (or any other society) may be at a particular point, the education of the child needs to include not just utilitarian subjects – the transmission of practical information and know-how – but subjects which foster inventiveness and the imagination, and the methodology employed needs to be of a kind that will teach children to think creatively. The moral issues – in relation to drugs, violence, sex, religion – need to be addressed not in a spirit of hysteria and hypocrisy, but openly accepting that more than one perspective is possible, that conflicting attitudes are natural, and that the emphasis needs to be laid, above all, on having consideration for others.

Savater sees education as fundamentally conservative, in the sense of preserving, of keeping what is valuable: 'En una palabra, la educación es ante todo transmisión de algo y sólo se transmite aquello que quien ha de transmitirlo considera digno de ser conservado' (ibid.: 148). In Savater's view, every society organizes education along lines that are meaningful to it and in ways which it considers most likely to maximize its chances of survival. But the totality of what any society is includes the longing for improvement of that society: '[L]a sociedad nunca es un todo fijo, acabado, en equilibrio mortal. En ningún caso deja de incluir tendencias diversas que también forman parte de la tradición que los aprendizajes comunican' (ibid.: 149). However, the educator is not just a neutral transmitter of a set of possible options being offered to the younger generation. Teaching is a subjective activity, and the teacher opts for a particular vision, normally one broadly in tune with that of the society in which he or she lives. For Savater, this means opting for democracy, for openness and for pluralism: '[E]l principal bien que hemos de producir y aumentar es la humanidad compartida, semejante en lo fundamental a despecho de las tribus y privilegios con que también muy humanamente nos identificamos' (ibid.: 153). He advocates an education which preserves and promotes what he calls *la universalidad democrática*, an education which valorizes common humanity over individual difference, an egalitarian education not devoted to excluding some people and including others but which is, above all, concerned to emphasize fundamental similarities among people of different groups, both sexes and any culture:

> [A]unque las etapas más avanzadas de la enseñanza puedan ser selectivas y favorezcan la especialización de cada cual según su peculiar vocación, el aprendizaje básico de los primeros años no debe regatearse a nadie ni ha de dar por supuesto de antemano que se ha 'nacido' para mucho, para poco o para nada.

> (ibid.: 154)

As a Basque, Savater is especially sensitive to issues of nationalism and ethnic identity; but, unlike the extremists – in the Basque Country or elsewhere – he argues for a way of looking at cultural identity which sees ethnicity as a very human reality that binds all members of the human race together, not as a distinction which divides them. This is because all cultures can be understood by those from outside that cultural milieu; none is either impermeable or impenetrable:

> Ninguna cultura es insoluble para las otras, ninguna brota de una esencia tan idiosincrásica que no pueda o no deba mezclarse con otras, *contagiarse* de las otras. Ese contagio de unas culturas por otras es precisamente lo que puede llamarse *civilización* y es la civilización, no meramente la cultura, lo que la educación debe aspirar a transmitir. (ibid.: 161; original emphasis)

This does not mean a bland homogenization – with the concomitant panic over globalization or Americanization – but it does mean breaking down 'the self-absorbed cultural myths which demand to be preserved intact without any change whatsoever' (ibid.: 161–2). On the one hand, the potential for universality exists in every culture; on the other hand, no culture is immune to provincialism:

> [L]a universalidad no es patrimonio exclusivo de ninguna cultura – lo cual sería contradictorio – sino una tendencia que se da en todas pero que también en todas partes debe enfrentarse con el provincianismo cultural de lo idiosincrásico insoluble, presente por igual en las latitudes aparentemente más opuestas.
>
> (ibid.: 162)

The danger is not bland homogenization or universalization but rather the opposite: the tendency to believe that only those who are from a particular culture – 'our' culture – can fully understand that culture and be a part of it: this is the danger of viewing the outsider as 'the other'. Such fundamentalism is alien to the task of education: democratic societies commit themselves – rightly, in Savater's view – to the preservation of democracy, which is a system and a way of living which does not occur naturally and which does not arise spontaneously in human society, but has to be achieved and implies the need for further effort and commitment to that very project.

Spain is a young democracy, and it may be that a country in the process of building a new society and establishing new cultural norms inevitably gives special attention to the way in which its young people are formed. Certainly, education has been of major concern to Spanish people in recent times, not only in terms of the increased quantity of education required for all sectors of the population, but also in terms of its quality and its nature. It is indicative of this intense interest in education in Spain that Savater's book was the best-selling book in the country for four months in 1997, selling hundreds of thousands of copies within six months of publication.

There are aspects of Spanish education which fall far short of the ideals enunciated by Savater and, presumably, favoured by the Spanish public. As in most societies, there are real educational and cultural advantages for the children of affluent parents, for example. The quality of education delivered in school can vary greatly, often relating to socio-economic factors, and even the average spend on education per pupil varies from one Autonomous Community to another (Andalusia, for example, having the lowest spend in 1998–99, according to *El Mundo* in November 1999). Again, from one Autonomous Community to another, the nature of the educational experience differs, in some cases in ways which seem natural and acceptable – the inclusion of classes in vernacular languages in Catalonia, the Balearic Islands, Valencia, Galicia or the Basque Country, for example – and in other cases in ways which strike the average Spaniard as anomalous: in one Autonomous Community, for instance, there have been complaints about a lack of local (regional) content in schoolbooks – including in mathematics textbooks! Certain specific elements of the system clearly need to be improved: pupil–teacher ratios, for example, tend to be higher than the average in OECD countries, while teachers' salaries are relatively low. Schoolchildren's performance in science and mathematics also needs improving: of over 20 countries surveyed by the OECD in the 1990s, Spain has generally come third last or fourth last in terms of attainment levels in those areas among 13-year-olds (OECD 1993, 1996, 1998).

In general, however, the standard of education in Spain is now high, at a level comparable to that of the most advanced countries in the world. Major challenges to the system include issues such as multiculturalism (which means not only the accommodation of cultural and linguistic diversity in the historical nationalities, but also the fair treatment of immigrants and of those belonging to minority cultures and minority religions), equity of treatment across the social classes and the Autonomous Communities, and the continued improvement in the general level of resources for education in the country.

FEATURE: YOUTH CULTURE

Although the primary formative influences on young Spaniards – as on young people elsewhere – are home and school, a third major factor contributes to moulding the young in Spain: youth culture. Spaniards themselves acknowledge this: according to a 1992 survey, they identify most with the following groups: 'las personas de su misma generación' and 'personas con sus mismas aficiones, gustos, costumbres, etc.' (CIS 1992: 17). It is only since the 1950s that the idea of youth culture as something having characteristics of its own, and existing separately from the culture of adults, has been appreciated. But the notion is a vague one, and can be misleading. It is certainly associated very strongly with the influence of the mass media – which play a central role in defining the parameters of youth culture – but it is also frequently considered to be synonymous with features such as a marked generation gap, low morals, mindless consumption of pop and rock music, alcohol and drugs. This image is itself a stereotype, of course, and the reality is that the generic label 'youth culture' covers a wide range of subcultures, which vary over time, across social classes and from place to place, both within the global context and in the context of any particular country.

It is noteworthy that young Spaniards in the 1960s and 1970s were relatively conservative compared with their counterparts in other European countries, especially in terms of their tastes in dress and music. The following (tongue-in-cheek) 'Ten Commandments' might suggest the priorities of the young in Spain today.

1. Smoke a lot, especially if you are male: in the EU, only the Greeks smoke more. 39% of Spanish men and 25% of Spanish women smoke (European Commission 1999b: 8).

2. Enjoy drink from an early age and continue to drink in moderation throughout your life, very rarely to the point of drunkenness.
3. Observe the latest fashions, and don't forget the strategic use of designer labels.
4. In music, combine consumption of major international acts with an interest in something local or folkloric – Celtic, for example.
5. Watch 207 minutes of television per day. Only the British (with 228 minutes) watch more TV than Spaniards do (*El Independiente*, December 1990).
6. *Some* experimentation with drugs is probably difficult to avoid.
7. In politics, be sceptical, if not cynical: all politicians are probably corrupt.
8. Take parents and family for granted, and stay as long as you want – *of course* they are the most important thing in the world; and remember the motto: *¡Vive de tus padres hasta que puedas vivir de tus hijos!*
9. Watch predominantly foreign films: about 90 per cent of cinema visits in Spain are to watch films from abroad – mainly from the USA (*Anuario El País* 1999: 278).
10. Sex is not worth dying or killing for, but then neither is virginity. And it's definitely *not* as important as money or a job!

READING: JOSEFINA R. ALDECOA, *HISTORIA DE UNA MAESTRA*

In the early 1930s, the Republican government undertook a programme aimed at bringing education to the towns and villages of Spain and improving the levels of literacy and culture among ordinary people, through the creation of thousands of new schools, libraries and cultural centres. The results were mixed, partly because the government alienated the Catholic Church from the process and had only limited resources. Not enough teachers were available, and those who dedicated themselves to this work were badly paid and poorly resourced.

The extract below is from the novel *Historia de una maestra*, based on the life of the author's mother. In it, Josefina R. Aldecoa (b. 1926) tells the story of one such idealistic teacher in rural Spain in the 1920s and 1930s, and recounts the deprivations that she and her husband suffered, and the hostilities they encountered in their efforts to provide education for the poor.

Si yo quisiera explicar lo que era entonces para mí la política, no sabría. Yo creía en la cultura, en la educación, en la justicia. Amaba mi profesión, y me entregaba a ella con afán. ¿Todo esto era política?

En Ezequiel encontré la continuidad de lo que mi padre me había enseñado, la austeridad, la mística del trabajo, la inagotable entrega. ¿Era eso política?

Ezequiel me leía fragmentos de discursos, artículos y noticias que tenían relación con la enseñanza. Yo apenas tenía tiempo para leerlos por mí misma, ocupada con la niña y con mis tareas habituales, pero al escuchar aquellas hermosas palabras, se me llenaban los ojos de lágrimas.

'Es deber imperativo de las democracias el que todas las escuelas, desde la maternal a la Universidad, estén abiertas a todos los estudiantes en orden no a sus posibilidades económicas sino a su capacidad intelectual', decía un decreto publicado en la Gaceta.

En un artículo se arengaba a los maestros: 'La República se salvará por la escuela. Tenemos ante nosotros una obra espléndida, magnífica. Manos pues a la obra.' ¿Era eso política? Al parecer lo era. No habían pasado quince días desde la proclamación de la República y ya teníamos a don Cosme en casa, ladino y conciliador. Venía a ver a la niña a advertirnos de los peligros que iba a encerrar para nosotros el apoyo incondicional a la nueva República.

—Dejarse de políticas. Las políticas que las hagan ellos en el Parlamento. Nosotros aquí, en el pueblo, paz y respeto para todos. —Y acto seguido—: Y no me diga, Gabriela, que con estas modas de la República no va usted a bautizar a la niña, que no me la va a dejar mora, tan preciosa como es la criatura . . .

La suerte estaba echada. Fuera o no política, estaba claro que nuestras ideas estaban en total acuerdo con las que la República proclamaba a los cuatro vientos.

'Tenemos el deber de llevar a las escuelas las ideas esenciales en que se apoya la República: libertad, autonomía, solidaridad, civilidad'.

—A la sobrina de Amadeo le han puesto el nombre de Libertad — me dijo Ezequiel cuando nació la niña.

—Está bien, allá ellos. Pero nuestra hija se va a llamar Juana como tu madre — le contesté yo.

El guardó silencio y yo me irrité.

—No empieces a engañarte con las palabras—le dije—. La libertad está ahí y hay que luchar por ella pero no empieces a conformarte con las palabras. Las palabras se gastan y pierden brillo. Los hechos no . . . .

La niña se llamó Juana y no fue bautizada. Después de la nuestra, habían nacido dos niños más y sus padres tampoco quisieron bautizarlos.

—El Cura debe estar furioso—le comenté a Ezequiel—. Lo único que temo es que crea que es obra nuestra.

Así que en la próxima clase de adultos Ezequiel lo dejó todo muy claro: que nosotros habíamos decidido libremente no bautizar a la niña, pero que ellos consideraran, también libremente, su decisión, porque no se trataba de alardear de nada que no hubiese sido firmemente meditado. Que no se trataba de ir en contra de nadie ni de provocar a nadie y menos aún de perder el respeto a los que no pensaban como nosotros.

—Yo no pierdo el respeto a nadie—dijo uno de los padres rebeldes. Ellos son los que me lo tienen perdido desde hace mucho. Yo no voy a la Iglesia porque no quiero y no bautizo a mi hijo porque no quiero. Pero no voy a disimular porque a ellos les moleste. ¿Disimulan ellos cuando bautizan a los suyos por si me molesta a mí?

'Ellos' se había convertido en un vocablo cargado de misterios y suposiciones. Para los republicanos, 'ellos' eran don Cosme y el Cura y los que compartían sus opiniones. A su vez 'ellos' éramos nosotros para don Cosme y sus aliados.

En los pueblos pequeños y alejados de las ciudades como los nuestros, las primeras reacciones frente a la República fueron el desconcierto y la desconfianza. En seguida la toma de posiciones se fue acentuando y se produjo una evidente división. Sin que nadie interviniese directamente, los vecinos se fueron agrupando en dos núcleos significativos, a favor unos y en contra otros del nuevo Gobierno.

Corrían rumores, comentarios socarrones. Se lanzaban unos y otros frases intencionadas. Era un tanteo, un ensayo general, una maniobra de fogueo.

—Don Cosme, vaya preparando las ovejas que me las voy a llevar un día de éstos—decía Pancho el pastor, que estaba en la casa desde la época del padre de don Cosme y mantenía con el amo unas relaciones de absoluta confianza.

—Antes de que te las lleves tú, las enveneno — replicaba riendo don Cosme.

—¿Y las viñas? — pinchaba el pastor.

—Antes de que me las quiten, las quemo — contestaba don Cosme.

Ya había desaparecido la broma. Se advertía un matiz de seriedad en la respuesta. Se vislumbraban ya las iras encendidas del desacuerdo.

Un día en la pared de la Iglesia apareció un letrero escrito con carbón: 'Abajo el clero'.

Al terminar la Misa salió el Cura con el pelo blanco revuelto, la sotana mal abotonada y empuñando un cepillo de raíces, que dirigió con fuerza contra el muro. Las palabras se borraron, pero la mancha negra quedó allí, informe y amenazante.

Los niños no eran ajenos al clima que empezaba a crearse en el pueblo. En la escuela fluían los comentarios, inocentes unas veces, intencionados otras.

—Dice mi padre que la República quiere quitar las iglesias . . .

—Será porque tu padre es el campanero y tiene miedo a quedarse sin oficio . . .

—Peor es el tuyo que nunca lo ha tenido . . .

Poníamos paz. Entre Ezequiel y yo habíamos preparado una lección histórica, llena de prudencia y moderación, en la que eludimos pronunciar una sola palabra de ataque a instituciones o personas.

Los niños la escucharon en silencio y no preguntaron nada.

Fue después, al discurrir de los días, cuando empezaron a surgir entre ellos las pullas, los pequeños ataques, las desavenencias que reflejaban las distintas posturas de sus padres. No obstante, poco a poco, una nueva normalidad se instaló en el pueblo. La calma presidía la vida del lugar. Aparentemente nada había cambiado a pesar de los continuos informes de la prensa.

Reforma agraria, reforma sanitaria, reforma de la enseñanza. Las reformas discurrían por la tinta fresca, pero todavía no se veían señales de su realización.

Entre el deslumbramiento por los cambios políticos del país y el desconcierto de nuestra nueva situación familiar, el tiempo fue pasando y sin darnos cuenta el verano se nos echó encima.

Yo estaba deseando llegar a casa de mis padres para que conocieran a su nieta y para encontrar alivio a la crianza de Juana con la ayuda de mi madre.

La víspera de las vacaciones un suceso vino a empañar nuestra alegría. Amadeo, el carpintero, nuestro amigo, fue asaltado una noche cuando volvía andando, solo, de visitar a unos parientes en un pueblo cercano. En la oscuridad no pudo reconocer a sus atacantes; aunque, decía él, 'seguro que no eran de aquí'.

Le pegaron una buena paliza y dice que sólo una palabra pronunciaban: masón, masón, masón, mientras le golpeaban.

(Aldecoa 1996: 107–11)

FURTHER READING

Alberdi, Inés, *La nueva familia española* (Madrid, Taurus, 1999).
A comprehensive sociological examination of a wide range of issues of relevance to the family in modern Spain.

Boyd-Barrett, O. and O'Malley, P. (eds), *Education Reform in Contemporary Spain* (London, Routledge, 1995).
Sets education in contemporary Spain in its historical context and offers many details about developments in education.

Centro de Investigaciones Sociológicas (CIS), *Homepage*, http://www.cis.es
An excellent source of information on social attitudes in Spain.

Jordan, Barry and Morgan-Tamosunas, Rikki (eds), *Contemporary Spanish Cultural Studies* (London, Arnold, 2000).
Part V of this book offers an interesting series of chapters on youth culture and popular culture in contemporary Spain.

OECD, *Education at a Glance: OECD indicators* (Paris, OECD, 1999).
Published every three years, this is a useful starting point for the comparative study of the educational systems of the OECD countries, including Spain.

9

Faith: What do Spaniards Believe?

9.1 INTRODUCTION: RELIGION AND IDEOLOGY

Spanish Catholicism is an integral part of Western European Christianity, and, as such, is related to a tradition based around questions of ultimate meanings, the consolation of the individual human being who faces the inevitability of death, and the conviction that there is one Supreme Being to whom the details of the lives of individual human beings are not trivial. As part of that tradition, it also shares whatever militant dimension is associated with the struggles between competing religious beliefs, whether in the context of Christianity's historical competition with Islam or Judaism, or in terms of the rival versions of Christianity that have vied with each other in Europe, especially since the sixteenth century.

Spanish people have a complex relationship with the Catholic Church. The traditional strength of Catholicism means that the vast majority of Spaniards have identified fairly automatically with that Church as the repository of their religious beliefs and practices; this tendency, however, coexists with quite a low level of regular religious observance (just 21 per cent of Spaniards attend mass at least once a week – CIS 1995a: 29), and with an increasing trend towards various forms of agnosticism and atheism. The latter trend should not be exaggerated, however. Despite the growth of non-Catholic religions and sects, from New Ageism to Islam, and the predominant acceptance of religious pluralism, the vast majority continue to hold certain fundamental religious beliefs. In a 1992 survey (CIS 1992: 34), 66 per cent of the people surveyed were happy to state their belief in the existence of the soul, and 80 per cent professed faith in God (although less than half said they believed in a life after death).

To suggest that the Catholic dimension of Spanish culture is becoming obsolete would be to ignore the reality of the large numbers of people who are in fact *católicos practicantes*, the much wider preservation of customs associated with rites of passage (baptism, communion, church weddings and funerals) and the strength of traditional festivals aimed at venerating Jesus Christ, the Virgin Mary and a wide range of saints.

In a sense, then, Spanish Catholicism is paradigmatic of European Christianity generally, but, in another sense, the Catholic Church in Spain has displayed characteristics peculiar to itself, cultural characteristics which make it unavoidable as an object of study for those who want to know Spain better. In an increasingly secular world, the Spanish Church has lost the prominent position it once occupied in society and, although the voices of bishops and priests are occasionally raised in protest at the weight given to materialistic values in Spain, the majority of Spaniards confine their contact with the Church to attendance at mass for rites of passage and occasional involvement in popular religious *fiestas*.

In this chapter, the topic of faith is addressed by focusing on certain specific aspects of religion and belief in Spain, including the orthodoxy which has been so deeply embedded in the Spanish Church (examined in section 9.2), the role of the institutional Church in modern times (9.3), the religious *fiestas* and *romerías* which are such a central part of the culture of the south of Spain (9.4), the expression of a desire to believe on the part of Miguel de Unamuno (9.5) and a brief outline of the views of a classic Jewish thinker, Maimonides, along with a text on the topic of non-belief by a contemporary Spanish writer, Rosa Montero.

9.2 THE SPANISH CHURCH AND THE EMERGENCE OF ORTHODOXY

In a 1995 survey (CIS 1995a: 29), only 2.6 per cent of Spaniards professed a faith other than Catholicism. We should not, of course, take this as an indication that the Catholic Church has the kind of hold on people's thinking which it has had in the past, or that Spaniards as a whole accept uncritically either the moral teachings of the Church or the notion that it has a role to play in social or political life. It is a reminder, however, of the fact that Catholicism is deeply rooted in Spanish life and that there is still a strong allegiance among many towards the customs and practices associated with Catholic traditions.

Until relatively recent times, most Spaniards would identify readily with the assumption that being Spanish meant also being Catholic: 'soy español, claro que soy católico'. It was a feature associated with national identity, and was seen as a core value, and – at least at an official level, though often also at a personal one – an inescapable aspect of Spanish ethnicity, so that one could no more avoid the condition of being a Catholic than one could deny the colour of one's skin.

We may question whether this aspect of Spanish national identity was a natural outcome of a shared history of conflict with other religious viewpoints (especially the Islamic one), or merely an attempt at retrospectively creating a quasi-mythical common interpretation of cosmic realities which would contribute to the soldering together of an 'imagined community'. But there is no doubt that Catholicism functioned as a means of asserting commonality in the face of a range of centrifugal cultural forces. While the union of the Crowns of Castile and Aragon in 1479 could be said to have yoked together disparate cultures, the institutionalization of religious orthodoxy facilitated both the extension of a centralized system of power based on the monarchy and the implantation of a sense of shared identity across the Peninsula.

A shared identity frequently revolves around, among other things, a sense of having a shared enemy. It is as if communities need to find an enemy to abhor, and if they do not already have one, they will invent one. The principal candidate for the role of despised 'other', in the case of medieval Spain, was 'the Moor', the Muslim 'infidel' whose powerful religious culture had spread so successfully from northern Africa in the course of the eighth century. European Christendom in general perceived Islam as its chief enemy and major threat in the late Middle Ages, and mobilized its forces in the form of the Crusaders, who proceeded to undertake military action, with a limited degree of success, against the Muslim presence in the Holy Land. They captured Jerusalem, for example, at the end of the eleventh century, but, less than a hundred years later, were expelled from the city, and by the end of the thirteenth century, their presence in the region had been more or less comprehensively neutralized.

The Islamic Empire at its height included territories from Asia Minor in the east to the Iberian Peninsula in the west. As Edward Said (1978) has argued so persuasively, the presence of this well-developed social and cultural order just beyond the boundaries of Europe was instrumental in itself in defining those boundaries and in establishing the characteristics of the entity called 'Europe'.

Also taking this line, Roger Ballard argues as follows:

> In the face of the emergence of an overwhelmingly powerful Islamic order to its south and east, a sense of collective identity began to crystallize amongst the population of the territory which was subsequently to identify itself as Europe – and most especially as western Europe .... [T]he banner under which collective mobilization began to be organized was that of Christendom, while the other at whom this nascent power was directed was perceived as being Muslim, oriental and black. The foundations around which contemporary conceptualizations of Europe were to be constructed were now in place.
>
> (Ballard 1996: 26)

Ballard goes on to place the Spanish Reconquest within the context of this wider European enterprise. In Al-Andalus (the Islamic territory on the Peninsula) there existed a thriving, prosperous society, which reached its zenith in the tenth century, within the unified 'caliphate' of Abd al-Rahman III, centred in Córdoba. The social and political character of Al-Andalus naturally shifted and evolved during the course of the centuries of Arab political dominance, but Al-Andalus came to be at the cultural heart of the Islamic Empire, rather than being just one more province of that Empire. Given that Christian and Muslim cultures coexisted on the peninsula for eight centuries, we can appreciate that there had to be at least some mutual tolerance and respect for differences between the two communities, whether in Al-Andalus or in the remaining territory under Christian control. In spite of this, in that Christian territory, the dominant perception of Al-Andalus was that it was alien, different and, at least among the political powers who ruled the kingdoms and principalities which comprised the Christian area, that it was a legitimate zone in which to conduct a 'crusade', without the bother of having to traverse eastern Europe and Asia Minor in order to reach one's battleground. Thus, the recognition of the 'difference' inherent in Islamic culture and the belief that this 'other' was a legitimate target of military attack were not mutually incompatible ideas. Both Christianity and Islam were proselytizing faiths, and their adherents believed in the rightness of their cause and the prerogative of spreading the Word. But for a variety of pragmatic reasons, mainly the need for the skill or labour of the members of the other community, both were for a long time willing to offer each other a protected position within their respective societies.

The reasons for the dissolution of this attitude of tolerance on the part of Christian Spain are many and complex. Nevertheless, it seems clear that any explanation would have at least two dimensions. On the one hand, the Muslim population in Christian Spain was gradually growing out of its position as a more or less impoverished minority, and its increasing economic strength thus made it seem more threatening. On the other hand, the very fragility and heterogeneity of the Christian territory being united by Ferdinand and Isabella made it imperative to identify a real or invented 'cultural unity' upon which political power could be based, and which could serve as a rallying cry for expansion and conquest, first in northern Europe and subsequently in the New World. In this way, the projection of a cultural 'other' became a political and military necessity. The change of attitude which transformed the Peninsula from a series of mutually hostile but internally quite tolerant states to an increasingly intolerant and aggressive zone of competition appears to have begun in earnest around the beginning of the fifteenth century, but it is towards the end of that century, with the unification of the territory under the Catholic Monarchs, that the process is accelerated and the intolerance becomes more vicious.

The role played by the Spanish Inquisition in the imposition of the new orthodoxy must not be overlooked. From the moment when the Catholic Monarchs entered into an agreement with Pope Sixtus IV to establish the inquisitorial process in Spanish territory, the interlinking of political power and religious orthodoxy was made evident.

9.3 THE CHURCH IN THE MODERN AGE

During the course of the nineteenth century, and for much of the twentieth, the Spanish Church was identified more or less closely with the establishment powers of the military and the landowners. If the numbers of men and women attached to religious orders and the level of observance of Church rites are reliable indicators, Spain was then a highly 'religious' country. The Church's role in Spanish society was underpinned by the constitutional position which it held and by the special agreement (or *Concordat*) between the Spanish government and the Vatican which was entered into in 1851. Even the relatively liberal constitutions of 1812 and 1869 recognized the special position of the Church, while the Constitution of 1876 – a highly influential document which formed the legal basis on which Spain moved into the twentieth century – contained an article on the Church's position which opened with the words: 'La religión católica apostólica romana es la del Estado'. Even though the same article then went on to assure members of other religions that they would not be 'molestados en el territorio español por sus opiniones religiosas ni por el ejercicio de su respectivo culto', the thrust of the legislation was to the effect that, once again, being Spanish meant being Catholic.

Religions other than Catholicism held little sway with Spaniards and the minuscule numbers of Protestants or Jews in the country tended to be discreet about their convictions; indeed, for much of this period, they were forbidden to proselytize, even if they were theoretically free to practise. But opposition to the Church as an institution was by no means non-existent, and resentment of the Church's power led to occasional outbursts of violent anticlericalism even in the nineteenth century, just as it did with even more tragic consequences in the twentieth. Massacres of monks and nuns took place, for instance, in the 1830s in Madrid, Zaragoza and Barcelona. The biggest material blow suffered by the Church around that same period, however, was the *desamortización*, or expropriation of lands owned by the Church, which took place in 1835–36 under the guidance of the Finance Minister Juan Alvarez Mendizábal. In the course of the succeeding decade or so, these Church lands were then sold off by the government. The object of this exercise was both to weaken the economic power of the Church itself and to encourage the development of a class of small landowners. Those who could afford to buy the expropriated lands, however, were already relatively affluent, so that few new landowners were brought into the sector. In its turn, the Church's wealth was sufficient for it to be able to withstand the effects of this measure, which, in any case, were temporary since most of the property was later restored to it. Support for the Church among the bourgeoisie and the aristocratic classes continued to be strong for most of the century, as religious observance became an indispensable aspect of social superiority for large sectors of the population.

By the end of the century, the Church was increasingly focusing its attention on what it saw as a fundamentally important element of its activities, namely education. Education in Spain was an elitist pursuit, controlled for the most part by the Church, with the majority of both primary and secondary school students attending Catholic schools (see 8.3). A church such as this, an institution based largely around traditionalist ideology, pious hypocrisy and snobbery, was, not surprisingly, distinctly unattractive to liberal intellectuals influenced by general European thinking, notwithstanding the fact that Catholicism at the popular level continued to find support among the population. But resentment of the institutional Church's identification with the rich, and its apparent willingness to collude in the exploitation of working people, combined with its general indifference to cultural and educational deprivation, provoked ordinary Spaniards into a reaction which crystallized in the measures taken against the Church in the course of the Second Republic.

It was during the first two years of the Republican period (1931–32) that serious attempts at reform were undertaken. The Republican authorities were convinced that what most needed changing in Spain was the mindset of the people. Undertaking this project entailed making a serious attempt at educational reform, on the one hand, but in tandem with this and closely associated with it was the need to address the issue of the hold of the Catholic Church on people's thinking. Thus, the new Republican constitution of 1931 officially separated Church and State in Spain, stating, in Article 3: 'The Spanish State has no religion'; beyond that, however, legislation was introduced which banned the compulsory teaching of religion and brought about the removal of religious symbols such as crucifixes and statues of the Virgin from the classrooms of state schools. Provoked by such measures and appalled at the sporadic violence perpetrated against nuns, priests and monks in various parts of the country, the Church and its allies gradually hardened their anti-Republican stance. When the Civil War began in 1936, therefore, the Church was inevitably partisan, and, with the exception of the Basque clergy, sided with the Nationalist forces under the rebelling generals. In turn, these forces – the eventual victors in the war – capitalized on the opportunity offered by this support for their belligerence by characterizing the cause they espoused as a 'crusade', i.e. a struggle against the heathen forces of the Republic, who were depicted as wanting to destroy the traditional morality of Spain and undermine the supposedly pure spirituality of her people. In this respect, the Nationalists were not just associating with natural conservative allies within Spain, they were also aligning with anti-democratic Catholic opinion internationally, a fact emphasized by the support which came from such institutions as the Irish Catholic Church and indeed, the Vatican itself. At the end of the war, in April 1939, Pope Pius XII went so far as to send a telegram of congratulations to General Franco on his victory.

The alliance between Church and State was once more institutionalized under Franco, with heavy Church involvement in a wide range of political and social matters during the dictatorship, including control of the educational system and the exercise of restrictions on publications and the media through censorship. The closest the Franco regime came to articulating anything like an ideology was the profession of the principles of 'National Catholicism', and the mutual commitment of Church and State to each other was copper-fastened in a new Concordat (a revision of the 1851 agreement), signed by the Vatican and the Spanish government in 1953. In it, the state undertook to protect the Catholic Church in Spain and to give it precedence in matters pertaining to morality, as well as to continue to pay the salaries of priests. The principal political advantage to the regime, derived from the Concordat, was the fact that the Church had to have government approval for the nomination of any bishops. This measure had the effect of allowing Franco to veto these appointments and thus to ensure the exclusion of liberal-minded priests from the ranks of the hierarchy.

The cosy relationship between the Church and the regime began to weaken as early as the 1950s, as younger priests, and especially Basque priests with nationalist leanings, questioned the support given to an autocratic regime by the Church. Meanwhile, in the early 1960s, the Catholic Church worldwide undertook a reassessment of its role. The Second Vatican Council (1962–65) was a forum out of which emerged a much more socially aware church, concerned at the offensive contrasts between rich and poor in certain countries, and committed to principles of justice as well as to civil and religious liberties. Spanish priests ministering in working-class communities were increasingly inclined to put such principles into practice by becoming politically active and identifying with left-wing groups (such as the illegal Communist trade union *Comisiones Obreras*). Numbers affiliating to Catholic workers' organizations such as *Hermandades Obreras de Acción Católica* (HOAC) and *Juventud Obrera Católica* (JOC) swelled, at least partly because these groups had the advantage of being fairly immune from the threat of repressive action on the part of the authorities.

From being one of the regime's staunchest supporters, the Church moved to a position where it was an increasingly outspoken critic of the regime, even to the extent that a special prison was set up for priests in Zamora in the late 1960s (mainly to accommodate nationalistic Basque priests). Under a liberal cardinal-primate, Vicente Enrique y Tarancón, the Spanish hierarchy gave voice to views that were implicitly or explicitly critical. For example, in a proposition supported by a majority of the bishops and priests gathered at a special Assembly in September 1971, there was a clear expression of regret at the pro-Franco stance which the Church had taken in earlier decades. From the following text, which was contained in one of the documents debated at the Assembly, we can infer how far their thinking had already changed by then. The extract starts with a quotation from St John the Evangelist:

'If we say that we have not sinned, we make God out to be a liar, and his word is not in us' (John I, 1:10). And so, let us humbly acknowledge this and ask forgiveness because at that time we, as ministers, did not know how to bring about reconciliation within the bosom of our people, who were divided by a great fratricidal war.

(quoted in Díaz-Salazar and Giner 1993: 29; my translation)

In the new democracy, the Church has striven to preserve what it can of its moral authority, to encourage – with very modest success – allegiance to religious practice, and to preserve its hold on a significant part of the private sector in the educational system. With Archbishop Tarancón's retirement in 1982, the Church's new leadership has been less liberal and more concerned to uphold 'traditional' values, emphasizing the importance of the family and of Catholic teaching in the area of sexual morality. It has lost the battle against contraception, abortion and divorce, however, and educational reforms (LODE and LOGSE in particular) have ensured that there is increasing state monitoring of the private education offered in Catholic schools.

9.4 POPULAR MANIFESTATIONS OF FAITH? ANDALUSIAN *FIESTAS* AND *ROMERÍAS*

As suggested earlier, systems of faith and ideologies are appropriated by different societies in different ways. The particular character of the religious practice which predominates in any community thus reflects its preferences and prejudices. The potentialities of any particular religion – its symbols and systems of meanings, its metaphysics and its organizational structure – are used by members of that community in distinctive ways.

In Spain the dominant religious system is Catholicism, much of which is recognizably part of a wider pattern of Christian belief, including its monotheism, its sacred rituals, the way in which sacramental powers are vested in specially trained ministers, and the veneration of saints. We have already seen some of the ways in which the Spanish Church is culturally distinct, in terms of its close association with the state and the tradition of a strong determination to ensure dogmatic orthodoxy and the enforcement of a repressive moral code, and even, at times, its tolerance of, or complicity in, acts of violence. One other important feature of Catholicism in Spain is the high level of significance attaching to the ritual practice of devotion to particular images, statues and other representations of Jesus Christ, the Virgin Mary and a panoply of saints, male and female, associated with specific places or groups of which they are deemed to be patrons.

Pilgrimages and processions are the most striking manifestation of this popular culture, the culmination of this dimension of Spanish Catholicism. They are particularly abundant in Andalusia and, indeed, are often thought of as a defining element of Andalusian culture. But just as Spanish Catholicism generally cannot be understood without an appreciation of the wider context of European Christendom from which it emerged, this 'processional culture' needs to be seen as a regional variant on the general Spanish practice of public veneration of the deity and the saints. And just as the theology and liturgy of the Spanish Catholic Church is necessarily linked to the social and political activities of the Church as an organization, so these Andalusian 'religious' practices have to be appreciated as vehicles which carry meanings relating to the socio-economic and political context in which they are encountered – all of which is not to deny the fact that, for many younger Spaniards in particular, these festivities are little more than an excuse to *pasarlo bien*!

The principal organizational nexus on which the processions and pilgrimages are based is the *hermandad*, or brotherhood, and there is a vast array of such groups, some of which have existed for several centuries. Most are based in Andalusia itself, although some can be found beyond Andalusian frontiers, especially in places where large numbers of Andalusians have gone to work, such as Madrid or Barcelona. The membership of these brotherhoods, their organizational structures and the activities they undertake, constitute a rich and complex commentary on a whole range of issues relating to social exclusivity, group identity and internecine rivalry, as well as being an instrument for the profession of faith and a system of charitable support for the needy members of the community. The ostensible purposes of the brotherhoods are the latter: their declared aims are typically to articulate a community's veneration of Christ, Mary or a patron saint, thereby contributing to the development of their members' spirituality, to perform acts of charity towards the poor in the community and to provide mutual support in times of need for their own members. The high point of their activities – frequently the only activity they organize – is the principal annual procession (sometimes associated with a pilgrimage) in honour of the image of Christ or the Virgin, or the particular saint, who happens to be their patron. A large number of these processions take place during Holy Week (in which case the particular brotherhood concerned would be one devoted to the cult of a Christ figure or a specific Virgin), and the resultant atmosphere and spectacle can be extremely impressive. This is especially the case in large Andalusian cities such as Seville, Málaga or Granada, where the numbers of brotherhoods taking part in processions during this period can rise to over 50. Each brotherhood carries at least one *paso*, or float, bearing the image of Christ and/or of the Virgin to which it is devoted, and each solemn procession can last for several hours, at the end of which the images are returned to their respective churches, where they are kept until the following year.

The rivalry between the various brotherhoods to produce an impressive float and to process with solemnity and in reverential silence is intense. The large floats may be carried by as many as 80 *costaleros*, the select group – mainly men – who are allowed the privilege of bearing the float on these occasions. The act of bearing the float is both a privilege and an expression of penance: in theory at least, the men offer to undertake this task as reparation for their sins.

In smaller towns and villages, fewer brotherhoods process, although the devotional tradition associated with particular small towns can occasionally attain a status of major importance which transcends the limits of the district in which the town is located. This is the case, for instance, of the famous *Rocío* pilgrimage, which takes place in the town of Almonte (Huelva) every year around Whitsunday (the Christian feast of Pentecost, usually in May). *El Rocío* currently attracts the attention of many thousands of people, both pilgrims and tourists, and is given wide media coverage not just in Andalusia but also in Spain generally, and even abroad. On one level, this is a festival of devotion to Christ's mother, Mary, embodied in the image of the *Virgen del Rocío* (the Virgin of the Dew), a statue which is located a few kilometres outside the town of Almonte. The resonances of this *romería*, however, extend well beyond the confines of this little town and popular piety. For instance, individual participants in the rituals can be distinguished according to how significant or insignificant they are to core activities of the pilgrimage, and particularly to the Whit Monday procession of the *Virgen* which is the central act of the festival. Tourists and various onlookers are the most marginal, while *almonteños*, and especially members of the brotherhood which organizes the event, are of central importance. As Michael Dean Murphy (1994) demonstrates, although the pilgrimage may appear to 'bring together' people of diverse origins and varied social backgrounds, the fact is that social and class distinctions are inherent in the way in which the rituals are carried out: they are revealed in the position that one occupies in the procession, in the details of the traditional costume worn by the various participants, and even in the difference between being mounted on horseback or going on foot in the procession. Beyond this, *El Rocío* has attained a special significance in relation to various aspects of Almonteño and Andalusian identity. As Murphy (1994: 54) puts it: 'Almonteños ... resist vigorously any attempt to expropriate an event in which they are monumentally outnumbered by more socially powerful outsiders.'

Although other local pilgrimages have in fact suffered this fate, the Almonteños are determined to maintain the town's primacy in the huge event, and this despite the fact that most Almonteños only grudgingly accept that this is achieved through the control exercised by the elite group who make up the principal brotherhood within the town. All social classes are represented in the event, but the egalitarian spirit which this might suggest masks the fact that those who are familiar with the details of behaviour and dress can judge other people's class and background and the extent of their familiarity with the rituals. The traditional costumes worn by participants fall into two categories, one (comprising *traje corto* for men and the *traje de gitana* for women) being traditionally associated with the middle and upper classes, the other (the *camisa caqui*) deliberately chosen because of its resemblance to the traditional attire of the farm labourer. This provides two options, namely 'dressing up' like the *señoritos* or 'dressing down' like a *jornalero*, but in turn each of these alternatives has been extended in significance, mainly by outsiders from beyond Almonte, to suggest 'typical Andalusian costume' (in the case of the *traje corto*) and 'genuine Almonteño' (in the case of the *camisa caqui*). Choices about which costume to wear and exactly when to wear it, or deliberately to desist from wearing either, are complex judgements which carry social significance relating to the participants' sense of how closely they belong to the pilgrimage and to the various social groups taking part in it. While the Almonteño habitué is likely to have strong opinions on the appropriateness of the dress code which is suitable for any particular aspect of the festival, interpretations of what is 'authentic' will vary over time and from one individual to another, so that:

> [t]he Almonteño critique of what they regard as the misguided constructions of those who glean their pilgrimage for meaning . . . [confirms] that just as outsiders have yet to learn how to participate effectively in the procession, so have they failed to decode properly its inherently ambiguous symbols.
>
> (Murphy 1994: 58)

In *El Rocío*, as in the *Semana Santa* festivals, as well as in the myriad *fiestas* held to honour patron saints in towns and villages all over Andalusia, the task of organizing the main processional activity is the responsibility of a local 'brotherhood'. These *hermandades* (known also as *cofradías* if they happen to organize Holy Week processions) are nominally lay associations whose activities are sanctioned and regulated by the church authorities. Tensions and disputes between lodges of these brotherhoods and their local priests and bishops are quite common, however, and the brotherhoods have a high level of autonomy over their own activities, the more prominent of them wielding a great deal of influence in the communities where they are based. As outlined above, their explicit aims are devotional and charitable, but, as Isidoro Moreno Navarro (1985) has suggested, there is a latent purpose which they serve and which helps to explain the deep significance they have for so many Andalusians. The two principal aspects of this deeper rationale are, first, that they offer a means of *socialization*, a means for people to establish social relations within the context of a formal association, and secondly, they provide a means to achieve at least a symbolic *integration into a social group*. This latter purpose will take different forms, depending on the composition of the brotherhood: some groups are highly exclusive, with a membership based on social class or restricted to those practising a particular profession, while others allow membership to all those living in a particular district or town. This implies that, beyond any religious aim that the brotherhoods have, an important function they serve is to foster a feeling of group identity, so that membership of a particular lodge and participation in the annual procession reinforces a sense of belonging to a community that is identifiably one's own. Of course, even with the *hermandad*, some members are perceived as being more central to the group than others: thus, more affluent members are more inclined to be prominent and to sit on management committees, etc., while members from lower socio-economic backgrounds occupy more marginal positions.

One particular category of *hermandades*, which Moreno Navarro (1985: 69) labels the *semicomunales,* are those in which membership may be automatic, with each new generation affiliating by right to either their father's lodge or their mother's lodge. These brotherhoods divide communities vertically, in that all members of a town or village will belong to either one or other of the two 'semi-communal' associations existing in it. The rivalry between the two can be intense, as each strives to outdo the other in the range and impact of its charitable works and other activities, although the competition between them naturally reaches a peak at times of processions. If both brotherhoods are *cofradías*, they will hold two rival processions (in the one small town, village or district), with members making enormous efforts and spending large sums of money to ensure that their own floats are elaborately decorated and that their procession takes place with appropriate dignity and solemnity, while the competing procession, perhaps held just a few hours earlier or later on the same day, is completely ignored by them. Each of the two hostile brotherhoods will venerate their particular 'Christ' (*el Cristo de la Santa Cruz, el Cristo de la Buena Muerte*, etc.) and their particular 'Virgin' (*la Virgen de los Dolores, de las Angustias, de la Soledad*, etc.), but while one group will give prominence to their Christ-figure, the other will place more emphasis on their Virgin. One consequence of this is that, while the group with Christ as prominent will be more masculine in tone and expression, the 'Virgin-oriented' group will be more likely to emphasize feminine qualities.

The thrust of this activity, and of the activities of the *hermandades* generally, is to ensure that the association which you belong to is seen to be as important and as successful as possible. It evinces commitment to a principle of 'egalitarianism' based on the concept of *no ser menos*, of asserting one's right to be deemed as worthy of respect as anyone else. The impressive, and often very moving, results achieved in the emotionally charged processions and displays are the outcome of a huge investment by many people in terms of both time and resources. Families may make significant sacrifices in order to participate, and poor families often make proportionately larger sacrifices than others out of a perceived need both to contribute and to maintain a certain social standing by so doing.

9.5 'MI RELIGIÓN ES LUCHAR CON DIOS': FAITH, IN MIGUEL DE UNAMUNO

Both the politics of Church–State relations and the social significance of religious festivals are aspects of the public dimension of the issue of faith, in the Spanish context. Faith is essentially an intimate, personal issue, however, and one Spanish writer who wrote extensively about the personal dimension of religious conviction is Miguel de Unamuno (1864–1936). For Unamuno, faith sprang from mankind's desire to survive beyond the grave; it was something precious and uplifting, and the longing for eternal life was a natural aspiration, characteristic not of the weak but of the strong, something which reflected the conviction that life should be lived to the full and that, therefore, total annihilation of the self should be resisted. In Unamuno's case, however, this was combined with an intellectual scepticism, an appreciation of the fact that, on a rational level, it is impossible to be fully certain of the existence of either God or an afterlife.

Unamuno's chief statement of his philosophy is the book *Del sentimiento trágico de la vida* (1913), which consists of a series of essays reflecting on the conflict between reason and faith that preoccupied the author for most of his life. It starts from the position that man is not an abstraction whose core meaning can be apprehended merely through a process of philosophical analysis: a theoretical knowledge of the truth of the human condition is not enough, because those who analyse, as well as those analysed, are human beings, not abstract entities. Man – the 'hombre concreto, de carne y hueso' – is what should concern all philosophers who wish to understand the human condition. But an essential part of the human condition is the imperfect state of our knowledge: human reason tells us only that we cannot know for certain if God exists, while, on an emotional level, we still long for faith. What Unamuno wished for was the simple faith of his childhood which he thought of as the traditional faith of Spanish Christianity.

Unamuno lost his faith as a young man, but his visceral attachment to it and his concern with life after death were such that he could never reconcile himself to that loss. The mode of religious belief that he had left behind was essentially Catholic; the way of thinking about faith which he developed in his intellectual career was characteristic of Protestantism. The influences he betrays are Protestant also: in particular, his form of 'despairing Christianity' is closely related to that of the Danish philosopher Søren Kierkegaard. Both he and Kierkegaard were doubters: both realized that no philosophical system invented by human beings was capable of fully explaining human existence. Unamuno drew from this doubt the conclusion that rational philosophizing was insufficient to explain human beings to themselves; therefore rational philosophy, and along with it, positivistic thinking, were to be dismissed as inadequate. Ultimately, for Unamuno, reason leads to death, in that rational thinking leads to the conclusion that human beings are born in order to die:

[L]a razón, la razón humana, dentro de sus límites, no sólo no prueba racionalmente que el alma sea inmortal ... sino que prueba más bien ... que la conciencia individual no puede persistir después de la muerte del organismo corporal de que depende. Y esos límites, dentro de los cuales digo que la razón humana prueba esto, son los límites de la racionalidad, de lo que conocemos comprobadamente.

(Unamuno 1951, II: 823)

To transcend reason means to turn to irrationality, and entails inverting the kind of logical thinking which others believe is normal. Thus, for instance, he criticizes the thinking of Descartes, whose dictum *Cogito, ergo sum* ('I think, therefore I am') had laid the basis for rational philosophy since the eighteenth century. Unamuno suggests that all we can deduce from the fact of thinking is that we are thinking beings, not that we are living beings. Reversing the Cartesian expression, he says: 'La verdad es *sum, ergo cogito,* soy, luego pienso.' The most basic fact, therefore, is that we live, not that we think, and what we want, more than anything, is for that life to continue. This is the *hambre de inmortalidad* that Unamuno says everyone desires. Some satisfy that desire by turning to religious faith, but such an option is not open to everyone, only to those who are simple enough to be able to accept traditional faith.

This 'tragic sense of life', the awareness of the conflict between reason (which terminates in scepticism and relativism) and faith (which, despite the evidence, leads to belief in the supernatural), served as the basic underlying theme for the novel *San Manuel Bueno, mártir,* which Unamuno wrote in 1930. In it, the conflict is embodied principally in the character of Don Manuel, who is parish priest of the little town of Valverde de Lucerna. He is considered by his parishioners to be such a holy person that they think of him as a saint, but he has lost his faith. His way of coping with this loss of faith is to immerse himself in his life as a priest and to ensure that the people of Valverde continue to have the consolation of religion in their lives. The Marxian idea of religion as 'the opium of the people' is embraced by Don Manuel, who believes that people need the reassurance of eternity that religion gives them, since life is meaningless if it is confined to the span of a person's life on earth. As Unamuno put it in *Sentimiento,* 'Si del todo morimos todos, ¿para qué todo? ¿Para qué?' ('If we are all going to die completely, what is the point of it all?') (ibid.: 767). Although Unamuno himself was a professor at Salamanca University and not a priest, the novel is clearly autobiographical. Don Manuel embodies the philosophical struggle between faith and reason that Unamuno lived out in his own life. He is devoted to the people whom he considers his 'flock', and is kind and generous with all. He is regarded as a hero by all those around him, including the person through whose eyes the story is told, Angela Carballino. She is depicted as passive and submissive, loyal to her faith and selfless in the maternal interest she takes in Don Manuel's well-being. In this sense, she has many of the characteristics of traditional Spanish Catholics as Unamuno conceived of them. The faith that Angela seems to stand for is the simple faith of the loyal Spanish Catholic, which Unamuno would have liked to but could not maintain. And yet, Angela herself emerges at the end of the novel as someone who is now unsure about her own faith, since she has realized that Don Manuel himself has ceased to believe. Thus, Angela, more than the protagonist, represents the modern doubter, the agnostic who does not know what to believe.

Faith, for Unamuno, rests on a paradox: it is not enough simply to say that we cannot know about transcendental truths: to live a full life, we need, he says, to struggle perpetually to believe. Man's need for God is a natural one; without God and the supernatural, man's life is a pointless struggle. Hence, faith means the creation by man of that supernatural being which we so desperately crave. He defines faith as a process summarized in the phrase 'crear lo que no vemos' and maintains that 'to believe in God is, at least in the first instance, to want him to exist, to crave the existence of God' (ibid.: 897).

Unamuno's philosophical position was similar to that of the existentialists of the early twentieth century, in that it was concerned with the realities of man's daily life, with the actualities of everyday existence. It differed, however, from the thinking of atheistic existentialists – and was perhaps all the more representative of Spanish attitudes in this respect – in that it sought to maintain a Christian faith despite the odds.

FEATURE: MAIMONIDES – A GUIDE FOR THE PERPLEXED?

The expulsion of the Jews in 1492 cut short the influence of an important sector of the population of Spain, many of whom had been involved for generations in the professions and in skilled craftwork. For centuries, Spanish Jews had contributed to the social and cultural life of the Peninsula, in both Al-Andalus and Christian Spain. Hebrew was a significant language of scholarship in Toledo during the time of Alfonso X in the thirteenth century, as it had been in Seville and Córdoba in earlier centuries.

One of the most important Jewish philosophers to come out of Spain was Mosé Ibn Maimón (known as Maimonides), born in Córdoba in 1135. His family were obliged to leave Córdoba to escape religious persecution, and lived successively in a number of different towns in Al-Andalus, before fleeing to Fez in North Africa in 1160, moving eventually to Cairo where they were free to live openly as Jews. Maimonides studied medicine, and in 1171 he became the personal doctor of Alfadel, the vizier of Saladin, and was named head of the Jewish community in Egypt.

Maimonides had a vast knowledge of the Old Testament, of the writings of the ancient Greeks, and of Arab philosophy and science, which was the most advanced of his time. He wrote in both Hebrew and Arabic; in Hebrew he composed, for example, the *Mischné-Torah*, a compendium of Jewish law and religion, while in Arabic he wrote his best-known work, *The Guide of the Perplexed*, which was composed around 1190. The *Guide* is a scholarly explanation of Judaism, aimed at those who, like himself, wished to reconcile religious belief with a rational understanding of the world. He strove for a compromise between blind faith and scepticism, encouraging enquiry but always convinced that there were religious mysteries which were simply not amenable to rational explanation. His major contribution was to bring rational thinking, especially the philosophical approach of Aristotle, to bear on religious thinking, contrary to the approach which had been adopted by earlier Jewish writers who had claimed that there could be no reconciliation between the two. For Maimonides, reason and faith were best seen as complementary ways of seeking a common truth, and neither was inferior or superior to the other in terms of that purpose.

For Maimonides, man's ultimate aim in life was to know and love God, and this process could be assisted by achieving greater understanding through reflection and study. What was studied, however, should be appropriate for the individual concerned, and should correspond to the level of development of that person's intellect. We should not broach issues which are too complex or too advanced for us, and there will always be more challenging questions to be addressed as we proceed through the levels of understanding.

In the *Guide*, Maimonides offered his readers a variety of detailed proofs for the existence of God, proofs which were standard for the period in which he was writing. For example, the fact of motion proves the existence of God, since all motion on earth was understood to be caused by the movement of the planets and stars, the celestial spheres, which in turn could only be moved by a Prime Mover – who had to be God.

What his thinking lacked in originality, Maimonides made up for in his insistence on balance and compromise. If beauty is harmony, he argued, and virtue is the medium between two extremes, grace and virtue will both be found in a virtuous soul. Life should be lived in such a way that we take proper account of the physical, spiritual and intellectual dimensions of our existence. He advocated a moderate lifestyle, eating healthy foods, sleeping not more than eight hours a day, bathing at least once a week and avoiding the company of calumniators! Evil, he said, comes from people ignorantly believing that the universe exists only for themselves, so that when things do not go their way, they think that the whole world is a bad place; truth, on the other hand, comes most clearly to those who realize how large the universe is and how small a part of it we are.

READING: ROSA MONTERO, 'EL MÁS ACÁ'

Rosa Montero is a journalist who has written extensively about modern Spanish life and values. She is also a novelist and short-story writer, whose works include *Amado amo* (1988) and *El nido de los sueños* (1991) and the collection of stories *Amantes y enemigos* (1998). Some of her newspaper articles are collected in the volume *La vida desnuda* (1994), and it is from that collection that the following extract is taken. In it, Montero reflects on the notions of belief in God and religion, and asserts that these are not essential for us to be able to appreciate the mystery and beauty of life.

[N]o es necesario creer en ninguna divinidad ni en ninguna religión para saber oír el canto oscuro de la vida profunda. Esto es, de aquello que no tiene palabras, que carece de forma; que está fuera del tiempo y del espacio. De todo lo que no sabemos sobre el mundo y sobre nosotros mismos, que es muchísimo más que lo que conocemos. La existencia entera es un misterio, pero vivimos de espaldas a él: nuestra sociedad es demasiado simplista y positiva.

Antes, cuando las religiones formaban parte de la vida cotidiana y eran el marco obligado de la realidad, la gente convivía con el misterio: creían en milagros y demonios, en ángeles y apariciones, en rituales y magias. No echo de menos esa época de la humanidad: era inculta, carnicera y fanática. O más inculta, carnicera y fanática que la época actual, que aún lo es en exceso. Pero es cierto que hoy no existe lugar para el misterio (o sea: para el enigma radical de nuestras vidas) en esta sociedad de computadoras y ejecutivos. Como tampoco hay lugar para lo maravilloso. Y, sin embargo, hasta el niño más pequeño, sabe que lo maravilloso está por todas partes: maravillosa es una mosca, que vuela y zumba y se las arregla para buscarse la existencia en el calor de la tarde; maravillosas son nuestras manos, que se abren y se cierran tan obedientemente, que acarician, sienten, escriben a máquina, sujetan objetos. Maravilloso es mirar y ver, y pensar, y soñar. Y caminar sin caerse, y que haya nubes en el cielo, y recordar todas las mañanas, al despertar, tu propio nombre.

De modo que lo que la gente suele entender hoy por realidad no es más que un aspecto muy limitado de la vida real: es sólo lo tangible, lo mensurable, lo sujeto a cómputos e impuestos. Cuando se habla en literatura de realismo, por ejemplo, a menudo sólo se están refiriendo a una suerte de costumbrismo testimonial y chato. Pero la realidad es mucho más que eso. En la realidad están las cosas y su ausencia, la fantasía y el miedo, lo imaginario y lo que ni tan siquiera somos capaces de imaginar. Esa es una de las razones, me parece, por las que la gente va al cine, y al teatro, y lee libros: porque necesita dejar un lugar en su vida para lo misterioso, lo mágico, lo fantástico. No debe de ser casual que el auge de la novela empezara en el siglo XIX, coincidiendo con la decadencia social de las religiones.

Ahora bien: reconocer que vivimos en la punta de un iceberg y que a nuestros pies se abren esos abismos de incertidumbre, tierra incógnita de lo que es la vida y el universo, no implica la fe ciega (porque toda fe es, por definición, irracional) en ninguna religión concreta. A decir verdad, es difícil que la idea de un dios justiciero y antropomórfico te quepa en la cabeza: es demasiado simple, demasiado cándida, demasiado parecida a la necesidad que los humanos tenemos de una figura semejante. Lo digo para esos lectores tan amables que parecen empeñados en convertirme: una no está hambrienta de dogmas y divinidades, de paraísos y de infiernos. Es más: cuando me hablan los creyentes de glorias metafísicas, de milagros ultraterrenales y de los arcanos insondables del más allá, siempre me asombra su falta de percepción de la realidad. Porque el enigma reside en nuestras vidas cotidianas. El verdadero misterio está en el más acá.

(Montero 1994: 44–6)

FURTHER READING

Campo, Salustiano del, *Tendencias sociales en España (1960–1990)* (Bilbao, Fundación BBV, 1993).
Volume II offers useful information on Spanish attitudes to religious belief, values and ideologies.

Díaz-Salazar, Rafael and Giner, Salvador, *Religión y sociedad en España* (Barcelona, Planeta, 1993).

Chapter 1 ('Religión y política en España') is an excellent summary of Church–State relations in the twentieth century.

Gibson, I., *Fire in the Blood: the new Spain* (London, Faber/BBC Books, 1992).

Chapter 2 is a useful discussion of the historical relationships between Christians, Muslims and Jews in Spain.

Graham, H. and Labanyi, J. (eds), *Spanish Cultural Studies: an introduction* (Oxford, Oxford University Press, 1995).

Chapters 3, 9 and 15 set the Spanish Church in its social and cultural context.

10

Death: ... *acercándonos al hoyo ...*

10.1 DEATH, CULTURE AND SOCIETY

For Spaniards, as for most westerners, death is an uncomfortable – if not altogether 'taboo' – topic on a personal level, a cause of grief and an issue often addressed by recourse to the consolation of religious rites and, possibly, a belief in the survival of the soul. There are occasions, however, when it seems that the reality of death is deliberately not avoided by Spaniards, and at certain times and in certain contexts death is placed centre stage in the most spectacular way. Death is often said to be the invisible protagonist of the bullfight, and the graphic representations of the suffering and death of Jesus Christ in Holy Week can be interpreted as elements in a public drama depicting the ongoing struggle between life and death. Artistic and literary representations of death emanating from Spain over the centuries have become famous throughout the world. In relatively recent times, the destruction and horror of belligerent conflict are themes which have had a special resonance in the context of the Spanish Civil War.

One version of the Spanish stereotype sees Spaniards as people with two very distinct sides to their nature: one side is happy-go-lucky, devoted to the business of living life to the full; the other side is a dark and brooding personality, obsessed with violence and death. The sources of the stereotype can only be guessed at, and presumably they include historical factors such as the infamous Inquisition, the violence committed against the indigenous peoples of the New World or the various wars which Spain was involved in down the centuries, such as the European wars of Charles V and Philip II, the Peninsular War against Napoleon at the beginning of the nineteenth century, and, of course, the Civil War in the twentieth. The nature of Spain's Holy Week processions, with their images of bloody Christs and their reminders of mortality, and, inevitably, the bullfight, are also relevant if we wish to explain this apparent fascination with death. It is possible, on the basis of this evidence, to construct an image of the Spaniard as a person with an experience of death which is different from that found in other cultures, someone for whom death is a familiar and integral part of life and mortality a constant presence.

However, death is presumably no more or no less 'real' for Spaniards than it is for other people. In modern times, it might be argued that the opposite is the case: in the – outwardly, at least – optimistic and prosperous Spain of today, people seem more devoted than ever to living life to the full and enjoying the material benefits of a consumer society, and, in their private lives at least, ignoring death as much as people in any other advanced society do.

What Spain does, as every society does, is find ways of making death manifest in public, whether through literary and artistic creation or public spectacle of one sort or another – film, drama, festivals. In Spain, some of the more significant ways that people have found of confronting the reality of death are through the spectacle of the bullfight, the theme of 'honour' (especially in the plays of the Golden Age), and creative expression. It is these areas, and the experience of the Spanish Civil War, that we shall discuss in the main sections of this chapter.

10.2 BULLFIGHTING

By far the most spectacular way in which death is made manifest in public in Spain is through bullfighting. In the summer months every year, thousands of bullfights take place around the country, and tens of thousands of bulls are killed as part of these public spectacles. Newspapers report daily on the seasonal progress of the *lidia*, and television stations broadcast the more important fights to Spanish homes and internationally. It is clearly a major economic activity, but one which is sustained by the commitment of the professionals taking part and the support of the *aficionados* who attend.

Countering the zeal of the fans, there is strong criticism of bullfighting both within Spain and abroad. With mottoes such as 'La tortura no es ni arte ni cultura', opponents of bullfighting dismiss it as a cruel and barbarous activity, one which harks back to a violent past and which ought to be eliminated if Spain is to be a fully modern, humane and forward-looking society. Clearly, killing an animal for entertainment is a practice which raises a moral issue, and we are forced – at least on an individual level – to make up our own minds about whether we approve of it or not, and, at the very least, about whether we want to attend such a spectacle or not. Whatever decision we make, it is probably important to bear in mind that, while bullfighting itself is a specially Spanish activity (despite the fact that versions of it exist also in France, Mexico and some other countries), the various elements of the bullfight are present in one form or another in many other cultures. Thus, the act of killing animals itself is probably universal, even if the motive is usually the provision of food; the killing of animals for entertainment is certainly a feature of many societies (taking the form of hunting, cock fighting or coursing, for example); the

Figure 6: Ramón Masats, *Toro sentado, Pamplona,* 1960. This image of bullfighting is by one of Spain's most respected and influential photographers, Ramón Masats (b. 1931), who took a series of photographs which documented with freshness and originality the changes in outlook that were taking place in Spain during the 1950s and 1960s. (*Carta de España,* no. 536, February 1999.)

general act of publicly inflicting injury is a part of the 'sport' of boxing, as it is a matter of daily routine in certain countries where legal amputations or public executions of criminals take place – and in both these latter cases, of course, the violence is inflicted on human beings. Even the process of constructing a spectacle out of witnessing a human being confront imminent mortality – which happens when bullfighters expose themselves to the danger of death by goring – is a fundamental part of, for example, motor sports, which are thought of as thrilling and dangerous, but not as immoral. This is not an argument in favour of the *corrida*; but it suggests that, if we are to condemn bullfighting because it appears to legitimize violence or because it encourages young people towards violence, we must surely ask similar questions about a wide range of activities that take place in other cultures.

Needless to say, neither the supporters nor the detractors of bullfighting attempt to label it a 'sport'. For its supporters, it is quite different from the normal concept of sport and is implicitly superior to it; it is more likely to be thought of as an art-form or a dramatic spectacle. It has had ardent support along these lines from artists and intellectuals: Lorca thought it was the most cultured festival that existed anywhere in the world and described it as an 'auténtico drama religioso donde, de la misma manera que en la misa, se adora y se sacrifica a un Dios' (García Lorca 1965: 118); Menéndez Pelayo referred to it as 'this huge and terrible pantomine of fierce and tragic beauty' (quoted in Delgado Ruiz 1986: 8). Whatever it is, it is certainly more than mere entertainment, although, at a minimum, the crowd at a bullfight will want to be entertained also. But if it is about more than just experiencing the frisson of a close encounter with death, its possible meanings are multiple and ambiguous.

Delgado Ruiz (1986), for instance, defends the view propounded by Lorca (above) and argued also by others, including the anthropologist Pitt-Rivers (1984), that the bullfight is a sacrificial rite, a 'religious' event in which a key player with special abilities and qualifications (the torero/matador) sacrifices a valuable animal of superior quality and bloodline in a ceremonial act involving a large crowd or congregation, the latter having certain types of limited participation in the events taking place. Delgado Ruiz points out that *fiestas* involving the running or fighting of bulls not only have an ancient popular tradition in Spain, but have also been attacked and disapproved of for centuries. This disapproval has taken the form of bans and restrictions on such activities, since they were seen as conducive to disorder and subversive of civic and political authority. The custom of organizing bull festivals was eventually appropriated by the Spanish authorities in the eighteenth century, when the concept of bullfighting as the *fiesta nacional* was born. Since then, bullfighting as a cultural phenomenon has been pressed into service as a nation-forming element in Spain, i.e. as another cultural reality which serves to unite and centralize the country, in opposition to the linguistic and cultural diversity of the Peninsula, and to its centrifugal political tendencies. Although there are parts of Spain where bull festivals hardly take place at all, such as Galicia, and although there is one part of Spain which is more clearly identified with bullfighting than anywhere else (Andalusia), the way in which bullfighting is organized, with its administration centred in Madrid, and with the season of major bullfights taking place in a sweep around the capital over the summer months, contributes to its force as a unifying symbol for the country as a whole. As one of its opponents, Eugenio Noel, has put it, bullfighting 'is the sole link which unites the regions and transforms an Andalusian into a Basque, a Spaniard from Extremadura into one from Catalonia, a Catalonian into an Andalusian' (quoted in Douglass 1984: 255).

Bullfighting is also frequently taken as a metaphor for sexual activity and male–female courtship, or, at least, as an activity which has sexual connotations, as witnessed in any number of poems and literary texts, or in films such as Carlos Saura's *Carmen* (1983) or Pedro Almodóvar's *Matador*

(1985). Several different interpretations along these lines have been offered in serious commentaries on the bullfight. In one version (in Delgado Ruiz 1986, for instance), the matador is seen as a female – or at least androgynous – figure seducing and taming the wild, male bull who symbolizes virility and the chaotic disruption of accepted social norms.

For Pitt-Rivers (1984), the torero – and, by extension, the people he represents – is rewarded for his sacrifice of the bull by having his sexuality reinforced. The masculine strength of the bull, a paragon of virility, is transferred at the moment of his death to the one who slays him:

> He aquí el sentido del rito: a través de la representación de un intercambio de sexo entre el torero y el toro y la inmolación de este último, que transmite su capacidad de engendrar al vencedor, se efectúa un trasvase entre la Humanidad y la Naturaleza: los hombres sacrifican el toro y reciben a cambio la capacidad sexual de aquél. Emblema de la masculinidad bestial, que es la fuente de la virtud del macho entre los andaluces – manso quiere decir castrado, pero también falto de valor, domado, despreciable –, el toro da su vida para que los hombres puedan recuperar las fuerzas de la naturaleza que han perdido en su condición de civilizados.
>
> (Pitt-Rivers 1984: 39)

The version offered by Carrie Douglass (1984) sees the bullfighter as a male figure – whose tight trousers emphasize his masculinity – wooing and enticing the bull, who alternately is attracted to and flees from him in a simulated courtship ritual, only to be eventually 'penetrated' by the torero's sword in an orgasmic union resulting in death. The bull, on this reading, is not seen as having female sexuality, but is taken as a metaphor for the female dimension of the rituals of courtship. One of the features of the bull which reinforces this interpretation is that a great deal of importance is attached to the bull's being a 'virgin' on arrival at the ring, both literally a physical virgin and also a virgin to the cape, since thoroughbred bulls are not meant to have been used for bullfighting until they make their one and only entrance into the ring.

The material result, in either case, is the death of the bull, and there is also the constant danger of death for the bullfighter. Death is therefore at the heart of the ritual, and perhaps the most pointed feature of death in the bullring is the fact of its inevitability; as soon as the bull enters the ring, we know that within about twenty minutes he will be dead. Leaving aside the issue of possible cruelty to the animal, the fact of the inexorability of the bull's death means that what is being acted out – at least in good-quality *corridas* – is a tragedy. After all, this is not the slaughter of a meek and humble animal, but the emotionally charged death of a proud, strong, fierce *toro bravo*, with qualities which the audience admire and relish: courage, breeding, bravura, athleticism. The bull may be seen as a 'god' by some, but he is also a kind of 'monster', huge, threatening, uncontrolled, violent and extremely dangerous. Colour is also symbolic: the *black* bull represents brute animal nature, which is overcome by the brightly attired torero, who stands for the intelligent, 'civilized' aspect of human nature.

The threat that the bull is seen as representing for the people is emphasized in the many *encierros* that take place in Spain during the year. These are the festivals which entail having a bull – often young bulls or animals of inferior quality – run through the streets, preceded by the young men of the town. The monster racing through the streets is at once an emblem of the threat posed to the social order by wild and uncontrolled energy (especially masculine energy), and a symbol of the destruction (often illogical and arbitrary) caused by death itself among the living population. The outcome is inevitably that the bull ends up being coralled in the ring – which is often a makeshift structure erected for the period of the *fiesta* in the town's main square – and normally the routine terminates in either a mock-bullfight (a *tanteo*), in which the bull is not killed, or in a serious bullfight, in which he is.

10.3 DEATH AND HONOUR IN GOLDEN AGE DRAMA

Violent death is a standard element in the 'honour' plays of the Golden Age. These plays ultimately revolve around the willingness to defend one's honour by killing the person who has besmirched it.

The system of honour was traditionally understood as having both a social dimension – in terms of a person's social standing – and a moral dimension, in that honourable behaviour was meant to be synonymous with morally correct behaviour, in particular with correct sexual behaviour on the part of women. The image of an 'ideal' gentleman – with impeccable morals and perfect manners – lay at the heart of the notion of honour, this image itself harking back to the figure of the medieval knight: brave, gallant, generous to friends and family, an implacable foe to his enemies. By the sixteenth century, Spaniards were very clear both about who could be deemed to have *honor* and about how someone deemed honourable should behave, the assumption being that honour was associated, by right of birth, with the aristocracy, and that a true gentleman could not accept the slightest affront to his honour without exercising his right to defend that honour, if necessary by challenging the offender to a duel.

While nobles were obliged to protect and defend their honour, peasants had no such obligation. Honour was not expected of the peasantry, although, under certain circumstances, it was possible for them to attain it. Similarly, although in a sense a woman could lose her honour by 'losing her virtue', the social stigma was attached principally to the male who was deemed responsible for her – her husband, father, brother or fiancé – and it was he who was obliged to take vengeful action in response to the affront. The ultimate response in defence of one's honour, no matter how that honour was impugned, was of course to kill the offender.

The system clearly relates to imbalances in social power, both in the sense of the distinction which is assumed to exist between *labradores* and *nobles*, and in the sense of the submissive role in which it placed women. Remnants of the honour system persisted in Spanish legislation until the time of Franco: male and female adulterers were treated differently under the law, with males, for example, being punishable for adultery only if a public offence was caused. The honour code underpinned much of Spanish social behaviour – both legal and extra-legal – for centuries, and it is still perceived as a significant factor in people's treatment of each other in the Mediterranean region generally (Peristiany 1968). It is only in certain restricted contexts, however, that the 'point of honour' is now treated as a serious alternative to the regular legal system anywhere in the world: we can perceive its influence in the 'honour killings' of women who transgress strict sexual codes in a country such as Pakistan (where hundreds of women are brutally murdered by their own fathers or brothers every year), or in the criminal underworld of the Italian Mafia, for example, where legal authority is ignored.

Where honour themes receive the most extensive literary treatment is in the plays of the Spanish Golden Age, written mainly during the latter half of the sixteenth century and the first half of the seventeenth. Perhaps the clearest depiction of the 'honourable gentleman' in Golden Age drama is the figure of Don Alonso, the protagonist of the play *El caballero de Olmedo* by Lope de Vega (1562–1635). Here we have an ideal portrait of the gallant hero: Don Alonso is brave, honest, noble, loyal to his king and a paragon of Christian virtue. He falls madly in love, however, with the beautiful Doña Inés, who – unfortunately for both of them – is promised by her father in marriage to another nobleman, Don Rodrigo. The latter is as evil as Don Alonso is good, and even after Alonso saves his life (by rescuing him from an attack by a bull), Rodrigo still resolves to kill Alonso out of his feelings of jealousy over Inés. When Alonso is returning from Medina (where Inés lives) to Olmedo, Rodrigo attacks and kills him, justifying his actions to himself by claiming that he has been jilted by Inés, whose affection for Alonso is clear. In terms of the honour code, Alonso's death is 'justified' on the grounds that Inés' father has broken his promise to allow Rodrigo to marry her, and by the fact that Alonso was willing to bend the rules of social behaviour in order to see Inés and court her: although his love for Inés is pure and the two lovers were chaste in their relationship, Alonso had enlisted the aid of a Celestina-like figure, the half-witch, half-procuress Fabia, in order to convince Inés of his love and get her to respond to him, and he had also transgressed by meeting Inés at night and without her father's permission. The underlying motivation for the killing, of course, is not honour at all: Rodrigo is merely invoking damaged honour to justify a crime which is the result of his envy and jealousy.

As is so often the case, issues of honour are here intermingled with the themes of love and jealousy, and the mix heightens dramatic tension and intensifies the emotional appeal of the characters, who must seek fulfilment for their feelings of love within the strict bounds of prescribed social behaviour. The result is a fast-paced tragicomedy, which ends with the impending execution of the murderer, Rodrigo, and his henchman, Fernando. Such an outcome reinforces the conventional values of the time, while providing a colourful and convincing account of a traditional story.

Although Lope was far from being a revolutionary, and rarely forced any depth of thought from the audience, one of his best-known plays takes a relatively unconventional angle on the theme of honour, in that it hinges on the notion that honour is something which is of concern not just to nobles but also to the peasantry. *Fuente Ovejuna* is a play in which a malevolent aristocrat commits an offence not against one individual, but against the entire community of the town which gives the play its title. The individual in question is the *Comendador*, Fernán Gómez, Grand Commander of the Order of Calatrava, a historical character who, in 1476, had been attacked and killed by his own feudal vassals because of his tyrannical behaviour towards them. This knight takes an excessive interest in the local peasant women, acting as if he had a right to force his attentions on any of them. The prime object of his lust is Laurencia, the daughter of Esteban, whom we witness gradually responding to the amorous overtures of another of the peasants, Frondoso, and eventually marrying him. The Commander, however, arrests Frondoso and abducts Laurencia, but when she escapes from his clutches, she harangues the gathered townsfolk, scorning them for their lack of valour and urging them to react to the Commander's behaviour. Despite the general willingness amongst them to recognize the impropriety of taking violent action against a nobleman – who, in their estimation, and in that of the people of Lope's time, had a natural responsibility to protect his vassals and a concomitant right to their respect – the villagers rise against the Commander and kill him. When the king hears of the events, his initial response is to condemn the killing; however, the townsfolk refuse to name any individuals who may have carried out the actions. As the judge who questions them reports:

> . . . everyone,
> with fearless fortitude,
> when I demanded who had done the deed,
> replied with one accord: 'Fuente Ovejuna'.

(Lope de Vega 1989: 209)

The king, while insisting that a crime has been committed, allows the people to go unpunished.

Here, the honour theme applies to the right that the townsfolk have to defend themselves against Fernán Gómez's outrages generally, and the specific affront to the virtue of the ravished peasant women. The outcome is the death of a character seen as villainous in the extreme, although his villainy is linked not just to the people's response to his immoral behaviour, but also to the need for the peasant people to seek the approval and protection of the king.

Other important 'honour plays' of the Golden Age include Tirso de Molina's *El burlador de Sevilla* (see 5.3.4) and the three plays called *El médico de su honra*, *El pintor de su deshonra* and *A secreto agravio, secreta venganza* by Pedro Calderón de la Barca (1600–81).

10.4 *UN MILLÓN DE MUERTOS*: THE SPANISH CIVIL WAR

Death on a vast scale is characteristic of human history since the early twentieth century, and the events of two world wars in particular have impressed upon people's minds the sheer horror and waste attendant on belligerence between nations. But typical also of the twentieth century was the 'civil war' or conflict within a nation, and no such conflict was as ruthlessly destructive, or had so much international resonance, as the Spanish Civil War.

The war began, in July 1936, when a group of generals rebelled against the Spanish government, a government which had been elected by popular vote in February of that year. The mayhem that resulted brought violent death to hundreds of thousands of Spaniards over the years that followed. Although the war ended officially on 1 April 1939, executions and reprisals continued for years after that: some estimates place the total number of dead at up to 1 million.

The war progressed through three main phases. During the first phase, rebel troops (*los nacionales*, the so-called 'Nationalist' side of the conflict) advanced towards Madrid, from the south (under General Franco) and from the north (under General Mola), quickly dominating most of Andalusia and occupying the mountains in the southern part of the northern meseta. With the assistance of the International Brigades, Madrid held out against the rebels and a front was established there in October. The Brigades consisted of individuals who had defied their own governments to come to Spain from France, Germany, the USA, Britain, Ireland and other countries, to assist in the defence of the Republic. The French and British governments, sensitive to the high level of tension in Europe at the time, and wishing to avoid a generalized conflict in the continent, had committed themselves to not assisting either side in the war, with the object of confining the conflict to the Peninsula. The result of this was to weaken the position of the legitimate Republican government of Spain, which had official assistance only from the Soviet Union. Germany and Italy supplied arms and expertise to the Nationalist side, and in November 1936, these countries recognized the Nationalist government. General Franco had taken over sole command of the Nationalist forces in October.

In the second phase of the war, major battles took place as each side tried to gain the upper hand, although a greater unity of command on the Nationalist side meant that their efforts were more successful. The battle of Guadalajara was the Nationalists' attempt to completely surround Madrid by gaining control of the area to the east of the capital. When this failed, they concentrated instead on gaining territory along the north coast, taking Vizcaya in June 1937. The Republican government, having relocated from Madrid to Valencia, launched the battle of Brunete with the aim of striking at the vanguard of their enemies' attack on Madrid; this too was a costly failure. By 21 October 1937, all of the north was in the hands of the Nationalists, which meant that they now had access to the coal mines, iron deposits and other resources in that area.

In the third phase, an initial victory by the Republican forces at Teruel was quickly reversed as the Nationalists retook the town. In April 1938, the Nationalists managed to cut Catalonia off from the rest of the Republic. An offensive by Republican forces on the Ebro line aimed at cutting Nationalist forces in two also failed; the Republicans found themselves exposed to a devastating battle which lasted three months and which virtually destroyed their army: some 90 000 men were lost.

The Nationalists launched an offensive in the east in December 1938, and by the end of January 1939, General Yagüe was able to enter Barcelona – where the Republican government was now based – in triumph: the members of the government fled across the border to France. Although there were still large areas of the country, from the centre down towards the south-east, in Republican hands, morale among their troops was low, their command structures were fragmented and they had little armed strength. German and Italian assistance meant that the Nationalist side had superior forces, especially in terms of aviation. The final collapse came at the end of March 1939 as Madrid was occupied, followed by the capitulation of the remaining parts of Spain. Franco signed his last war dispatch on 1 April 1939.

The Spanish Civil War was about many things: in the period 1931–34, the Republican government had attempted to change Spain radically, introducing a constitution which downgraded the status of the Catholic Church, conceding autonomy to Catalonia and the Basque Country, and undertaking land reform and an educational and cultural revolution. In February 1936, another left-oriented government had come to power; but, with law and order breaking down, attacks on churches and clergy increasing and economic pressure building up, the military – supported by the Church, the landowners, monarchists and Falangists – took matters into their own hands and decided to seize power. Three years of fighting ensued, at the end of which the country was virtually destroyed: ruined shells of houses, bombed roads and bridges, a collapsed infrastructure, the grief of those who had lost family members and the exile of many thousands of Republican sympathizers, remained.

Atrocities had been committed on both sides, with summary executions and massacres of civilians occurring in both the Nationalist and Republican camps, each side outdoing the other in its mistreatment of civilians. As towns and villages were captured, those suspected of having sided with the enemy would be incarcerated or executed. The Nationalist forces were particularly noted for their ruthlessness; as General Franco's army advanced from the south in the summer of 1936, they wreaked a rapid revenge on villagers and townspeople who were identified, correctly or incorrectly, as Republican sympathizers. Collins and Lapierre (1968), for example, give an account of how, in the town of Palma del Río (Córdoba), the people seized some prize fighting bulls belonging to the local landowner, Don Félix Moreno, at the start of the war. The bulls were slaughtered and their meat was eaten by the villagers, but, within weeks, Don Félix was to exact his revenge. The Nationalist army took the town as its defenders fled, leaving 4000 of its 12 000 inhabitants at the mercy of the advancing troops and their supporters. Don Félix was one of the landowners who had the opportunity to select men to be executed, which he did; those unfortunate enough to be picked out for death were herded to a wall and machine-gunned in groups of 25. One of those selected to die lived to tell the tale. He was given a reprieve because he was a distant relation of Don Félix's; his name was José Sánchez, and the authors depict the scene through his eyes:

> Don Félix stepped back from the line of men against the wall, some shocked to silence, some sobbing, some shouting to him for forgiveness. He turned to the soldiers crouched behind their machine gun.
>
> ¡*Fuego*! he ordered.
>
> The clanging metallic roar of the machine gun beat against Sánchez's ears. His head shook with its reverberations. He watched the gun pick its way along the wall from left to right. It moved very slowly, chest-high, its bullets tearing puffs of white mortar from the wall exposed between its victims. He saw them fall, these men whose sweat and sorrow he had so often shared, their bodies twitching in disjointed movements as the machine gun's cartridges tore them apart. Then it was over. The echo of the machine gun hung for an instant on the still, stifling air of midday. From the heap of men at the base of the wall a new sound rose to join it, the pathetic groans of the dying. Some of their bodies jerked their way toward death with a few last convulsive fits of energy. Sánchez saw an officer kick his way through that pile of bodies, firing a rapid *coup de grâce* into each form that moved or from which rose a last dying protest.
>
> (Collins and Lapierre 1968: 83–4)

The Civil War was to change everything in Spain for decades to come. There was no process of healing or forgiveness at the end of the war, no reconciliation between victors and vanquished. The bitterness continued, and the so-called 'Reds' on the Republican side were rooted out and subjected to imprisonment, and in some cases executed as traitors by those in power. People whose sympathies were with the Republic were 'purged' from the public service and left to starve, or manage as best they could, in the harsh economic conditions of the 1940s and 1950s.

It took more than 20 years for Spanish economic and agricultural output to return to pre-war levels. Those who could claim allegiance to Franco and the National Movement prospered, while the 'enemy within' was suppressed by the might of the army and the Civil Guard. Those liberal intellectuals who had flourished in the pre-war era to such an extent that the 1930s were referred to as the 'Second Golden Age' went into exile or were imprisoned and censored.

Eventually economic recovery began to happen in the 1960s, but the shadow of the war continued to loom over Spain even then. The playwright Antonio Buero Vallejo (1916–2000), who had spent several years in jail for his left-wing views, managed to convey the continued sense of significance of the war in his play *El tragaluz* (1967). In it, he presents a Spanish family, living in Madrid, who were typical of the many families who had lived for decades with the memory of the awful events of the war. The Father in *El tragaluz* is a *cesante*, removed from his civil service post in the wake of the war, and now suffering from dementia. The cause of his dementia is the trauma he suffered during the war when his baby daughter died of starvation brought about by the loss of all their provisions when their own son, Vicente, ran off with the bag containing their food. Much of the action of the play is motivated by the guilt felt by Vicente, now a grown man proving himself successful in business in 1960s Spain, who returns ever more frequently to the family home. The family has attempted to repress the memory of Vicente's betrayal, not acknowledging that this was what caused the Father's mental illness, although the truth has remained in the air of the family flat in Madrid. Mario, Vicente's brother, despises him for what he did, but also for his complete dedication to material success and for his willingness to sacrifice any moral principle in order to achieve and sustain it.

The themes of exploitation and materialism are interwoven with a concern about the human condition and the issue of individual identity. The Father, in his strangely lucid madness, focuses on unknown people whose pictures he cuts out of magazines and postcards, as he asks: '¿Quién es ese?' His God-like mission is to 'save' as many of the people in old photographs as possible. The answer to his question is given as 'Ese eres tú': human beings share an identity, so that hurting someone else is tantamount to hurting oneself. Buero seems to suggest that the 'otherness' which we think we perceive in other people – the 'difference' which we see between ourselves and them – is what allows us to dehumanize them, to treat them as less valuable than ourselves, to treat them violently, to kill them. At the end of the play, the Father kills Vicente, his own son, expiating the guilt which the son felt and which the Father perceived, even though the play does not suggest that Vicente is simply to be condemned for his actions. 'Toda acción es impura', Vicente claims in the play: no one can lead a completely blameless life, but the violence which is part of our human nature, this play suggests, needs to be contained, and needs to be counterbalanced by generosity and acts of reconciliation. Buero, in the late 1960s, was presenting a Spanish audience, typically composed of members of Franco's successful middle classes, with a reminder of the horror of the war which had taken place

30 years earlier, and with a statement of the need for reconciliation between the victors and the vanquished. There is an indirectness about Buero's criticism of the Spain of his time, which comes about because of the censorship practised during the dictatorship, and which he, and others of an independent frame of mind, suffered. Despite the restrictions on his writings, however, and despite his imprisonment, Buero remained in Spain all his life, and produced a steady output of excellent plays from the late 1940s onwards. Many other writers – especially those of an older generation than Buero's, people such as the poet Rafael Alberti (1901–99) or the novelist Ramón J. Sender (1901–82) – had already been committed to left-wing causes or were identified as Republican sympathizers when the Civil War broke out, and therefore had had to flee the country.

The Spanish war was both a national and an international conflict. It was fought on Spanish soil but, as we have seen, people came from many countries to participate, mainly in defence of the Republic. The International Brigades were made up of idealistic young men who believed that Spain was the theatre for a battle between totalitarianism – which was gaining strength in Germany and Italy, and which was influential among many sectors of the populations of other countries – and democracy. They risked their lives, and many made the ultimate sacrifice, in defence of the principles of freedom and equality. On their return, they often continued to suffer the opprobrium of their compatriots, being branded 'left-wing sympathizers' and 'communists' and treated with suspicion in the 1940s and 1950s, especially those who returned to the USA.

There were idealists on the Right, also: those Spaniards who believed in Catholicism and faithfulness to an ideal of Spanish nationalism, and people from outside Spain who saw the Spanish Republic as a threat to European democracy and as an extension of the influence of 'godless' Soviet-style Communism. It would have been difficult to know, in 1936, that the victory of the Right in the Spanish war would lead to four decades of oppressive dictatorship in Spain and that such a victory would be the prelude to the savagery imposed on the world by Nazi totalitarianism in World War II.

The reverberations of the war on Spaniards were to last for a long time. It was probably the most traumatic event in the history of Spanish society, and it generated a sense of fear and oppression which coloured Spanish life for most of the twentieth century. Clifford Geertz suggests that such events cause 'a failure of nerve, a constriction of the sense of possibility' in a society, along with

the sort of muffled panic we associate with psychic trauma more generally: obsession with signs, most of them illusory, that 'it is about to happen again'; perfection of elaborate precautions, most of them symbolic, to see that it doesn't; and irremovable conviction, most of it visceral, that it is going to anyway – all resting, perhaps, on the half-recognized desire that it do so and to get it over with.

(Geertz 1993: 324)

Republican Spain experienced a revolution during the 1930s which ended in catastrophic failure; when the second major change in twentieth-century Spain – the transition to democracy – was starting to happen in the 1970s, there was a real fear that the process could degenerate into violence, that old wounds could open and that the result could be another traumatic orgy of violence. Perhaps the very memory of the Civil War helped to ensure that such violence was not the outcome.

10.5 LITERARY PERSPECTIVES ON HUMAN MORTALITY

The one absolute certainty about life is death. Even if we believe in an afterlife, we know that our own physical mortality is inevitable. Death is, therefore, not just one basic dimension of life but the most fundamental fact about life, a fact which overrides all others. How we deal with it varies from one person to another and from one culture to another, but, even if we try, we cannot escape the inexorability of our own end. The huge fascination that death exercises is reflected in the extent to which it has been addressed in literature and art through the ages, in Spain as elsewhere. Here we look first at two of the best-known writers on death, and then at some other places where the issue has been addressed in Spanish literature.

10.5.1 Manrique and Lorca: two versions of death

Two classic interpretations of death are those offered by the writers Jorge Manrique and Federico García Lorca. Separated by over 400 years, they offer two distinct visions of the relationship man holds with death, one steeped in the Christian vision of his time, on the cusp between the medieval world and the Renaissance, the other an avant-garde artist of the early twentieth century, seeking to articulate a sense of the power of mythic forces operating within, and at times against, man, in his struggle to come to terms with his own mortality. Both are consummate poets, revelling in the power of language, and find a voice with which to express subtleties of feeling in an accessible idiom, producing work with which the reader can appreciate the delights of life and explore the ambiguities of human attitudes to death.

Jorge Manrique (1440?–79) was a Castilian nobleman from a family which was heavily involved in the various political and military conflicts of its time. Both Jorge himself and his father, Rodrigo, were 'warrior-poets' and both died of injuries received in battle. It was in the wake of his father's death that Jorge composed the poem for which he is famous and which is generally known now as the *Coplas por la muerte de su padre*.

Looked at from the perspective of the twenty-first century, the poem surprises us by the didactic tone which the poet adopts in many of the verses, and by the apparent lack of personal anguish experienced by the son who has just lost his father. We sense that we are attending a funeral sermon rather than listening to a personal outpouring of grief, and we realize that this is a public poem, written about the death of a significant public figure of his time, and aimed at conveying the importance of remembering our own mortality:

> Recuerde el alma dormida,
> avive el seso y despierte,
>   contemplando
> como se pasa la vida,
> como se viene la muerte
>   tan callando;

Our modern sensibilities may lead us to expect a more intimate, more private response to the death of a close relative. Manrique, however, clearly sees this death as more than just the death of a beloved individual; he sees it also as an instance of the end which awaits us all and as the termination of an exemplary life. Manrique draws out the lessons to be learned: that death can come and sweep us away at any time; that rich and poor are equal before death; that time will cause power and beauty to decay and disappear; that we should not put our trust in the ephemeral things of this world, and that the good Christian should accept death with dignity and in good grace.

Manrique's main point is a religious one: the world in itself is neither a good nor a bad place; what matters for the good Christian is the attitude one adopts towards it, because an obsessive concern with material things is ultimately futile:

> Este mundo bueno fue
> si bien usásemos dél
>   como debemos,
> porque, segund nuestra fe,
> es para ganar aquél
>   que atendemos.

Moreover, all are equal before death the conqueror. The course of our lives flows like a river, and no matter whether we are powerful rivers or quiet streams, our fate is to flow into the sea which is death:

> Nuestras vidas son los ríos
> que van a dar en la mar
>   que es el morir:
> allí van los señoríos
> derechos a se acabar
>   y consumir;
> allí los ríos caudales,
> allí, los otros medianos,
>   y más chicos;

allegados son iguales,
los que viven por sus manos
    y los ricos.

Manrique urges us not to be deceived by time; everything passes away, and we must realize that 'lo presente . . . en un punto se es ido y acabado'. Past heroes have fallen to the ravages of time: Manrique presents a long list of kings, princes and knights, all of whom were famous in their day for their achievements and who nevertheless have now gone 'the way of all flesh'. Death is personified as an all-powerful enemy manifestly able to dispose of such people at will, and the poet rhetorically addresses Death, asking where it has sequestered away these illustrious individuals:

Tantos duques excelentes,
tantos marqueses y condes,
    y varones
como vimos tan potentes,
di, Muerte, ¿do los escondes
    y traspones?

He conjures up a powerful image of a great medieval army with flags and pennants flying:

Las huestes innumerables,
los pendones y estandartes
    y banderas . . .

But the arrow of death can pass cleanly through any army, defeating and destroying seemingly at will:

Que si tú vienes airada
todo lo pasas de claro
    con tu flecha.

The hero of the poem, however, is the knight and warrior on whose death this elegy was written, Don Rodrigo Manrique, and he is depicted as a great and virtuous man, a famous hero who was loyal to his friends and kind to his subordinates. Although he did not leave behind great wealth, we are told, he undertook battles against the Moors, 'ganando sus fortalezas / y sus villas', and thereby earned a justified reward of lands and vassals.

But death comes to call at Rodrigo's door and, in the poem, we witness the visitation of Death, who enters into a dialogue with Rodrigo to remind him of the ephemeral nature of human life and of the worthlessness of the things of this world and to urge him to summon his strength and courage to confront this one last challenge. It is Death who then articulates the life-philosophy of the medieval nobleman, setting out the three types of life that can be experienced, which are (1) the mundane life lived out by those obscure souls who are forgotten after their death; (2) the life of fame which affords a kind of survival beyond the grave, a *vida de honor*, which is superior to ordinary temporal life since it is longer lasting, although it is still not eternal; and (3) the everlasting life, gained in one of two ways – either by prayers and lamenting (if you are a monk), or by undertaking battles against the infidel – 'trabajos y afliciones / contra moros' – (if you are a noble warrior).

Rodrigo answers death's call by accepting in a businesslike manner the imminence of his own death, and by assuring Death that his will is in harmony with the divine will, since 'querer ombre bivir / cuando Dios quiere que muera / es locura'.

Death in the *Coplas* is a moral issue intimately linked to a strong religious conviction. It has the medieval flavour of death as a phenomenon with a public, communal dimension: we can learn a useful lesson from an individual death, and we can rely on a shared faith in an afterlife to help us conquer the fear of our own death. There is no dramatic defiance of death here, and there is no railing against the unfortunate loss. We see a warrior who is prepared to welcome his inevitable end, which in turn heralds the beginning of a life of fame and of the everlasting life he will surely achieve in Heaven; Rodrigo is prepared to slip quietly into death, as the rivers in the poet's earlier metaphor merge silently with the sea.

While Jorge Manrique's own death – the result of a wound received in battle – was fitting for a man who devoted much of his life to military activity, the early death of Federico García Lorca was a tragedy which shocked the literary world of his time and which continues to fascinate readers of his work today. It was also a crime: Lorca was murdered by Nationalist forces in Granada in August 1936, shortly after the Civil War broke out. He had been an active intellectual during the period of the Republic and one of the most celebrated Spanish writers of his day. Although he held no strong political convictions, he was identified with left-wing politics, having been a member of the touring theatrical group *La Barraca*, which had brought cultural activities to the small towns of Spain during the Republican period. Exactly why he was singled out to be killed is not clear, but he was clearly perceived to be a Republican sympathizer, obviously an intellectual (and, as such, already a 'degenerate' in the eyes of many) and, to add to these 'crimes', he was a known homosexual. Thus, despite the fact that he had influential friends on the Nationalist side, he was taken away and brutally murdered by the side of the road on the outskirts of Granada.

In Lorca's poetry and plays, death is a frequent presence. His three major dramatic works from the 1930s exemplify this. In the play *Bodas de sangre*, two rivals are in love with the same girl (simply called 'La Novia'), and on the day she is to marry one of them (just called 'El Novio' in the play), the other (Leonardo), to whom she is irresistibly attracted, carries her off. The play ends with a confrontation between the two rivals, who end up killing each other in a knife-fight, itself prefigured by various references to knives and daggers during the play. In *Yerma*, set against a similarly ill-defined but very Andalusian rural background, the eponymous heroine cannot endure not being able to bear children, and, consumed by frustrated passions, she eventually kills her own husband. Frustration is the theme of *La casa de Bernarda Alba* also. Bernarda, the oppressive matriarch who imposes total isolation on her five daughters as a means of mourning her dead husband, is a symbolic figure, representing the forces of narrow conventionalism, suppressing vital instincts out of a concern with *el qué dirán*. Two of the daughters love the same man, Pepe: the eldest, Angustias, to whom he is betrothed, and the young and beautiful Adela. Pepe, in turn, is attracted to Adela, but Bernarda discovers their relationship, and, out of a sense of shame, kills him. On discovering that Pepe is dead, Adela cannot control her anguish and kills herself.

These plays connect with vital forces. References to the earth, to the moon, to the vigorous growth of plants, to water, to the desolation of a barren countryside and to the stiflingly oppressive heat of an Andalusian summer, are all suggestive of powerful energies at work in the world and in human beings. Lorca is renowned for being able to conjoin the mythical with the local. The plays have the feel of the small rural communities of the south of Spain and are clearly set in that context, but the dramas that unfold are stories of human conflicts which seem to relate to the basic instincts and core passions of people anywhere.

In his collection of poems *Romancero Gitano*, published in 1927, Lorca presents a series of ballads set in a similar world, a world which seems to be under the sway of death. The *romances* in this collection tell stories of love, of passion, of deceit and loss, in a language which displays Lorca's consummate verbal skill, while still being relatively direct, and employing ancient metrical forms which are engagingly simple. Despite this apparent simplicity, Lorca's verbal artistry can be highly original, and the surrealistic conjunctions of images which he achieves can startle the reader even as they resonate with suggestions of ominous forces at work in the world. There are frequent references to named places in and around Granada, but these are mythologized: as well as actual places, they are the locus for universal human conflicts, and they become places where 'primitive' passion meets social control and order.

Examined analytically, outside the context of the work itself, the details in the poems can easily be ridiculed, but, when set within the world of the *Romancero*, the powerful symbolism combines with the masterful language to offer us a moving poetic experience. For example, in 'Romance sonámbulo', Lorca evokes a dead gypsy girl who has committed suicide, presumably out of despair at the thought that her gypsy lover has been taken and killed by the Civil Guard. She has drowned in an *aljibe*, a stone water-fountain, typical of the old Moorish area of Granada, and the moon lights up the water so that her image can be seen on its surface:

> Sobre el rostro del aljibe
> se mecía la gitana.
> Verde carne, pelo verde,
> con ojos de fría plata.
> Un carámbano de luna
> la sostiene sobre el agua.

But her lover has not been killed, only wounded. He is a smuggler and has been injured by the Civil Guards who have pursued him from Córdoba. He arrives at the girl's house, knowing that he is going to die from his injuries. He is met by the girl's father and asks to be taken to her. The father seems to know that his daughter is dead, but is slow to come out with the devastating truth. The 'dark roses' in his reply to the smuggler probably stand for the young man's blood which is staining both his white shirt and the sash around his waist:

> —Trescientas rosas morenas
> lleva tu pechera blanca.
> Tu sangre rezuma y huele
> alrededor de tu faja.
> Pero yo ya no soy yo,
> ni mi casa es ya mi casa.

His world is no longer what it was, and it is as if powerful primeval forces were at work, subverting the gypsies' security and demolishing an ancient way of life. An eerie green light, at once suggestive of both the vitality of nature and the naturalness of mortality, hangs over the universe inhabited by these characters:

> Verde que te quiero verde.
> Verde viento. Verdes ramas.
> El barco sobre la mar.
> Y el caballo en la montaña.

Perhaps the greatest of Lorca's poems on the theme of death, however, is a long poem written some years after the publication of the *Romancero*, a lament on the death of one of Lorca's friends, a bullfighter who was killed in the ring. The *Llanto por Ignacio Sánchez Mejías* was composed in the autumn of 1934, after the death of Sánchez Mejías, who was gored in Manzanares bullring on 11 August and died of his injuries two days later. Sánchez Mejías was a well-educated man who had been heavily involved in the artistic and cultural life of his time; for example, he financed a major homage to the poet Góngora in December 1927 and brought a number of surrealist plays to the stage in 1928.

The poem is an elegy in four sections: 1. La cogida y la muerte; 2. La sangre derramada; 3. Cuerpo presente; 4. Alma ausente. In different parts of the poem, Lorca expresses a profound sadness, achieves brilliant avant-garde verbal effects, praises his dead friend, mourns his loss and sets himself the challenge of never letting the bullfighter's memory die. There are echoes of Manrique's *Coplas* in his listing of the hero's virtues and in the ambition to overcome death through the achievement of fame. There is a mythologizing element in the references to bulls and a universalizing dimension in that this death is seen as an instance of the mortality which awaits us all. The tone varies from one section of the poem to another. In the first section ('La cogida y la muerte'), we hear the declamatory, ominous repetition of the line 'A las cinco de la tarde', the hour when the bullfight traditionally begins:

> A las cinco de la tarde,
> Eran las cinco en punto de la tarde.
> Un niño trajo la blanca sábana
> *a las cinco de la tarde.*
> Una espuerta de cal ya prevenida
> *a las cinco de la tarde.*
> Lo demás era muerte y sólo muerte
> *a las cinco de la tarde.*

By the end of the poem, however, Lorca is addressing his dead friend in an intimate voice:

> El otoño vendrá con caracolas,
> uva de niebla y montes agrupados,
> pero nadie querrá mirar tus ojos
> porque te has muerto para siempre.
>
> Porque te has muerto para siempre,
> como todos los muertos de la Tierra,
> como todos los muertos que se olvidan
> en un montón de perros apagados.
>
> No te conoce nadie. No. Pero yo te canto.
> Yo canto para luego tu perfil y tu gracia ...

The poem speaks to us of the inevitability of death and of the defeat of human endeavour. It focuses on the courage and vitality of the man who faces death in the bullring. But the drama of Sánchez Mejías' death is a paradigm for the common challenge faced by all of us: we are all obliged to grapple with the business of living and strive to make a success of our lives, only to look death in the eye at the end of it.

10.5.2 Approaching the end

One dimension of dealing with death is accepting the transience of life, and focusing, at least temporarily, on the loss that that transience implies. Such a focus can lead us to lament the human condition, bearing witness, in what we say or write (or depict in one artistic form or another), to the contrast between the fulness that life can hold and the decay and destruction that time wreaks on our lives.

In the shadow of the Spanish Civil War, a writer such as Blas de Otero (1916–79) picked up this theme of human mortality, echoing Manrique's metaphor of life as a river, in the poem 'Lo eterno' (published in the 1950 collection *Angel fieramente humano*), in which he refers to 'ese río del tiempo hacia la muerte'. In the poem, Otero expresses his horror at the solitude of man, pitted against time and the universe:

> Sólo el hombre está solo. Es que se sabe
> vivo y mortal. Es que se siente huir
> – ese río del tiempo hacia la muerte –.

The 'eternity' of the title is a condition desired by all; but, as was the case with Miguel de Unamuno (see 9.5), this condition is seen as unattainable:

> Es que quiere quedar. Seguir siguiendo,
> subir a contra muerte, hasta lo eterno.
> Le da miedo mirar. Cierra los ojos
> para dormir el sueño de los vivos.

The eyes in the poem see with the clear light of reason, and what they see is mortality. This human rationality is pitted against the notion of the simple faith in the afterlife that both Otero and Unamuno sought in vain.

The phrase *sueño de los vivos* is itself intertextual, as it echoes another classic Spanish text, Pedro Calderón de la Barca's play *La vida es sueño*. This, too, is a poetic expression of the fleeting nature of human life: but, unlike in Otero, the flimsiness of life in Calderón is compensated for by the belief in a life beyond the grave. Calderón, a seventeenth-century priest, presumably had that consolation, even if it did not annul the sense of loss associated with his perception of life's brevity, as in this extract from the play:

> ¿Qué es la vida? Un frenesí;
> ¿qué es la vida? Una ilusión,
> una sombra, una ficción,
> y el mayor bien es pequeño;
> que toda la vida es sueño,
> y los sueños, sueños son.

The *sueño* in Calderón is not just a reference to brevity, of course, but to the way in which human beings live under an illusion of solidity and permanence which ultimately leads to the disillusionment of death. In the play, King Basilio's son, Segismundo, is kept locked away in a castle because his father fears that he may revolt against him, as has been predicted by his clairvoyants. Having been reared in the castle in ignorance of his true identity, he is drugged and taken to Court where, on awakening, his violent behaviour shocks his father, who has him put to sleep again and taken back to the castle.

Segismundo now believes that his visit to court has been a dream, and it is only when the people, outraged at what has happened, revolt against the king that Segismundo conquers his father. The play and shift of identities experienced by Segismundo lead him to ask how real an understanding we have of our own selves. In terms that foreshadow contemporary psychological theory, Calderón depicts man as a creature who dreams that he is who he thinks he is, so that, in order to be themselves, people must play the role of being themselves:

> Sueña el rey que es rey y vive
> con este engaño mandando,
> disponiendo y gobernando;
> y este aplauso, que recibe
> prestado, en el viento escribe,
> y en cenizas le convierte
> la muerte, ¡desdicha fuerte!:
> ¿que hay quien intente reinar
> viendo que ha de despertar
> en el sueño de la muerte?

The message that life is brief, and that death and life are inseparable, is a central theme in the contemporary novel *Las afueras de Dios* (1999), by Antonio Gala (b. 1936), set in an old people's home, at the point where life comes closest to being death. Gala explores the relationship between life and death through the eyes of a nun working in the home, who reflects on human mortality:

> ¿Es la muerte el estado normal, contra el que la vida sobreviene y lucha, o lo normal es la vida, que sufre el asalto exterior y artificial de la muerte? ¿Quién fue primero? ¿Qué lo advenedizo: la gallina o el huevo? ¿Quién resiste a la otra? O acaso todo es uno y lo mismo, y somos vida y muerte a la vez. Porque la vida está llena de muertes, pero también la muerte está llena de vida, y es aquélla la que más nos impulsa a vivir, a seguir vivos.
>
> (Gala 1999: 29)

The presence of the threat of death is seen as making life more intense:

> *¿Qué importa más, la muerte que dura tanto o la vida que dura tan poco? ¿Quién gana la batalla? . . . En definitiva, las dos son la misma cosa. No dos siamesas de distintos colores, no la doble cara de la misma moneda, sino un fruto que madura, una imbricación inseparable. La vehemencia, la intensidad, el regusto de la vida dependen de la muerte: sólo existen porque ella existe.*
>
> (Gala 1999: 110)

In a more domestic setting, the poet Luisa Castro presents the stark reality of death as it is experienced in everyday life. She evokes the banality of the presence of death among the living through reference to the death of a pig, in her poem 'El cerdo'. Here, the slaughtered animal exudes a smell which replaces the smell of eau de cologne for the young girl who witnesses the events; the smell of the pig's blood ends up clinging forever to the poet's memory:

'EL CERDO'

Me habían puesto una falda nueva porque llegaba gente,
el agua de colonia,
rescatada de la profundidad de los armarios,
resbalaba por mi frente
una vez al año, por diciembre,
tibia.

Tengo una capacidad de olvido propia de la niñez,
pero mi casa no tenía un lugar para la muerte,
así que había que morir en el pasillo,
improvisar un ataúd de sal,
una roldana de muerte
en el rellano de la escalera.

Y atravesar la escena
sólo para beber agua.

Las tripas, el riñón, el corazón, el hígado,
desaparecen pronto de mis sueños.
Su llanto en mi cabeza reproduce débiles resonancias.

Pero el olor a sangre
adherido para siempre en las bombillas tan tenues,
alimentaba todos mis malos pensamientos.

(Castro 1990: 19–20)

Death in this poem is a familiar presence, part of the ordinary reality of the family situation: 'había que morir en el pasillo'. The rich ambiguity of the poetic expression manages to suggest both horror at the ominous otherness of the animal's death and a sense of how that mortality is somehow a shared, communal experience, the defining experience of all living creatures.

On a similarly mundane level, although with less subtlety of sentiment, a piece of verse like the following – an epitaph on a child's gravestone – conveys with disarming directness that sense of the closeness of death to life, the quotidian intrusion of mortality into the world of the living:

Padres cuyo desconsuelo
tregua no da a la aflicción
cese vuestro triste duelo
porque lloráis una flor
que presta ya aroma al cielo.

The piece is quoted by Janine Fribourg (1979: 145), who suggests that it is characteristic of a certain kind of Spanish sense of the proximity between the space occupied by the living and the space occupied by the dead. Fribourg notes the frequency of such epitaphs in Spain and the abundance of instances where the composers of the epitaphs adopt a dialogic format to express their conviction that death has not succeeded in separating the deceased from the bereaved, as in these lines also: 'Duerme sin miedo hijo mío / tu madre te aguarda aquí' (ibid.: 145).

According to Fribourg, this is of a kind with the popular Spanish tendency to depict supernatural beings – Christ, the Virgin, patron saints – as ordinary human figures, often presented in songs and other invocations as going about the world of the living, carrying out everyday tasks which resonate with the normality of living people's lives.

Whether or not arguments such as Fribourg's overstate the Spaniard's sense of the propinquity between living and dead, between the natural and the supernatural, it often seems as if the Spaniard is more willing than most to treat death lightly, to refuse to be overawed by mortality. In everyday speech and in the media, we often witness a fine sense of macabre humour. Expressions and sayings mentioning death abound in Spanish: from an ironic phrase such as *acercándose al hoyo* (literally, 'approaching the hole in the ground') as a synonym for dying, to the grisly humour of a proverb such as *De aquí a cien años, todos calvos* ('In a hundred years' time, we'll all be bald'). In the same vein, a media story which amused the nation in October 1999 told of how the mayor of the town of Lanjarón (Granada), on learning that the town cemetery was full, decreed that no one in the town should die until the council had finished work on extending the graveyard. In the same month, the national daily *El País* published a serious story on the booming Spanish funeral industry, complete with a photograph of several coffins, under the tongue-in-cheek headline 'Un negocio que va de muerte' (approximately, 'Dying trade finds new lease of life').

Thus, lamentation over the brevity and inevitability of death is balanced with a wry, humorous resignation at the common fate of all mankind. Death can even be seen as a welcome fate, and the dead apparently envied. St Teresa's 'muero porque no muero' was the expression of a conviction that only in death would she achieve her ultimate goal of union with God.

In our time, or perhaps always, death represents the ultimate otherness: it is something which we think of as happening to other people, not to us – and, in a literal sense, whenever we hear about a death taking place, that is always the death of another. And yet, as we progress through life we are reminded of human mortality, and, as we grow older, the awareness of death increases and becomes a sense of the inevitability of our own personal mortality. This is as true in Spain as it is elsewhere, although the ways in which the Spaniard's sense of mortality is expressed often seem to suggest a greater willingness to confront death than in other cultures.

Figure 7: Pablo Picasso, 'Guernica', 1937 (Museo Nacional Centro de Arte Reina Sofía). © Succession Picasso/DACS 2001.

FEATURE: PICASSO'S 'GUERNICA'

This legendary mural by Pablo Picasso (1881–1973) was painted as the centrepiece of the pavilion built by the Spanish government for the Universal Exposition held in Paris in 1937. Picasso chose as his theme for this commission the destruction of the Basque town of Guernica, which had been carried out on 26 April 1937 by the Nazi air force on behalf of the Nationalist side in the Spanish Civil War.

The bombing, which shocked and horrified the entire world, was the first ever saturation bombing of a civilian town, and was a precursor of later blitzes that took place during World War II. For three hours, the town was bombed to the point of annihilation. According to an eyewitness (quoted in Oppler 1988: 162), the first wave of bombing took place some time after four o'clock in the afternoon, with heavy bombs and hand-grenades being dropped to stampede the population. This was followed by a spate of machine-gunning which drove the people to seek shelter. Next, more heavy bombs and incendiaries were dropped, in order to wreck the houses and burn them on top of the victims. People who fled to the hills were pursued by the German pilots, who strafed them with machine-gun fire. Two days later, Franco's troops took control of the town and the surrounding area. When Picasso learned what had taken place, he adopted the bombing of Guernica as the subject for his picture, which was substantially completed by June 1937, and which attracted enormous attention during the six months that the Exposition lasted.

This picture is probably the most famous anti-war image of all time. Its effect is dramatic: on the one hand, the overall symbolic intent is clear, as befits a painting which was composed not for an intellectual elite but for the general run of visitors to the Paris exhibition. The anguish and terror of the victims of war is conveyed through the expressions on the faces of the human figures in the painting, the effect being heightened by the muted colours which are employed in the composition: black, white and two greys. The injured horse, the figure of the bird and the various human figures are violently dislocated, further emphasizing the anguish and terror experienced by the 7000 inhabitants of Guernica on the fateful day in question, and by victims of war in any era.

The precise significance of the various elements of the picture is open to interpretation, and the possible meanings of the individual components and their relationship to the overall composition have been debated at length. For example, does the bull on the left – the only 'serene' figure in the painting – represent the brute strength of military oppression or the resistance of the Spanish people to the forces of Franco? What purpose is served by the inclusion of two lights, the violent revelatory central one and the more homely image of an old-fashioned lamp, and what direction is the overall lighting meant to be coming from in the picture? Does the horse represent the threat of violence or is it meant to depict victimhood? Whatever the answers to these questions, the huge painting, which measures nearly 8 x 3.5 m, stands both as an unequivocal condemnation of a specific crime which took place in 1937 and as a universal expression of outrage at the violence of which human beings are capable.

Picasso stipulated that the picture should never return to Spain until democracy had been restored to the country. Resisting overtures made by Franco's government, Picasso kept his resolve in this regard and the picture only came back to Spain in 1981, six years after the death of the dictator. The painter himself lived outside Spain for almost all his adult life, residing mainly in Paris, despite his own deep sense of Spanishness. As a creative artist, he transcended geographical boundaries and became a major figure in modern culture. He is generally considered to have been the most outstanding artist of the twentieth century.

READING: CAMILO JOSÉ CELA, *LA FAMILIA DE PASCUAL DUARTE*

The novel *La familia de Pascual Duarte* caused a sensation when it was published in 1942. Its dispassionate portrayal of the violent central character, Pascual Duarte, struck a chord with the Spanish people, who had just been through the nightmare of a devastating war, and set the tone for much of the writing of the succeeding years. The author, Camilo José Cela (b. 1916), is a prolific novelist and short-story writer who has also become a major personality in Spanish society. He won the Nobel Prize for Literature in 1989. In the extract below, from Chapter 5 of the novel, Pascual describes, in brief unemotional terms, the death of his younger brother, the reaction of his unfeeling mother and the hypocritical behaviour of his neighbours in the aftermath of the little boy's death. The person being referred to at the beginning of the passage is his brother, Mario.

[C]omo al que el destino persigue no se libra aunque se esconda debajo de las piedras, día llegó en que, no encontrándolo por lado alguno, fue a aparecer, ahogado, en una tinaja de aceite. Lo encontró mi hermana Rosario. Estaba en la misma postura que una lechuza ladrona a quien hubiera cogido un viento; volcado sobre el borde de la tinaja, con la nariz apoyada sobre el barro del fondo. Cuando lo levantamos, un hilillo de aceite le caía de la boca como una hebra de oro que estuviera devanando con el vientre; el pelo que en vida lo tuviera siempre de la apagada color de la ceniza, le brillaba con unos brillos tan lozanos que daba por pensar que hubiera resucitado al él morir. Tal es todo lo extraño que la muerte de Mario me recuerda ...

Mi madre tampoco lloró la muerte de su hijo; secas debiera tener las entrañas una mujer con corazón tan duro que unas lágrimas no le quedaran siquiera para señalar la desgracia de la criatura. . . . De mí puedo decir, y no me avergüenzo de ello, que sí lloré, así como mi hermana Rosario, y que si tal odio llegué a cobrar a mi madre, y tan deprisa había de crecerme, que llegué a tener miedo de mí mismo. ¡La mujer que no llora es como la fuente que no mana, que para nada sirve, o como el ave del cielo que no canta, a quien, si Dios quisiera, le caerían las alas, porque a las alimañas falta alguna les hacen!

Mucho me dio que pensar, en muchas veces, y aún ahora mismo si he de decir la verdad, el motivo de que a mi madre llegase a perderle el respeto, primero, y el cariño y las formas al andar de los años; mucho me dio que pensar, porque quería hacer un claro en la memoria que me dejase ver hacia qué tiempo dejó de ser una madre en mi corazón y hacia qué tiempo llegó después a convertírseme en un enemigo. En un enemigo rabioso, que no hay peor odio que el de la misma sangre; en un enemigo que me gastó toda la bilis, porque a nada se odia con más intensos bríos que a aquello a que uno se parece y uno llega a aborrecer el parecido. Después de mucho pensar, y de nada esclarecer del todo, sólo me es dado el afirmar que la respeto habíasela ya perdido tiempo atrás, cuando en ella no encontraba virtud alguna que imitar, ni don de Dios que copiar, y que de mi corazón hubo de marcharse cuando tanto mal vi en ella que junto no cupiera dentro de mi pecho. Odiarla, lo que se dice llegar a odiarla, tardé algún tiempo – que ni el amor ni el odio fueran cosa de un día – y si apuntara hacia los días de la muerte de Mario pudiera ser que no errara en muchas fechas sobre su aparición.

A la criatura hubimos de secarle las carnes con unas hilas de lino por evitar que fuera demasiado grasiento al Juicio, y de prepararlo bien vestido con unos percales que por la casa había, con unas alpargatas que me acerqué hasta el pueblo para buscar, con su corbatita de la color de la malva hecha una lazada sobre la garganta como una mariposa que en su inocencia le diera por posarse sobre un muerto. El señor Rafael, que hubo de sentirse caritativo con el muerto a quien de vivo tratara tan sin piedad, nos ayudó a preparar el ataúd; el hombre iba y venía de un lado para otro diligente y ufano con alguna tabla, tal vez con el bote del albayalde, y en su diligencia y ufanía hube de concentrar todo mi discurrir, porque, sin saber ni entonces ni ahora por qué ni por qué no, me daba la corazonada de que por dentro se estaba bañando en agua de rosas. Cuando decía, con un gesto como distraído:

—¡Dios lo ha querido! ¡Angelitos al cielo! . . . me dejaba tan pensativo que ahora me cuesta un trabajo desusado el reconstruir lo que por mí pasó. Después repetía como un estribillo, mientras clavaba las tablas o mientras daba la pintura:

—¡Angelitos al cielo! ¡Angelitos al cielo! . . . y sus palabras me golpeaban el corazón como si tuviera un reló dentro ... Un reló que acabase por romperme los pechos ... Un reló que obedecía a sus palabras, soltadas poco a poco y como con cuidado, y a sus ojillos húmedos y azules como los de las víboras, que me miraban con todo el intento de simpatizar, cuando el odio más ahogado era lo único que por mi sangre corría para él. Me acuerdo con disgusto de aquellas horas:

—¡Angelitos al cielo! ¡Angelitos al cielo!

¡El hijo de su madre, y cómo fingía el muy zorro! Hablemos de otra cosa.

Yo no supe nunca, la verdad, porque tampoco nunca me diera por pensar en ello en serio, en cómo serían los ángeles; tiempo hubo en que me los imaginaba rubios y vestidos con unas largas faldas azules o rosa; tiempo hubo también en que los creía de la color de las nubes y tan delgados como ni siquiera fueran los tallos de los trigos. Sin embargo, lo que sí puedo afirmar es que siempre me los figuré muy distintos de mi hermano Mario, motivo que a buen seguro fue lo que ocasionó que pensara que detrás de las palabras del señor Rafael había gato escondido y una intención tan maligna y tan de segundo rebote como de su mucha ruindad podía esperarse.

Su entierro, como años atrás el de mi padre, fue pobre y aburrido, y detrás de la caja no se hubieron de juntar, sin exageración, más arriba de cinco o seis personas: don Manuel, Santiago el monaguillo, Lola, tres o cuatro viejas y yo. Delante iba Santiago, con la cruz, silbandillo y dando patadas a los guijarros; detrás, la caja; detrás, don Manuel con su vestidura blanca sobre la sotana, que parecía como un peinador, y detrás las viejas con sus lloros y sus lamentos, que mismo parecía a quienes las viese que todas juntas eran las madres de lo que iba encerrado camino de la tierra.

FURTHER READING

Cunningham, Valentine, *Spanish Front: writers on the Civil War* (Oxford, Oxford University Press, 1986).
Offers a range of texts on the Civil War by various authors.

Pitt-Rivers, Julian, 'Honor', in *Encyclopedia of the Social Sciences* (New York, Macmillan, 1968), Vol. VI, 503–11.
This article explains the concept of honour and its relevance to literature and social behaviour.

Salinas, Pedro, *Jorge Manrique, o tradición y originalidad* (Barcelona, EDHASA, 1962).
A comprehensive introduction to the writings of Jorge Manrique.

Wilson, Edward M. and Moir, Duncan, *The Golden Age Drama: 1492–1700* (London, E. Benn, 1971).
Chapter 3 ('The drama of Lope de Vega') and Chapter 6 ('Calderón') offer reliable introductions to the two most significant Golden Age dramatists.

Bibliography

Alberdi, Inés. 1999. *La nueva familia española*. Madrid: Taurus.

Alberdi, Juan Bautista. 1999. Reacción contra el españolismo. In *Antología del ensayo*, http://ensayo.rom.uga.edu/antologia/XIXA/alberdi3.htm

Aldecoa, Josefina R. 1996. *Historia de una maestra*. Barcelona: Anagrama.

Aleixandre, Vicente. 1977. *Antología poética*. Madrid: Alianza.

Álvarez Junco, José. 1996. The nation-building process in nineteenth-century Spain. In Mar-Molinero, Clare and Smith, Angel (eds), *Nationalism and the nation in the Iberian Peninsula: competing and conflicting identities*. Oxford: Berg, pp. 89–106.

Anderson, B. 1983. *Imagined communities*. London: Verso.

Arcipreste de Hita, eds Criado de Val, Manuel and Naylor, Eric W. 1976. *Libro de Buen Amor*. Madrid: Aguilar.

Arendt, Hannah. 1958. *The human condition*. Chicago: University of Chicago Press.

Austen, John. 1939. *The story of Don Juan: a study of the legend and the hero*. London: Martin Secker.

Ballard, Roger. 1996. Islam and the construction of Europe. In Shahid, W. A. R. and van Koningsveld, P. S. (eds), *Muslims in the margin: political responses to the presence of Islam in Western Europe*. Kampen, Netherlands: Pharos, pp. 15–51.

Banks, Gordon. 1989. *Don Juan as psychopath*, http://www.pitt.edu/~gebanks/pubs/DonJuan.html

Bariaud, Françoise. 1983. *La genèse de l'humour chez l'enfant*. Paris: Presses Universitaires de France.

Barna, Laray M. 1993. Stumbling blocks in intercultural communication. In Samovar, Larry A. and Porter, Richard E. (eds), *Intercultural communication: a reader*. Belmont, CA: Wadsworth, pp. 337–46.

Beardsell, P. R. 1996. *Europe and Latin America: the identity of the Other*. Manchester: Manchester University Press.

Borges, Jorge Luis. 1972. *Ficciones*. Madrid: Alianza.

Boyd-Barrett, O. and O'Malley, P. (eds) 1995. *Education Reform in Contemporary Spain*. London: Routledge.

Bozal, V. 1973. *Historia del arte en España*. Madrid: Istmo.

Brassloff, Audrey. 1986. Spanish education in the state/Church context. In McNair, J. et al. (eds), *Education in Spain*. Papers given at Trinity and All Saints College, 22–23 November 1985. Leeds: Trinity and All Saints College, pp. 21–42.

Brenan, Gerald. 1970. *The literature of the Spanish people: from Roman times to the present day*. London: Cambridge University Press.

Brooksbank Jones, Anny. 1997. *Women in contemporary Spain*. Manchester: Manchester University Press.

Brown, P. and Levinson, S. 1987. *Politeness: some universals in language usage*. Cambridge: Cambridge University Press.

Burke, James. 1985. *The day the universe changed*. Boston: Little, Brown.

Bustos Tovar, José Jesús de (ed.) 1983. *Poema de mio Cid*. Madrid: Alianza.

Calvo Serraller, Francisco. 1995. *La imagen romántica de España: arte y arquitectura del siglo XIX*. Madrid: Alianza.

Campo, Salustiano del. 1993. *Tendencias sociales en España (1960–1990)*, Vols I–III. Bilbao: Fundación BBV.

Castro, Luisa. 1990. *Los hábitos del artillero*. Madrid: Visor.

Castro Lingl, Vera. 1998. 'La dama y el pastor' and the Ballads of the Cancionero General: the portrayal of the experienced woman. In Deyermond, Alan (ed.), *Cancionero studies in honour of Ian McPherson*. London: Queen Mary and Westfield College, pp. 133–46.

Cela, Camilo José. 1971. *La familia de Pascual Duarte*. Barcelona: Destino.

CIS. 1992. *Encuesta. Actitudes y valores, Estudio 2001*. Madrid: Centro de Investigaciones Sociológicas.

CIS. 1994. *Barómetro de abril, Estudio 2087*. Madrid: Centro de Investigaciones Sociológicas.

CIS. 1995a. *Encuesta. Actitudes y conductas interpersonales de los españoles en el plano afectivo, Estudio 2157*. Madrid: Centro de Investigaciones Sociológicas.

CIS. 1995b. *Encuesta. Perfiles actitudinales en la sociedad española, Estudio 2203*. Madrid: Centro de Investigaciones Sociológicas.

CIS. 1997a. *Encuesta. Juventud e identidad nacional, Estudio 2257*. Madrid: Centro de Investigaciones Sociológicas.

CIS. 1997b. *Encuesta. Juventud y entorno familiar, Estudio 2262*. Madrid: Centro de Investigaciones Sociológicas.

CIS. 1998. *Barómetro de mayo: Unión Europea, Estudio 2288*. Madrid: Centro de Investigaciones Sociológicas, http://www.cis.es/baros/ mar2288.htm

Clarke, John. 1984. 'There's no place like . . .': cultures of difference. In Massey, Doreen and Allen, John (eds), *Geography matters: a reader*. Cambridge: Cambridge University Press, pp. 54–67.

Collins, Larry and Lapierre, Dominique. 1968. *Or I'll dress you in mourning: the extraordinary story of El Cordobés and the new Spain he stands for*. London: Mayflower.

Cordella, Marisa. 1996. Confrontational style in Spanish arguments: pragmatics and teaching outlook. *Language, Culture and Curriculum* **9** (2): 148–62.

de Miguel, Amando. 1990. *Los españoles: sociología de la vida cotidiana*. Madrid: Temas de Hoy.

de Miguel, Amando (ed.) 1992. *La sociedad española 1992–93: informe sociológico*. Madrid: Alianza.

Delgado Ruiz, Manuel. 1986. *De la muerte de un dios: la fiesta de los toros en el universo simbólico de la cultura popular*. Barcelona: Península.

Delibes, Miguel. 1981. *Los santos inocentes*. Barcelona: Planeta.

Derhak, Dean. 1999. *Muslim Spain and European Culture*, http://www.xmission.com: 8000/~dderhak/index/moors.htm (accessed 5 June 1999).

di Febo, Giuliana. 1988. *La santa de la raza – Teresa de Ávila: un culto barroco en la España franquista*. Barcelona: ICARIA.

Díaz-Plaja, Fernando. 1966. *El español y los siete pecados capitales*. Madrid: Alianza.

Díaz-Salazar, Rafael and Giner, Salvador. 1993. *Religión y sociedad en España*. Barcelona: Planeta.

Díez, Miguel. 1977. *Las lenguas de España*. Madrid: Ministerio de Educación y Ciencia, Instituto Nacional de Ciencias de la Educación.

Documentación Social. 1987. '*Los inmigrantes en España*', *Documentación Social – Revista de Estudios Sociales y de Sociología Aplicada*. Madrid: Cáritas.

Dostoevsky, Fyodor. 1984 [1876]. *The diary of a writer*. Haslemere: Ianmead.

Douglas, Mary and Isherwood, Baron. 1979. *The world of goods: towards an anthropology of consumption*. London: Routledge.

Douglass, Carrie B. 1984. Toro muerto, vaca es: an interpretation of the Spanish bullfight. *American Ethnologist* **11**: 242–58.

Eco, Umberto. 1984. The frames of comic 'freedom'. In Eco, Umberto, Ivanov, V. V. and Rector, Monica, ed. Thomas A. Seboek, *Carnival!* Paris: Mouton, pp. 1–9.

Eriksen, Thomas H. 1995. *Small places, large issues: an introduction to social and cultural anthropology.* London: Pluto.

European Commission. 2000. *Eurobarometer* **52**. Brussels: European Commission.

Eurostat. 1998. *Facts through figures: Eurostat Yearbook at a glance.* Luxembourg: European Commission.

Eurostat. 1999a. *Demographic statistics data 1960–99.* Luxembourg: European Commission.

Eurostat. 1999b. *Key figures on health – pocketbook.* Luxembourg: European Commission.

Eurostat. 2000. *Eurostat news release,* 1 March 2000. Luxembourg: European Commission.

Fernández-Armesto, Felipe. 1996. *Columbus.* Oxford: Oxford University Press.

Fletcher, Richard A. 1992. *Moorish Spain.* London: Weidenfeld & Nicolson.

Ford, Richard. 1898. *Handbook for travellers in Spain.* London: John Murray.

Fribourg, Janine. 1979. Conception espagnole de l'espace séparant le monde des vivants du monde des morts. In Alvarez Pereyre, Frank (ed.), *Aspects de l'espace en Europe: étude interdisciplinaire.* Paris: SELAF, pp. 143–55.

Gala, Antonio. 1999. *Las afueras de Dios.* Barcelona: Planeta.

Gallagher, Michael Paul. 1998. *Clashing symbols: an introduction to faith and culture.* New York: Paulist Press.

Gallagher, Patrick. 1969. Luis de León's development, via Garcilaso, of Horace's Beatus Ille. *Neophilologus* **53**: 146–56.

García Lorca, Federico. 1965. *Obras completas.* Madrid: Aguilar.

Garcilaso de la Vega, ed. Navarro Tomás. 1970. *Garcilaso: Obras.* Madrid: Espasa Calpe.

Garrido, Luis J. 1993. *Las dos biografías de la mujer en España.* Madrid: Ministerio de Asuntos Sociales.

Geertz, Clifford. 1993. *The interpretation of cultures.* London: Fontana.

Gibson, Ian. 1992. *Fire in the blood: the new Spain.* London: Faber/BBC Books.

Gilmore, David G. 1998. *Carnival and culture: sex, symbol and status in Spain.* New Haven, CT: Yale University Press.

Graham, H. and Labanyi, J. (eds). 1995. *Spanish cultural studies: an introduction.* Oxford: Oxford University Press.

Green, J. R. 1968. *A gesture inventory for the teaching of Spanish.* New York: Chilton Books.

Hall, Edward T. 1959. *The silent language.* Greenwich, CT: Fawcett.

Hall, Edward T. 1976. *Beyond culture.* Garden City, NY: Anchor Press.

Heywood, Paul. 1995. *The government and politics of Spain.* New York: St Martin's Press.

Hickey, L. 1991. Comparatively polite people in Spain and Britain. *ACIS Journal* **4** (2): 2-6.

Hill, Clifford. 1982. Up/down, front/back, left/right: a contrastive study of Hausa and English. In Weissenborn, J. and Klein, W. H. (eds), *Here and there: cross-linguistic studies on deixis and demonstration.* Amsterdam: John Benjamins.

Hobsbawm, Eric J. 1990. *Nations and nationalism since 1780: progress, myth, reality.* Cambridge: Cambridge University Press.

Hofstede, Geert. 1991. *Cultures and organizations: software of the mind.* London: McGraw-Hill.

Hooper, J. 1987. *The Spaniards*. Harmondsworth: Penguin.

Hooper, J. 1995. *The new Spaniards*. Harmondsworth: Penguin.

Horrocks, Roger. 1995. *Male myths and icons: masculinity in popular culture*. Basingstoke: Macmillan.

Inner. 1988. *Los hombres españoles*. Madrid: Instituto de la Mujer.

Instituto de la Mujer. 2000. *Homepage*. Madrid: Ministerio de Trabajo y Asuntos Sociales, http://www.mtas.es/mujer/

Jones, R. O. (ed.) 1963. *La vida de Lazarillo de Tormes*. Manchester: Manchester University Press.

Keown, Dominic. 1999. The subversive presence of Ausías March. In Cruickshank, D. W., *A lifetime's reading: Hispanic essays for Patrick Gallagher*. Dublin: University College Dublin Press, pp. 153–65.

Kirby, Peadar. 1992. *Ireland and Latin America: links and lessons*. Dublin: Trócaire.

Lázaro Carreter, Fernando. 1997. *El dardo en la palabra*. Barcelona: Galaxia Gutenberg, Círculo de Lectores.

Levine, J. and Redlich, F. C. 1960. Intellectual and emotional factors in the appreciation of humour. *Journal of General Psychology* 62: 25–35.

Linz, Juan José. 1990. Reflexiones sobre la sociedad española. In Giner, Salvador (comp.), *España. Sociedad y política*. Madrid: Espasa Calpe, pp. 657–86.

Lope de Vega, ed. Victor Dixon. 1989. *Fuente Ovejuna*. Warminster: Aris & Phillips.

Machado, Antonio. 1971. *Poesías completas*. Madrid: Austral.

Maeztu, Ramiro de. 1941. *Don Quixote, Don Juan y la Celestina: ensayos en simpatía*. Buenos Aires: Espasa Calpe.

Maimonides, Moses, trans. Pines, Shlomo and intro. Strauss, Leo. 1963. *The Guide of the Perplexed*. Chicago: University of Chicago Press.

Mar-Molinero, Clare. 1997. *The Spanish-speaking world: a practical introduction to sociolinguistic issues*. London: Routledge.

Maravall, José María. 1995. The pre-history of educational reform in Spain. In Boyd-Barrett, O. and O'Malley, P. (eds), *Educational reform in democratic Spain*. London: Routledge, pp. 41–52.

Marías, Julián. 1970. *José Ortega y Gasset: circumstance and vocation*. Norman: University of Oklahoma Press.

Marías, Julián. 1986. *Hispanoamérica*. Madrid: Alianza.

Marina, José Antonio. 1998. *La selva del lenguaje: introducción a un diccionario de los sentimientos*. Barcelona: Anagrama.

Martín de Pozuelo, Eduardo, Bordas, Jordi and Tarín, Santiago. 1994. *Guía de la Corrupción*. Barcelona: Plaza y Janes.

Martín Gaite, Carmen. 1987. *Usos amorosos de la postguerra española*. Barcelona: Anagrama.

Martín-Santos, Luis. 1986 [1961]. *Tiempo de silencio*. Barcelona: Seix Barral.

McKendrick, Melveena. 1980. *Cervantes*. Boston: Little, Brown.

Montero, Rosa. 1994. *La vida desnuda*. Madrid: Aguilar.

Moreno Navarro, Isidoro. 1985. *Cofradías y hermandades andaluzas: estructura, simbolismo e identidad*. Seville: Biblioteca de Cultura Andaluza.

Murphy, Michael Dean. 1994. Class, community and costume in Andalusian pilgrimage. *Anthropological Quarterly* 67: 49–61.

Nash, Rose. 1970. Spanglish: language contact in Peru. *American Speech* 45 (3–4): 223–33.

Navarro, Ana (ed.) 1989. *Antología poética de escritoras de los siglos XVI y XVII*. Madrid: Castalia/Instituto de la Mujer.

O'Donnell, Hugh. 1994. Mapping the mythical: a geopolitics of national sporting stereotypes. *Discourse and Society* **5** (3): 345–80.

OECD. 1993. *Education at a glance: OECD indicators*. Paris: OECD.

OECD. 1996. *Education at a glance: analysis*. Paris: OECD.

OECD. 1998. *Education at a glance: OECD indicators*. Paris: OECD.

Oppler, Ellen C. 1988. *Picasso's 'Guernica'*. New York: W. W. Norton.

O'Reilly, Terence. 1995. The image of the garden in *La vida retirada*. In Wing, Helen and Jones, John A., *Belief and unbelief in Hispanic literature*. Warminster: Aris & Phillips, pp. 9–18.

Ortega y Gasset, José. 1946–47. *Obras completas*. Madrid: Revista de Occidente.

Ortega y Gasset, José. 1985. *Europa y la idea de nación (y otros ensayos sobre los problemas del hombre contemporáneo)*. Madrid: Alianza.

Padgud, Robert A. 1998. Sexual matters: on conceptualizing sexuality in history. In Parker, Richard and Aggleton, Peter (eds), *Culture, society and sexuality: a reader*. London: UCL Press, pp. 15–28.

Pérez, Janet. 1996. *Modern and contemporary Spanish women poets*. New York: Twayne.

Peristiany, Jean G. 1968. *El concepto del honor en la sociedad mediterránea*. Barcelona: Labor.

Pinillos, José Luis. 1974. La evolución de las costumbres. In Fraga, M., Velarde, J. and del Campo, S. (eds), *La España de los años setenta*. La Sociedad, Madrid: Moneda y Credito, pp. 341–81.

Pinillos, José Luis. 1987. *España y la modernidad*. Palencia: Centro Regional Asociado de la UNED.

Pitt-Rivers, Julian. 1984. El sacrificio del toro. *Revista de Occidente* **36**: 27–47.

Poyatos, Fernando. 1983. *New perspectives in nonverbal communication: studies in cultural anthropology, social psychology, linguistics, literature and semiotics*. Oxford: Pergamon.

Preston, Paul and Smyth, Denis. 1985. *Spain, the EEC and NATO*. London: Routledge & Kegan Paul.

Pritchett, V. S. 1984 [1954]. *The Spanish temper*. London: Hogarth.

Pujas, Véronique and Rhodes, Martin. 1998. Party finance and political scandal in Latin Europe. *Working Papers of the Robert Schumann Centre* **98/10**, San Domenico di Fiesole: European University Institute, http://www.iue.it/RSC/WP-Texts/98_10.html

Quesada Marco, Sebastián. 1987. *Curso de civilización española*. Madrid: SGEL.

Rank, Otto. 1975. *The Don Juan legend*. Princeton: Princeton University Press.

Relph, Edward. 1976. *Place and placelessness*. London: Pion.

Remland, Martin S., Jones, Tricia S. and Brinkman, Heidi. 1991. Proxemic and haptic behavior in three European countries. *Journal of Nonverbal Behavior* **15** (4): 215–32.

Richardson, Bill. 1998. Language influencing thought: cultural and cognitive factors in spatial expression. *SALIS Working Papers in Language and Society*. Dublin: Dublin City University.

Riding, Alan. 1985. *Mexico: inside the volcano*. London: I. B. Tauris.

Riera Mercader, Josep María and Valenciano, Elena. 1991. *Las mujeres de los noventa: el largo trayecto de las jóvenes hacia su emancipación*. Madrid: Morata.

Roca i Girona, Jordi. 1996. *De la pureza a la maternidad: la construcción del género femenino en la postguerra española*. Madrid: Ministerio de Educación y Cultura.

Rojas, Fernando de, trans. D. S. Severin. 1987. *Celestina*. Warminster: Aris & Phillips.

Rosetti, Ana. 1985. *Indicios vehementes*. Madrid: Hiperión.

Rubert de Ventós, Xavier. 1987. *Nacionalismos*. Madrid: Espasa Calpe.

Rubert de Ventós, Xavier. 1999. *De la identidad a la independencia: la nueva transición*. Barcelona: Anagrama.

Rudder, Robert S. 1995 [1973]. *The life of Lazarillo of Tormes, parts one and two*. Frederick Ungar Publishing Co., Inc., available at ftp://src.doc.ic.ac.uk/media/literary/collections/project_gutenberg/gutenberg/etext96/lazro10.txt

Ruiz Ramón, F. 1984. *Historia del teatro español: desde sus orígenes hasta 1900*. Madrid: Cátedra.

Said, Edward. 1978. *Orientalism*. London: Routledge & Kegan Paul.

Salmon, Keith G. 1995. *The modern Spanish economy: transformation and integration into Europe*. London: Pinter.

Savater, Fernando. 1997. *El valor de educar*. Madrid: Ariel.

Sedgwick, Henry Dwight. 1925. *Spain: a short history*. London: Harrap.

Shaw, Patricia. 1997. Sensual, solemn, sober, slow and secret: the English view of the Spaniard, 1590–1700. In Barfoot, C. C. (ed.) 1987, *Beyond Pug's tour: national and ethnic stereotyping in theory and literary practice*. Amsterdam: Rodopi, pp. 99–113.

Simonet, Julio E. 1996. *El Quijote censurado*. Ávila: Rubiños.

Smith, Colin (ed.) 1964. *Spanish ballads*. London: Pergamon.

Smith, Paul Julian. 1989. *The Body Hispanic: gender and sexuality in Spanish and Spanish American literature*. Oxford: Clarendon.

Sroufe, L. A. and Wunsch, J. P. 1972. The development of laughter in the first year of life. *Child Development* 43: 1326–44.

Tamames, Ramón. 1996. *La economía española*. Madrid: Temas de Hoy.

Teresa de Jesús, ed. de la Fuente, Vicente. 1915. *Escritos de Santa Teresa*, Vols I and II. Madrid: Imprenta de los Sucessores de Hernando.

Tirso de Molina. 1967. *El burlador de Sevilla y convidado de piedra*. Cambridge: Cambridge University Press.

Transparency International. 1998. *Corruption Index for Different Countries 1998*, http://www.GWDG.DE/~uwvw/icr.htm

Tusell, Javier. 1999. *Claves de Razón Práctica* 94: 22–33.

Ubieto, A., Reglá, J., Jover, J. M. and Seco, C. 1977. *Introducción a la historia de España*. Barcelona: Teide.

Unamuno, M. de. 1951. *Ensayos*. Madrid: Aguilar.

Vicent, Manuel. 1984. *Crónicas urbanas*. Madrid: Debate.

Vicent, Manuel. 1999. *Son de mar*. Madrid: Alfaguara.

Wierzbicka, Anna. 1991. *Cross-cultural pragmatics: the semantics of human interaction*. Berlin: De Gruyter.

Williams, Rowan. 1991. *Teresa of Avila*. London: Geoffrey Chapman.

Index

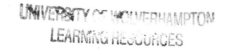